Making Nonfiction and Other Informational Texts Come Alive

A Practical Approach to Reading, Writing, and Using Nonfiction and Other Informational Texts Across the Curriculum

Kathy Pike

CAMBRIDGE CENTRAL SCHOOL
Cambridge, NY

Jean Mumper

WALLKILL CENTRAL SCHOOL
Wallkill, NY

PEARSON

AB

Boston ■ New York ■ San Francisco
Mexico City ■ Montreal ■ Toronto ■ London ■ Madrid ■ Munich ■ Paris
Hong Kong ■ Singapore ■ Tokyo ■ Cape Town ■ Sydney

SERIES EDITOR: *Aurora Martínez Ramos*
EDITORIAL ASSISTANT: *Katie Freddoso*
SENIOR MARKETING MANAGER: *Elizabeth Fogarty*
EDITORIAL-PRODUCTION ADMINISTRATOR: *Annette Joseph*
EDITORIAL-PRODUCTION SERVICE: *Colophon*
ELECTRONIC COMPOSITION: *Publishers' Design and Production Services, Inc.*
COMPOSITION BUYER: *Linda Cox*
MANUFACTURING BUYER: *Andrew Turso*
COVER ADMINISTRATOR: *Joel Gendron*

For related titles and support materials, visit our online catalog at
www.ablongman.com.

Between the time Website information is gathered and then published, it is not
unusual for some sites to have closed. Also, the transcription of URLs can result
in typographical errors. The publisher would appreciate notification where these
errors occur so that they may be corrected in subsequent editions.

LIBRARY OF CONGRESS CATALOGING-IN-PUBLICATION DATA

Pike, Kathy.
  Making nonfiction and other informational texts come alive : a practical
approach to reading, writing, and using nonfiction and other informational texts :
across the curriculum / Kathryn M. Pike, Jean Mumper.
     p.   cm.
  Includes bibliographical references and index.
  ISBN 0-205-36609-0 (alk. paper)
  1. Content area reading.   2. Literacy. I. Mumper, Jean.   II. Title.

LB1050.455.P54 2004
372.6—dc21   2003046372

Printed in the United States of America

10   9   8   7   6   5   4   3   2   1   CIN   08   07   06   05   04   03

To our families and to our colleagues in the Cambridge and
Wallkill School Districts, who helped make this book possible.
Special appreciation to Judy Woelfersheim, a wonderful friend,
who has made significant contributions to her students over the years.

and

To the wonderful teachers and students at Cambridge Central School
and in the Wallkill School District, whose work appears in this book,
and to our editors and reviewers for their feedback,
which helped make this text "come alive."

Contents

Preface   ix

1 A Journey into the World of Nonfiction and Other Informational Texts   1

Introduction   1
Nonfiction and Other Informational Texts   3
Role of Nonfiction   8
Pieces: A Year in Poems and Quilts, by Anna Grossnickle Hines   9
Using Nonfiction in the Classroom   11
  Class Environment   11
  Read-Alouds   12
  Whole Class Reading Instruction   13
  Models for Expository Writing   14
  Across the Curriculum   14
  Independent Reading   15
53½ Things That Changed the World and Some That Didn't, by David West   16
Nonfiction: The Challenges   16
INSTRUCTIONAL ACTIVITIES FOR THE CLASSROOM   17
AND BEYOND
  Let's Go Traveling, by Robin Rector Krupp   18
  Oh, the Things You Can Do That Are Good for You! All About Staying Healthy, by Tish Rabe   18

2 The Textbook and Beyond: Nonfiction Materials   19

Introduction   21
Types of Nonfiction Materials   21
  Textbooks   21

Trade Books   24
Periodicals   25
Primary Source Documents   26
Technology   28
Newspapers and News Magazines   30
Franklin D. Roosevelt: Letters from a Mill Town Girl, by Elizabeth Winthrop   32
Evaluating Nonfiction Materials   32
Text Structure   33
Fly with Poetry, by Avis Harley   42

INSTRUCTIONAL ACTIVITIES FOR THE CLASSROOM   42
AND BEYOND
  Mathematics, by Irving Adler   43
  Rescuing Endangered Species, by Jean F. Blashfield   43
STRATEGY AT A GLANCE
  Knowledge of Expository Text Structures   34
  Signal Words   34
  Paragraph Frames   39

3 Reading Nonfiction   44

Introduction   44
Reading Nonfiction Aloud   45
  Suggestions for Effective Nonfiction Read-Alouds   48
Guiding Readers through Nonfiction Text: Previewing and Overviewing   52
Literature Circles/Book Clubs and Nonfiction   53
A New England Scrapbook: A Journey through Poetry, Prose, and Pictures, by Loretta Krupinski   54
Key Features for Effective Literature Circles or Book Clubs   55
The Fossil Girl, by Catherine Brighton   72

INSTRUCTIONAL ACTIVITIES FOR THE CLASSROOM   78

AND BEYOND

Math Curse, by Jon Scieszka and Lane Smith   79

The Flag We Love, by Pam Munoz Ryan   79

STRATEGY AT A GLANCE

Interactive Read-Alouds   48

Say Something   49

Readers' Theater   49

Previewing and Overviewing   51

Literature Circles/Book Clubs   53

Fish Bowl   60

4 Strategies for Success   80

Introduction   80

Strategies for Success: An Overview   82

A Model for Strategic Instruction   83

A Burst of Firsts: Doers, Shakers, and Record Breakers, by J. Patrick Lewis   85

Strategies for Success   86

K-W-L and Variations of K-W-L (K-W-L-H and K-W-L Plus)   86

Anticipation/Reaction Guides   90

Question–Answer Relationships   93

Semantic Feature Analysis   96

Reciprocal Teaching   98

Reading for the Gist   100

Guess Whose Shadow?, by Stephen R. Swinburne   102

Vocabulary Development   102

List-Group-Label-Write   102

Previewing in Context   103

Contextual Redefinition   104

Concept/Definition Maps   105

Word Walls   105

INSTRUCTIONAL ACTIVITIES FOR THE CLASSROOM   108

AND BEYOND

Animal Homes: A First Look at Animals, by Diane James and Sara Lynn   108

Amazing Insects: Eyewitness Juniors 26, by Laurence Mound   109

STRATEGY AT A GLANCE

K-W-L (and Variants)   86

Anticipation/Reaction Guides   91

Question–Answer Relationships   93

Semantic Feature Analysis   97

Reciprocal Teaching   99

Reading for the Gist   100

List-Group-Label-Write   103

Previewing in Context   103

Contextual Redefinition   104

Concept/Definition Maps   105

Word Walls   106

5 Writing Nonfiction   110

Introduction   110

The Craft of Writing Nonfiction   112

A Framework for Teaching Nonfiction Writing—Persuasion   116

A Mountain Alphabet, by Margriet Ruurs   121

Patterned Writing   121

Writing to Learn   121

Journal Writing   122

Quick Writes   130

Possible Sentences   131

Two-Column Notes   131

Inquiry Charts or I-Charts   132

Technology in the Writing Classroom   133

A Street Called Home, by Aminah Brenda Lynn Robinson   136

The ABCs of Effective Nonfiction Writing   136

INSTRUCTIONAL ACTIVITIES FOR THE CLASSROOM   138

AND BEYOND

Wooden Teeth and Jelly Beans, by Ray Nelson, Douglas Kelly, Ben Adams, and Mike McLane   138

Postcards from Pluto: A Tour of the Solar System, by Loreen Leedy   139

STRATEGY AT A GLANCE

    Personal Journals   124

    Nonfiction Notebooks/Wonder Books   125

    Dialogue Journals   125

    Written Conversations   127

    Learning Logs   128

    Reading Response Logs   129

    Simulated Journals   129

    Class Journals   130

    Quick Writes   130

    Possible Sentences   131

    Two-Column Notes   132

    Inquiry Charts or I-Charts   133

6 *Graphic Organizers: Tools for Reading, Writing, Thinking, and Learning Nonfiction   140*

Introduction   140

Description of Graphic Organizers   142

Rationale for Using Graphic Organizers   142

Uses of Graphic Organizers   143

Types of Graphic Organizers   143

  Conceptual Graphic Organizers   145

  Comparison/Contrast Graphic Organizers   146

  Hierarchical Graphic Organizers   149

  Cyclical Graphic Organizers   150

  Sequential Graphic Organizers   151

  Apples, Bubbles, and Crystals: Your Science ABCs, by Andrea Bennett and James Kessler   152

A Final Word: Effective Use of Graphic Organizers   153

  Mapping Penny's World, by Loreen Leedy   153

INSTRUCTIONAL ACTIVITIES FOR THE CLASSROOM   154

AND BEYOND

  Ben Franklin and the Magic Squares, by Frank Murphy   155

7 *Showcasing Student Learning of Nonfiction, Using Creative Projects and Bookmaking   156*

Introduction   156

Literature Response Activities   157

Sharing Literature through Writing   158

  Letter Writing   158

  Newspaper Reporting   158

  Alphabetical Book Reports   158

  Personality or Characteristics Reports   159

  Silhouette Biographies   159

  Famous Quotes Report   159

  Shaped Book Reports   160

Sharing Nonfiction through Art   160

  Hung Up on Nonfiction   161

  Costume Designing   161

  T-Shirts, Quilts, and Tapestries   161

  Time Lines or Lifelines   161

Sharing Nonfiction through Drama   161

  Living Books   162

  How-to Demonstrations   163

  Role-Playing   163

  Mock Trials   163

  Yankee Doodle, by Stephen Kellogg   164

Sharing Nonfiction through Bookmaking   164

  Information in Cans   164

  Interlocking Plastic Bag Books   164

  Artifact-Bound Books   166

  Artifact Books   166

  Accordion Books   166

  Graduated Pages Books   167

  Framed Books   167

  Envelope Books   167

  Slit Books   171

  Flap Books   171

  Pocket Folder Books   171

Assessment of Bookmaking and Other Creative Projects   173

Conclusion   174

 The History of Counting, by Denise Schmandt-Besserat   175

INSTRUCTIONAL ACTIVITIES FOR THE CLASSROOM   176

 AND BEYOND ━━━━━

Richard Orr's Nature Cross-Sections, by Richard Orr   176

Bees Dance and Whales Sing: The Mysteries of Animal Communication, by Margery Facklam   177

8 *Assessment of Nonfiction Learning   178*

Introduction   178

Purposes of Assessment   180

 Erie Canal: Canoeing America's Great Waterway, by Peter Lourie   181

Measures of Assessment   181

Observation/Kidwatching   182

Rubrics   184

Retellings   185

Interviews, Surveys, and Inventories   186

Student Self-Evaluation   187

Think-Alouds   188

Student Products, Projects, and Other Work Samples   189

A Final Note   190

 A Kid's Guide to the White House, by Betty Debnam   191

INSTRUCTIONAL ACTIVITIES FOR THE CLASSROOM   191

 AND BEYOND ━━━━━

The Egyptian News, by Scott Steedman   192

Insects—Science Nature Guide, by Dr. George McGavin   192

Nonfiction Books: A Recommended List   193

Web Sites of Interest   204

Bibliography   205

Index   209

Preface

*W*elcome to a journey into the world of nonfiction. We have chosen the journey metaphor as a unifying theme for this text. In taking a journey, it is best to be selective about one's destination and to spend time to get to know the area visited and gain a thorough understanding of the place. We have chosen to be selective and take you on a journey to *one* part of the "literacy world"—the world of nonfiction. We emphasize that nonfiction is only one aspect of a student's voyage into literacy, and that students must be exposed to and provided a balanced, comprehensive literacy program. This means that all aspects of reading and writing receive appropriate emphasis—narrative and expository text, skills, and strategies alike. Along the way, students need "tour guides" who give instruction, demonstrations, opportunities for discussion, coaching, and investigation (Routman, 2000). The critical question to consider when planning for such an undertaking is: "What has to be in place to ensure that all students become literate?" This book is one route to developing literacy, because it focuses on the teaching and learning of nonfiction.

In writing this book, we have tried to mirror the features that are traditionally found in expository (nonfiction) texts, including illustrations, diagrams, insets, boxed materials, and so on, that help to clarify and explain the concepts being presented. Therefore, we have incorporated information and features in a variety of formats to be used in such a fashion.

In addition, we have included many nonfiction titles that can be used effectively in a balanced literacy program, and we have attempted to show the many uses that can occur with nonfiction texts. These include using them in literature circles, as models for writing, for research purposes, and so forth.

This "guidebook" is divided into eight chapters, with each having the following features:

- An initiating chapter activity, featuring a nonfiction trade book and extension activity
- A backpack graphic organizer, outlining the key topics in that particular chapter
- *Try This . . .* activities that can be undertaken in the classroom and are practical examples of the strategies or information being presented
- *Book Talks*, which are motivational messages about nonfiction books that are of special interest, placed in boxes or insets within the chapter
- *Book Talks and Beyond*, which not only raise the reader's interest in reading the book, but provide a meaningful extension activity
- End-of-chapter activities, which provide other activities for exploring nonfiction

Also, where applicable, we have summarized some of the strategies—each called *Strategy at a Glance*—so that they can be easily referenced when needed.

We have included many visuals throughout each chapter, as is done in expository texts. A variety of topics related to nonfiction are provided such as reading nonfiction, writing nonfiction, thematic studies, strategic learning in the nonfiction classroom, etc.—all designed to make your journey a comfortable and successful one.

At the end of your trip, you will find a professional bibliography and an extensive listing of nonfiction literature. Quality series that feature a wealth of nonfiction titles are also included.

At this time, we would like to thank our editors who "traveled" with us as we wrote this book—Aurora Martínez Ramos and Beth Slater. Their advice and "travel tips" were invaluable.

We hope you enjoy your journey and that you bring back some "souvenirs" that you can share with your students. Bon voyage!

Your fellow travelers,

Kathy Pike
Jean Mumper

1

A Journey into the World of Nonfiction and Other Informational Texts

Introduction

IMAGINE! Imagine being able to visit lands of long ago, explore the rain forest, take a trip down the Nile, and fly to outer space! All this—and more—can be accomplished simply by opening an informational book, also known as nonfiction or expository writing. That's what this resource book is all about—taking just such a trip into the world of nonfiction, where you will learn more about the

Inspired by Imagine by A. Lester
FROM THE CLASSROOM OF JEAN MUMPER
Grade 3, Wallkill, NY.

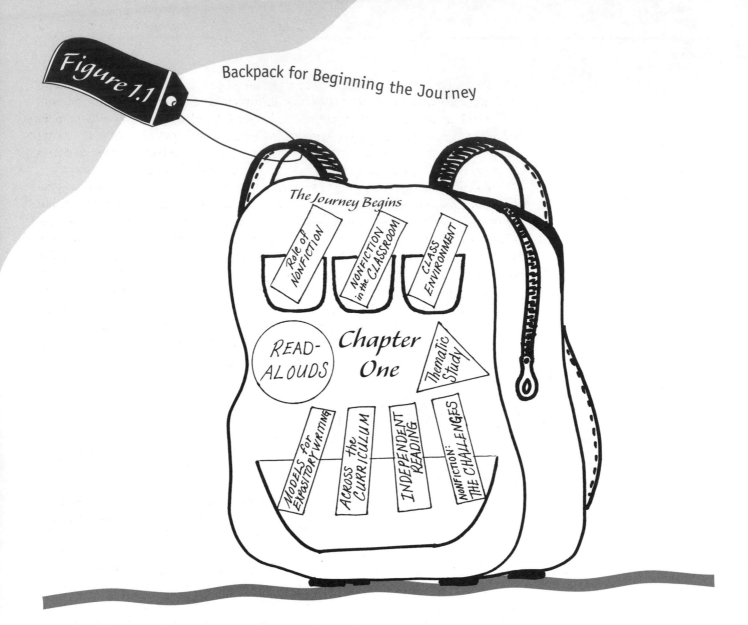

Figure 1.1 Backpack for Beginning the Journey

The Journey Begins

Role of Nonfiction

Nonfiction in the CLASSROOM

CLASS ENVIRONMENT

READ-ALOUDS

Chapter One

Thematic Study

Models for Expository Writing

Across the Curriculum

Independent Reading

Nonfiction: THE CHALLENGES

fascinating world of nonfiction, its role in the instructional program, and some exciting classroom nonfiction activities. As with any trip you might take, you could explore your destination without looking at maps and without careful planning; you could just roam around. At times, this spirit of adventure is fun and a great change of pace, but the trip that you will undertake in this book is a guided adventure, much like the trip that we advocate that your students take when you engage them in the reading and writing of nonfiction. We, as your tour guides, believe that if students are to learn, teachers must show them how. Therefore, this book is about the *how* as it pertains to the teaching and learning of nonfiction. So sit back and enjoy your trip—bon voyage!

This fantastic voyage into the world of nonfiction can be likened to a very popular literature series in elementary school—*The Magic School Bus* series, in which children are taken on amazing field trips by their teacher, Ms. Frizzle, to such places as inside a hurricane, a bee hive, the human body, and so on. More recently, Ms. Frizzle has taken on the role of tour guide during her summer vacation, leading her followers to Ancient Egypt.

To prepare for your journey, and to make sure you have an enjoyable and educational experience, several preparations should be considered beforehand. Prior to leaving, it would be helpful to become familiar with the term *nonfiction*, the differences between nonfiction and narrative text, the style of writing used in nonfiction, and so forth. The intent of this introductory chapter is to prepare you for the journey that you and your students will undertake.

To capitalize on the popularity of backpacks in student life, we will use the *backpack* metaphor throughout this text. Initially, such items as a description of nonfiction, a discussion of the role and challenges of using nonfiction in the classroom, and an explanation of the organizational structures that are used in writing nonfiction texts will be placed in your backpack. As you go through this text, other items (e.g., strategies, concepts, vocabulary, etc.) will be added to the backpack so that when you return from your trip, you will have enough "souvenirs" and "memories" to share with your students and your colleagues as you prepare and execute instructional lessons with nonfiction materials. Figure 1.1 illustrates the first items placed in your backpack as you embark on the magical journey into the world of informational texts.

NONFICTION AND OTHER INFORMATIONAL TEXTS

Many of the instructional materials found in elementary classrooms have been narrative (e.g., fictional) in nature. Narrative texts tell stories and are organized sequentially, with a beginning, a middle, and an end. The basic plan, or story grammar, of narrative texts consists of such elements as characters, setting, plot, and theme. The purpose of fiction is to be engaging and entertaining, and to involve the readers or listeners in stories about life, although occasionally, the purpose of fiction can be to inform or persuade (Fountas & Pinnell, 2001). Fiction is related to the world of the imagination and includes realistic stories, historical fiction, science fiction, plays, fantasy, and traditional literature such as myths, legends, folktales, fairy tales, and epics. Narrative texts, used in many read-alouds, shared reading, guided reading, and independent reading, both in and out of the classroom, are more familiar to students than are nonfiction texts. Used less frequently, but gaining in popularity, are expository texts (or nonfiction), which present information around a main idea. Due to the emphasis on narrative texts, students tend to be less familiar with expository writing, and are not as successful in reading and writing expository texts.

Not too long ago, the majority of nonfiction reading used in schools was found in textbooks, usually in such subjects as science, social studies, and math (known as the content areas). In general, students in grades four and beyond made the transition from predominantly narrative texts to content area materials. This transition was rather fast paced, with little instruction on how to effectively read expository text. Moreover, if textbooks were utilized in the primary grades in the content areas, the style of writing was still narrative in nature, although the material was factual. Today, however, this is no longer the case. Textbooks are still used, in both the primary and intermediate grades, but they have taken on new looks with many added aids and structural features that assist the learners in understanding and remembering the material. In addition, there are now many individual trade books used in teaching the content areas.

By having a greater variety of individual content area titles, as opposed to a single textbook, teachers have more flexibility and can provide more individualized, personalized instruction.

Informational books provide factual information using both text and visual images (Kerper, 1998). Because their primary purposes are to communicate and provide information and to explain, argue, and demonstrate, they must be accurate and up to date (Bamford and Kristo, 2003). The style used in nonfiction writing must be clear and interesting, enhanced with illustrations or graphics to facilitate understanding and clarity. Informational texts, which are the products of authors' research, are available in almost any area or topic, for example sports, cooking, history, geography, science, technology, crafts, art, and music, and can take many different formats: picture books, chapter books, documents, deeds, articles, letters, diaries, journals, brochures, manuals, photo essays, how-tos, notes, almanacs, world record books, newspapers, magazines, CD-ROMs, and the World Wide Web. Nonfiction is a genre that is quite versatile and appropriate for novices, sophisticated learners, and all those in between. Browsers and skimmers are welcome to nonfiction, as are those who read a text from cover to cover.

What do informational texts look like? Unlike narrative texts, which include long sections of intact text, informational texts are frequently broken up into sections: table of contents, headings, subheadings, glossaries, indexes, and so forth. In addition, there are visual aids that help focus readers and draw attention to important information. These include such textual features as boldface print, framed information, bullets, captions, the use of highlighted text or italics, labels, varied fonts, and so on. These basic features—*access features* and *visual features*—make the books more readable and accessible and facilitate a reader's locating of information. Figure 1.2 is a listing of the textual aids, text organizational features, and graphic features and visuals found in nonfiction.

Let's take a look at each of these types of features and see how they contribute to a reader's finding and understanding of the information provided in

Nonfiction, a carefully crafted genre, provides ideas, facts, and principles organized around main ideas, using both verbal and visual texts. The purposes of using informational texts are to inform, instruct, and enlighten. Therefore, nonfiction texts must be accurate and current and include essential information. Nonfiction texts include all books about the sciences (natural, social, and physical), history, sports, crafts, the arts, how-tos, newspapers, articles, the World Wide Web, and so on, that discuss factual information about a topic, as well as biographies, autobiographies, and memoirs. Informational texts include nonfiction materials and informational storybooks, which present both an engaging story, as well as pertinent facts.

nonfiction texts. *Access features*, or reference aids, are found scattered throughout nonfiction books: outside the body of the book (e.g., table of contents, glossary, index, bibliography, suggestions for further reading, and pronunciation guide); closer to the main body, serving as a frame for supporting the text (e.g., introduction, preface, author or illustrator notes, afterword, and appendix); and inside the text (e.g., bulleted information, headings, sidebars, and insets) (Kerper, 1998; Bamford & Kristo, 2000). Figure 1.3 describes the types of access features and their purposes and gives examples of books that contain the feature.

Access features support comprehension of nonfiction and often expand information about a topic. It should be noted, however, that there are excellent nonfiction titles that may not include every access feature. Also, access features may appear in sections of the book in which readers may not normally look for them—for example, pronunciation guides and glossaries, which may be embedded in the textual material itself.

Nonfiction authors present their information both verbally and visually, and they take as much care with their illustrations, photographs, charts, diagrams, and so on, as they do with the text. *Visual features* are selected that are best suited to convey the desired information and to support or explain the text (Moline, 1995; Kerper, 1998; Bamford & Kristo, 2000). Figure 1.4 describes some visual features, outlines their purposes, and gives some examples of books that utilize the particular visual feature.

Figure 1.2   What Do Informational Texts Look Like?

Text Features

headings	bullets	labels
boldface print	captions	varied type/font styles
use of capitals to indicate degree of importance	italics	changing colors in headings to indicate importance
titles	call-outs or side bars (information placed outside of regular text)	subheadings
framed information		highlighted information
		textual cues/signal words

Graphic Features/Visuals

diagrams	graphs	tables
cross-sections	timelines	maps
* photographs	figures	graphic organizers
* illustrations	charts	overlays
* can be color or black and white	word bubbles	cut-aways

Text Organizational Features

preface	glossary	appendix
table of contents	pronunciation key	
index		

Figure 1.3 Access Features in Nonfiction

Access Feature—Outside the Text	Description and Purpose	Book Examples
Table of Contents	A listing of the contents of a book designed to draw the reader's attention to what lies ahead and the content that will be covered	*How to Be a Friend: A Guide to Making Friends and Keeping Them* by Laurie & Marc Brown *How Do Bats See in the Dark?: Questions and Answers about Night Creatures* by Melvin & Gilda Berger *Lives of the Writers* by Kathleen Krull
Glossary	A listing of specialized words with their definitions, and sometimes pronunciations, that may not be clear in the text; can go beyond a simple definition by offering expanded information about key concepts	*Watchful Wolves* by Ruth Berman *The Summer Olympics* by Bob Knotts *The Vikings* by R. Nicholson & C. Watts
Pronunciation Guides	Phonetic spelling of words in the text provided to assist readers in pronouncing challenging words; can be found at the end of the book or inserted directly in the text	*Gone Forever! An Alphabet of Extinct Animals* by Sandra & William Markle *Navajo ABC* by Luci Tapahonso & Eleanor Schick
Bibliography and Recommendations for Further Reading	A listing of books and sources that the author used in his/her research; other books that relate, link, or connect to the topic to give readers the potential for obtaining additional information	*Uncle Sam and Old Glory: Symbols of America* by Delno & Jean West *Look What Came From Australia* by Kevin Davis *Benjamin Franklin* by Peter & Connie Roop
Access Feature—Around the Text	**Description and Purpose**	**Book Examples**
Introduction/Preface	Information that can elaborate on the writing of the book or provide assistance to the readers to understand the content	*The Buck Stops Here: The Presidents of the United States* by Alice Provensen *Girls Think of Everything: Stories of Ingenious Inventions by Women* by Catherine Thimmesh *The Barefoot Book of Heroic Children* by Rebecca Hazell
Afterword	Information provided at the end of the book that gives readers additional information about the topic, what might have happened to the event/topic, or other interesting data about the contents	*Eating Fractions* by Bruce McMillan *Welcome to the Green House* by Jane Yolen *On the River ABC* by Caroline Stutson
Author/Illustrator Notes	Notes provided about either/both the author and illustrator to give information about them, their research process, challenges in writing/illustrating the text, unanswered questions, etc.	*The Alphabet Atlas* by Arthur Yorinks *The Third Planet: Exploring the Earth from Space* by Sally Ride & Tam O'Shaughnessy *A True Book of Thanksgiving* by Dana Rau
Appendix	Variety of additional information found at the end of the book that expands upon the contents; might include Web Sites to visit	*A Mountain Alphabet* by Andrew Kiss & Margriet Ruus *Life in the Rainforest* by Lucy Baker *The Day We Walked on the Moon* by George Sullivan

Figure 1.3 Continued

Access Feature—Inside the Text	Description and Purpose	Book Examples
Sidebars	Information that is found usually on the perimeters of the page, outside the main body of the text; provide additional information, clarify, give examples and interesting tidbits, elaborate and extend what is in the text	*A is for America: An American Alphabet* by Devin Scillian *Eyes on Nature: CATS* by Jane Resnick *Insects—Science Nature Guides* by George McGavin
Bullets Asterisks, Stars	A way to list pertinent information and highlight facts	*The Flag We Love* by Pam Munoz Ryan *The Vikings* by Robert Nicholson & Claire Watts *50 Simple Things KIDS Can Do To Save the Earth* by Earthworks Group
Insets	A variation of sidebars, boxed information that allows the author to include additional text and illustrative material; can also include maps, charts, graphs, etc.	*Let's Go Traveling* by Robin Rector Krupp *In the Path of War: Children of the American Revolution Tell Their Stories* by Jeanne Winston Adler *Rivers and Oceans* by Barbara Taylor
Headings	Brief statements, questions, or phrases that alert readers to the most important aspect of the topic	*. . . If Your Name Was Changed at Ellis Island* by Ellen Levine *Mummies & Their Mysteries* by Charlotte Wilcox *Lives of the Artists* by Kathleen Krull

Figure 1.4 Visual Features in Nonfiction

Visual Feature	Description and Purpose	Book Examples
Illustrations and Photographs	Pictures, either artistic renditions or photo-images that support, clarify, or expand upon the content	*Kangaroos for Kids* by Judith Lehne *Sky Tree: Seeing Science through Art* by Thomas Locker *The World Beneath Your Feet* by the National Geographic Society
Captions	Phrases, sentences, or paragraphs that accompany illustrations or photographs; summarize portions of the text; expand on the topic or go beyond the text; enhance interest and motivation in the text	*Erie Canal: Canoeing America's Great Waterway* by Peter Lourie *Learning to Swim in Swaziland* by Nila Leigh *The Magic School Bus on the Ocean Floor* by Joanna Cole
Labels	Similar to captions, but generally limited to a single word or short phrases; accompany illustrations, diagrams, or photographs; sometimes arrows or lines are drawn from the label to the item being identified	*Deserts* by Gail Gibbons *North American Indians* by Anne Armitage *Desert Giant: The World of the Saguaro Cactus* by Barbara Bash
Diagrams	Artistic renditions of objects; help clarify, define, and support the text	*Starry Messenger* by Peter Sis *Rivers and Oceans* by Barbara Taylor *Mapping Penny* by Loreen Leedy
Time Lines	Visual pictorial features that are kinds of flow diagrams or graphs; visually depict information in chronological order and usually expand or elaborate on the text	*The Boston Tea Party* by Pamela Duncan Edwards *Follow the Dream: The Story of Christopher Columbus* by Peter Sis *The Life and Times of the Apple* by Charles Micucci

Figure 1.4	Continued

Visual Feature	Description and Purpose	Book Examples
Maps	Visual representations of geographic features that facilitate understanding of the text; often accompanied by keys and map scales	*Shipwreck at the Bottom of the World: The Extraordinary True Story of Shackleton and the* Endurance by Jennifer Armstrong *Celebrate the 50 States* by Loreen Leedy *Castle* by David Macaulay
Charts	Offer readers information in a condensed version within the text or adjacent to it; sometimes elaborate on the information	*Celebrations!* by Barnabus & Anabel Kindersley *Wooden Teeth and Jelly Beans* by Nelson, Kelly, Adams, & McLane *Hieroglyphs from A to Z* by Peter Der Manuelian
Graphs	Diagrams that represent ways to compare variable information, using a series of lines, bars, curves, or shaded areas	*Where Does the Garbage Go?* by Paul Showers *1000 Facts about the Earth* by Moira Butterfield *Endangered Birds* by World Conservation Monitoring Center

Informational texts were formerly books that were entirely factual in nature, but now they transcend the traditional barriers of both narrative and nonfiction texts, frequently containing elements of both. This genre of literature that is the focus of this resource book includes *informational texts*, with their expository text structures (the organizational writing styles used by authors of nonfiction), and *informational storybooks*, which are narratives that include both a story and information about the topic under study. Typical examples of informational storybooks include *The Magic School Bus* series mentioned previously.

ROLE OF NONFICTION

It is predicted that, by the year 2020, the amount of information will double every seventy-three days (Grolier, 1995). Will students be prepared for this

Try This

Features of Nonfiction

Compile some nonfiction texts that contain some of the access features used in nonfiction. Nonfiction big books work well for this activity. Divide the class into groups and give each group one or more of the nonfiction texts. Have the group examine the texts and write down the features they observe in the text. A chart of the groups' findings could be prepared and kept on display to remind students of the organizational aids that nonfiction authors use to help readers learn about a topic. The activity could be repeated, with students noting the visual features of nonfiction texts.

Pieces: A Year in Poems and Quilts
by Anna Grossnickle Hines

Can you visualize the seasons of a year beautifully described and illustrated using a patchwork pattern? Combining stitches that create unique quilting blocks with poetic language produces an extraordinary picture book that can be enjoyed by all. Each quilt is different, and each is paired with an original poem. Some of the poems are framed in the quilt blocks themselves, while others are accompanied by full-page quilt block interpretations of the seasons. The story behind the quilts concludes the book. This book can inspire budding poets, as well as those who wish to experiment with another art form.

amazing amount of information? Will they be able to use it and understand it effectively to meet the needs and demands they will encounter in their lifetimes? Most of the reading (approximately 80 percent to 90 percent) students will have to do in the future will be informational in nature; therefore, it is imperative that we, as educators, prepare our students for using and understanding informational texts.

To further demonstrate the importance of nonfiction in our lives, the SCANS report, prepared by the U.S. Department of Labor, identified the basic competencies necessary for success in the workplace (Secretary's Commission on Achieving Necessary Skills, 1991):

- Identifying , organizing, planning, and allocating resources
- Working with others
- Acquiring and using information
- Understanding complex interrelationships
- Working with a variety of technologies

As you can see, acquiring and using information are integral to performing effectively, not only in school, but also for succeeding at work and at home.

Preparing students for their future, whether it is further schooling or the workplace, begins in your classroom. Students need to learn how to learn. They

Nonfiction in Our Lives

Write down all the reading and writing you have had to do in the past week. Examine your list to determine how much of it was nonfiction, as opposed to fiction. Just take reading, for example—your list might look something like this: telephone messages; recipes; grocery list; memo from your principal or superintendent; letters from your students' parents or your own family members; the newspaper; an article in a news magazine; a schedule; a teachers' manual; announcements; attendance sheet; notes in your plan book; a novel; and so on. This list could even be compiled with your students to demonstrate how much of our lives is spent reading and writing nonfiction.

need to know how to read nonfiction successfully so that they can acquire, use, and apply the information that is presented. They need to learn how to research, organize their findings, and present them in interesting and understandable ways. Nonfiction needs to have a prominent place in teachers' instructional repertoires—nonfiction needs to be packed into teachers' instructional backpacks so their students can be successful on their journeys to becoming lifelong learners.

Although using nonfiction has a direct impact on students' futures, the primary reason for using nonfiction in elementary classrooms is to get information. Through nonfiction texts, in-depth, interesting information can be obtained on many ability levels. Today, nonfiction texts are engaging with informative illustrations or photographs, along with other organizational features that enhance the text—captions, charts, sidebars or call-outs (information that is set in the margins, at the bottom of the page, etc.), graphs, and so forth.

Nonfiction also can be a means for providing authentic literacy experiences and for developing reading and study skills that students will use throughout their lives. Through nonfiction, students can learn how to gather, organize, and summarize information. They can be given opportunities to determine fact from fiction, and fact from opinion. They can learn to detect bias and therefore become more informed citizens who can base decisions on rational data, as opposed to emotional, subjective information. Students' vocabularies and stores of knowledge can be increased through the reading of and listening to nonfiction texts. In addition, students can apply what they have learned and demon-

---

Figure 1.5	Benefits of Using Informational Books

Using nonfiction in the classroom:

- Builds background knowledge and develops concepts
- Provides in-depth, accurate information about a topic
- Allows teachers to provide more individualized instruction, a variety of topics, and reading levels
- Enhances vocabulary development
- Familiarizes students with the writing style of expository texts
- Provides models for writing succinctly
- Facilitates purposeful, authentic learning
- Promotes inquiry, discovery, and active learning
- Enhances visual literacy
- Utilizes visuals to clarify information
- Promotes student self-confidence and self-esteem since students can become knowledgeable about a topic
- Strengthens critical reading and writing skills
- Satisfies and increases curiosity
- Gives options to students who enjoy and prefer non-fiction
- Whets students' appetites for obtaining information, which can lead to further reading of additional informational texts

| *Figure 1.6* | The Role of Nonfiction in Developing Reading and Study Skills |

By exposing students to informational texts, students have the opportunity to develop the following reading and study skills:

- gather information
- organize and summarize information
- synthesize what they have learned
- analyze vocabulary
- locate facts
- determine fact from fiction
- determine fact from opinion
- compare/contrast information
- use information to determine accuracy of texts
- build vocabulary and knowledge for reading, writing, listening, viewing, and speaking
- relate what they have learned to previous learning/facts
- use research skills and technologies
- apply what they have learned and demonstrate the learning in a variety of ways, e.g., reports, oral or written presentations, computer simulations, etc.

strate the learning in a multitude of ways, from oral presentations to computer slide shows.

In addition to the necessity of using nonfiction for preparing students for their futures and for acquiring information, students enjoy nonfiction because these books are informative, exciting, and interesting. Nonfiction not only provides facts and information, but also nurtures students' excitement and imagination, sparks their curiosity, and enhances an interest in learning (Figure 1.5) (Burke & Glazer, 1994; Grolier, 1995; Harvey, 1998). Check out the library or local book store, and see how many children gravitate to the nonfiction sections to look at dinosaurs, airplanes, volcanoes, insect-eating plants, or the Civil War. Students deserve—and need—nonfiction so that they can learn, obtain, and use information effectively and successfully (Figure 1.6).

USING NONFICTION IN THE CLASSROOM

There are a variety of ways that nonfiction can be used in the classroom: for creating stimulating, inviting classroom environments; as read-alouds; for whole class reading instruction; as models for expository writing; to enhance any curricular area; in thematic units; and for independent reading.

Class Environment

To encourage students to live rich nonfiction lives, full of passion, wonder, and excitement, teachers need to set up their class environments to take advantage of the wide variety of nonfiction materials that are available (Harvey, 1998). The walls, halls, and shelves can invite exploration into nonfiction. Baskets of nonfiction books can be placed prominently in the library corner or in a section of the classroom devoted to a particular unit of study. Artifacts, resource books, charts, photographs, sign-up sheets, student work, announcements, nonfiction book reviews—all these and more can help create an environment that encourages and supports inquiry-based learning and invites students to learn about and enjoy informational texts.

The halls and display cases outside the classroom should not be forgotten as ways to "sell," promote, and celebrate nonfiction. Molly Oakley, a fifth-grade teacher preparing to take her students on a week long trip to Washington, D.C., filled the bulletin boards outside her classroom with maps of Washington, D.C., photographs, postcards, the itinerary, announcements of meetings and fundraising activities, and other information about the upcoming trip. In addition, students placed information about what they were learning about the United States government in the hallway for others to view. Figure 1.7 depicts the students' artistic renditions of *The Preamble to the Constitution*, which were displayed in the hallway. By showcasing the class learning in this way, the information was reinforced, the students' motivation for the trip and the learning were enhanced, and the entire school got to share the students' excitement and experiences.

Read-Alouds

> *Speaking of bugs, what was one of the first land animals to leave its tiny footprints on American soil? The lowly cockroach! With its six hairy legs and two little hairs on its rear end to tell if something is sneaking up from behind, this wily bug has survived 300 million years of history. (Who would have thought a hairy butt would come in handy?) They survived killer meteors and deadly ice ages. No ifs, ands, or but(t)s about it, cockroaches deserve the title, America's first settlers.* (Levy, 2000, p. 10)

And so begins a nonfiction book—*Who Are You Calling a Wooly Mammoth?: Prehistoric America*—from America's Horrible History Series, published by Scholastic Press. Don't you think students will be captivated as they learn some fascinating, humorous, horrible, weird, awesome, and wacky information about North America's prehistoric life?

Teachers tend to associate narrative text with reading aloud to students, but nonfiction texts make wonderful read-alouds as well. Nonfiction texts can build background knowledge for a topic of study, expand students' vocabulary, and motivate students, as well as provide them with fascinating facts and information. Reading nonfiction aloud helps students appreciate the style, the structure, and the language of well-crafted nonfiction. The beauty of using nonfiction as a read-aloud is that nonfiction does not have to be read in its entirety. Portions of the text can be read and discussed, photographs and their captions can be shared, and snippets of information can titillate and excite. Times for reading nonfiction aloud can be scheduled, or reading nonfiction can purposefully and educationally fill those moments between activities or while waiting for a special-area teacher to arrive.

Figure 1.7   Student Artistic Renditions of the Preamble to the U.S. Constitution

Whole Class Reading Instruction

Teachers frequently use a single textbook or piece of nonfiction with the entire class to address the teaching of science, social studies, or mathematics. It must be remembered, however, that if nonfiction is to be used for this purpose, teachers must be intentional about preparing students for the learning, showing them how to read nonfiction and how to use and apply what they have learned. As with narrative text, preparation and guided exploration should accompany the learning before, during, and after the reading.

Pre-Reading

- Activating and building background knowledge
- Motivating the learners
- Setting a purpose for reading
- Discussing the access features of the text (e.g., table of contents, index, glossary)
- Providing an overview of the text (e.g., perusing the text, noting the bolded information, illustrations, author's notes, questions at the end, etc.)

During Reading   Assisting learners with the following:

- Locating information
- Recording information
- Skimming the text
- Reading purposefully to answer questions or discover information
- Summarizing
- Visualizing
- Rereading
- Creating vocabulary lists
- Answering questions

After Reading   Assisting learners with the following:

- Answering questions
- Summarizing
- Recording what was learned
- Reporting what was learned
- Discussing the contents
- Applying/extending the contents (e.g., oral presentations, projects, PowerPoint or HyperStudio presentations, etc.)

Further information on reading nonfiction is presented later in this resource guide.

Models for Expository Writing

To assist students in their expository writing, teachers should share many exemplary nonfiction pieces, which include books as well as articles, news reports, memoirs, reports, and so forth. Nonfiction materials can be used for mini-lessons and shared reading to increase students' repertoires of models and writing styles, which can be used in their own written investigations.

Across the Curriculum

No matter which area of the curriculum is undertaken, there are nonfiction books available to enhance the learning. Nonfiction books are essential in the subjects traditionally considered the content areas—science, social studies, and math—but they can also be used in English Language Arts, art, music, health, and so on. Students can be "taught" how to read using nonfiction books, and how to respond to texts using nonfiction books. Using nonfiction materials in literature circles and book clubs is explored later in this book.

Independent Reading

Many teachers set aside a portion of the school day for the students to read silently and independently. Instead of always choosing a novel or a storybook, students can read a piece of nonfiction (e.g., a trade book, newspaper, informational magazine, etc.). Again, students do not have to read the entire piece, but can browse, read sections, examine the diagrams, and so forth. Sample titles of some nonfiction reading selections can be found in the listings at the back of this book.

Figure 1.8   Semantic Map for Thematic Study on Weather

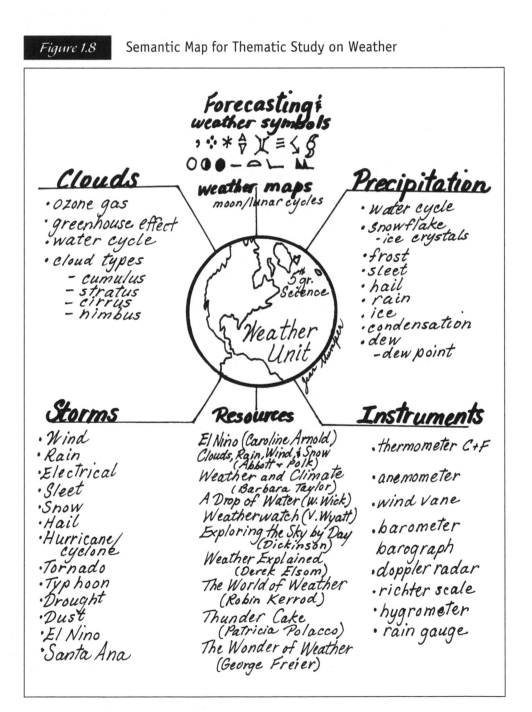

53½ Things That Changed the World and Some That Didn't

by David West

What would the world be without music, books, clothes, engines, and so on? Discover some amazing inventions that have changed the world, such as the sandwich, safety pins, the teddy bear, microscope, the sail, the toilet, clock, and more—and read about some that have not. Tinker with these creations that have made our lives easier, healthier, more comfortable, and more enjoyable. From primitive discoveries, such as the line and the wheel, to such modern inventions as rockets and computers—this book contains them all. It also includes some inventing disasters! Prior to young students reading this book, ask them to list some inventions that they could not live without in their daily lives. See how many of their inventions are described in this book, and learn about their fascinating histories. Who knows—you just might inspire one of your students to create another invention that could change the world!

NONFICTION: THE CHALLENGES

In the primary grades, children have many experiences with narrative text, and most have internalized the way that stories are organized. Children have had fewer experiences with nonfiction. Consequently, the organizational structure of nonfiction writing is unfamiliar. The style of writing changes, as well, becoming more compact and dense. The vocabulary of expository writing is technical and specialized, unlike that of narrative text, and students may have to remember multiple concepts while reading their nonfiction texts. In addition, the logical connectives and transition words that are necessary for understanding the relationships between ideas presented in the text are often implied rather than stated directly. When these connectives are included, students are not familiar with their use, because these signal words are generally not addressed in the instructional program. Moreover, in the elementary grades, many content area texts are written in a descriptive manner so that the organizational structure becomes less useful for understanding and retaining the information.

In addition to the style of writing and the organization of expository materials, there are other difficulties associated with content area learning. There is a great deal of information to be learned, and students may have little prior knowledge of the topics being addressed. Students also must be able to identify the important concepts and organize their learning efficiently and effectively. They have to discern key points, take notes, retain the information for further use, and demonstrate their knowledge in some meaningful fashion (e.g., tests, reports, projects, etc.) (Harvey, 1998; Allen, 2000). Unfortunately, many students are not prepared for these tasks. Many of the difficulties in content area learning arise from the fact that students are rarely taught how to read and write strategically. Figure 1.9 summarizes some of the challenges that content area reading may present.

| Figure 1.9 | Challenges of Informational Text |

- Readers have insufficient prior knowledge about content area topics.
- Readers are unfamiliar with the organizational text structures of expository writing.
- Authors of content area materials tend to use a dense style of writing and include many ideas in a short space.
- The writing can lack logical connectives and transition words, which hinder understanding.
- When logical connectives and transition words are included to show relationships of ideas, they are often not explained to students.
- The vocabulary is technical and specialized.
- Students may not understand how to use such organizational features as diagrams, timelines, and the like.
- Since the texts are written to inform, rather than to entertain, motivation and interest may be affected.
- Students are frequently required to apply or demonstrate what they have learned.

Sources: From Cudd & Roberts, 1989; Harvey, 1998; and Readence, Bean, & Baldwin, 2000.

Instructional Activities for the Classroom

1 Chapter-Beginning Activity

As noted previously, nonfiction can take students to places that they might otherwise not get to experience. A book similar to *Imagine* by Allison Lester can be shared as a read-aloud. In *Imagine*, the author takes her readers to such faraway places as the rain forest, the ocean, and the Antarctic. Detailed illustrations of the setting and the animals found in that environment are provided, framed by a border, and created with the names of all the animals found living in the particular area. The chapter-opening example was constructed by a third grader after completing a thematic study on cultures around the world. Instead of merely listing words from the country around the border, the student chose to provide symbols. This book, with its intriguing format, could be used as a means for students to apply what they have learned about other geographical places, a period in U.S. history, animals, plants, space, and so forth.

2 Activating Students' Prior Knowledge about Nonfiction

Give students the prompt *When I Read Nonfiction . . .*, and have them respond orally or in their journals. A class chart could be constructed listing the students' responses. This activity could be repeated later in the year after explicit instruction of informational texts has been undertaken and compared with the students' earlier thoughts.

Book Talk and Beyond

Let's Go Traveling

by Robin Rector Krupp

Ready for a trip to visit ancient lands? Want to see more of what's left of our mysterious past? Well, then, just pack your bags and climb aboard to visit the prehistoric caves of France, the pyramids of Egypt, the Great Wall of China—and more! As you venture off to visit six ancient sites, you will read about the young narrator's (Rachel Rose's) impressions, her diary entries, postcards she writes, and lists of new words she finds that provide an insight and a flavor to the site visited. Accompanying

the main body of the text are many other types of information, in a variety of forms, such as maps, illustrations, artifacts of the area, photographs, buttons, and so on. Her postcards and diary entries offer readers another perspective on the places she visits. With the abundance of ways utilized to present information about a place and/or culture, this book could be used as a model for travelogue extensions. If students are learning about areas throughout the United States, conducting an in-depth study of their own state, or exploring another country, they could present their findings in a similar fashion. They could make "suitcases" from large sheets of oaktag, and design travel stickers (similar to those found in airports or souvenir shops) to decorate the outsides of their suitcases. Inside they could place their "passports," maps of places visited, brochures, tickets to interesting museums or performances, and other mementos of their "virtual field trip." They could also send "postcards" from places visited to other classes, friends, and families.

Oh, The Things You Can Do That Are Good for You! All about Staying Healthy

by Tish Rabe

Written in the style of Dr. Seuss, this book, part of The Cat in the Hat's Learning Library, introduces readers to basic nonfiction, with the topic of this text being ways to stay healthy. This whimsical, rhythmical text, complete with Seuss-like illustrations, teaches children ways to stay healthy, for example, taking care of one's teeth, wearing helmets, getting enough rest, and so forth. In addition to the rhyming storyline text, there are inserts, also in rhyme, that provide additional information about the particular healthy habit being described. Did you know that sneezes can travel five feet and blast out at speeds over one hundred miles an hour? There is also a glossary, a section on further reading, and an index. This book, and other titles in the series—*Oh Say Can You Seed?*, *There's No Place Like Space!*, *Fine Feathered*

Friends, for example—can serve as models for other nonfiction pieces written in Seuss-like style. Individual students can write a page for the book dealing with some aspect of nonfiction. Of course, the student Dr. Seuss illustrators can add to the text with their interpretations of the content.

2

The Textbook and Beyond: Nonfiction Materials

And In That Universe . . .

Once there was 1 Universe.
In that Universe there were 2 Galaxies.
In those Galaxies there were 3 Star Systems.
In those three Star Systems there were 4 beautiful Planets.
On those 4 beautiful Planets there were 5 odd continents.
On those 5 odd Continents there were 6 weird Countries.
In each country there were 7 States.
In each State there were 8 counties.
In each County there were 9 sparsely populated Villages.
Now you will find out why.
In each of those 9 Villages there were 10 Volcanoes.
On each of those 10 Volcanoes there were 11 Cooled Chunks of Lava.
On each of those 11 Cooled Chunks of Lava there were 12 unique
  Flower Pots.
In each of those 12 unique Flower Pots there were 13 Plants.
Along with those 13 Plants there were 14 twisty Roots.

Inspired by: Anno's Mysterious Multiplying Jar by Anno

19

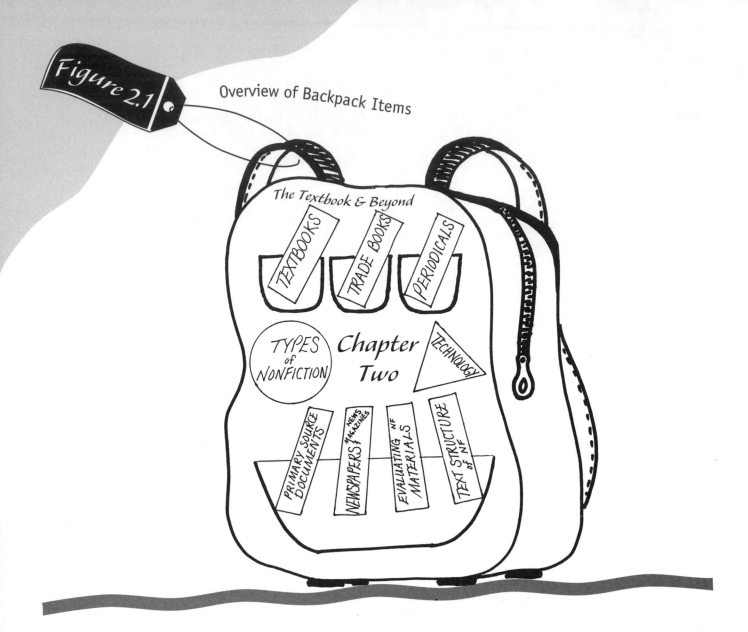

Figure 2.1 Overview of Backpack Items

In each of those 14 twisty roots there were 15 Waterways.

In those 15 Waterways there were 16 Drops of Water.

In all of those 16 Drops of Water there were 17 Micro-organisms

On each of those 17 Micro-organisms there were 18 Cilia.

Each of those 18 Cilia contained 19 Viruses.

Each of those 19 Viruses had 20 Ugly Bumps.

As to how many Bumps on each of those Viruses, the answer is surprising. It is 20! 20! is 20 Factorial. 20 Factorial, or 20! is equal to 2,432,902,008,176,604,000!

One day all the volcanoes erupted. That is how the dinosaurs became extinct. Millions of years from now the same thing is going to happen to the Universe again!!

by Laura Constantinides
    Grade 4
    Windham, N.Y.

INTRODUCTION

To return to our metaphor of a trip into the fascinating world of nonfiction, there are many avenues to take when considering learning in the content areas. Just as there are many roads and highways to get to a destination—for example, from New York City to Boston—the same can be said for helping students acquire the necessary skills and strategies to become successful using nonfiction. This chapter maps and explores the many possible materials that can be incorporated into a nonfiction instructional program. Figure 2.1 provides an overview of what you will "see" on this portion of your journey.

Not all nonfiction is found between the covers of books. Nonfiction is everywhere, in lots of different forms, shapes, sizes, and formats. Figure 2.2 is a listing of nonfiction materials that are authentic, readily accessible, and adaptable for classroom use. Not only are the possibilities for providing purposeful, enriching instruction with nonfiction endless, but students deserve to experience and learn about their world using these materials.

TYPES OF NONFICTION MATERIALS

Textbooks

The textbook industry is booming (Manzo, 1998), because textbooks are required and used in many content area subjects. Because textbooks can play an important role in content area instruction, their use and misuse must be understood by those using them. There are many quality textbooks that contain important information and are organized in an understandable and usable format. Some of the advantages of using textbooks include their ability to

- provide adequate coverage on a wide body of knowledge,
- specify the content to be covered and provide a framework so that teachers can easily plan for inquiry,
- save time for teachers by outlining topics and offering activities and assessment possibilities,
- provide common background knowledge for students, and
- serve as supplemental resources (Moore et al., 1998; Routman, 2000).

Try This

Showcasing Nonfiction Materials in Our Lives

Delegate a portion of your classroom to a collection of nonfiction materials, which could be showcased as a museum or used as a learning center. Encourage the students to bring in examples of these materials. List the variety on a chart that is readily accessible to students for reference and for possible future additions. The students will be amazed at the amount and variety of nonfiction reading that occurs in their lives and in the world.

Figure 2.2   Nonfiction Materials

advertisements	contracts	maps	responses to
advice columns	conversations	math writing	texts
alphabet books	coupons	story problems	resumes
agenda	debates	solutions to	reviews
almanac	definitions	problems	rules
anecdotes	deposit slips	learning logs	schedules
announcements	diagrams	math journals	science
apologies	dialogue	memoirs	observations
applications	diaries	memos	notebook
appointment	dictionaries	menus	lab reports
books	directories	messages	semantic mapping
articles	editorials	minutes of	signs
atlases	envelopes	meetings	slogans
autobiographies	essays	newsletters	songs and ballads
autograph books	fact sheets	newspapers	speeches
ballots	flyers	notes	statistics
banners	food packages	obituaries	study guides
bibliographies	glossary	opinions	summaries
biographies	graphs	outlines	surveys
book jackets	guidebook	petitions	tables
books	handbook	photo essays	telegrams
brochures	index	picture books	telephone
bumper stickers	Internet	poetry	directories
business cards	interviews	postcards	thesauruses
captions	invitations	posters	tickets
cartoons	itineraries	prescriptions	timelines
catalogs	journals	primary source	timetables
CD ROMS	junk mail	documents	travelogues
certificates	lab reports	questionnaires	want ads
chapter books	labels	questions	weather reports
charts	learning logs	quizzes	world record
comics	letters	recipes	books
commentaries	lists	requests	World Wide Web
computer	magazines	research reports	yearbook
programs	manuals		

In addition, publishers often package textbooks with a multitude of ancillary materials, which teachers find attractive and helpful: maps, blackline masters, manipulatives, primary source documents, problems of the day, and so forth.

Although the textbook has assumed a significant role for instruction, it should be noted that the textbook is only one source of information and that there are disadvantages to using it exclusively (which can hinder student understanding):

- The readability of textbooks may be too challenging for the intended students.
- Textbooks are often *inconsiderate;* for example, they are written in a style that is difficult for students to understand.
- There is no depth to the information provided, as many topics are covered in a cursory fashion.
- The style of writing is bland, with the contents watered down and "politically correct," and sometimes altered to meet the criteria for large statewide adoptions.
- Due to their expense, they are not replaced in a timely manner, and therefore can become outdated.
- Teachers rigidly follow the publishers' suggestions, go through the contents of the textbook from cover to cover, and therefore do not have time to incorporate other nonfiction materials.
- Teachers merely assign the content to be read and the end-of-chapter questions to be completed, many times without adequate preparation and discussion.
- Textbooks are frequently not motivating or interesting to students. (Cooper, 2000; Routman, 2000)

Some of the disadvantages are inherent in textbooks themselves, but others have to do with the way some teachers use them. To make textbooks more effective, teachers should examine them to see whether the publishers have incorporated features that will help make the text more *considerate*, that is, features that will facilitate the students' ability to construct meaning. Some of these features include the following:

- Previews or overviews of the chapter's contents
- Bulleted or sidebar information to make aspects of the text more understandable
- Focusing questions
- The use of special effects (e.g., changing fonts or font size, bolding text, color changes, etc.)
- Visual supports (e.g., charts, diagrams, photographs, timelines, etc., that are labeled, have captions, or other explanatory items)
- Summaries or questions that tie the information together
- Application or extending activities

Also, teachers should note the organization of the textbook, the style of writing, and the presentation of the ideas. These areas should be considered when adopting a textbook for a particular content area.

Another concern, mentioned previously, was the way textbooks have been used by some teachers. Obviously, teachers can use textbooks more effectively by preparing students for the learning by activating and building the students' prior knowledge, by providing scaffolds and supports as students read through the text, and building in opportunities for discussion, reflection, and application, areas that are addressed in other sections of this resource book. Used appropriately, textbooks still can be used as one resource to help develop strategic readers, ones who are successful in constructing meaning from text.

Many teachers use their textbooks selectively, guiding students through the appropriate parts of the text, pointing out relevant information and visuals, and using the text as a reference. Teachers also realize the *importance of using multiple materials* to increase their students' depth of understanding, their mo-

Try This

Collecting Trade Books on a Specific Topic

Select a topic that you will be teaching in the near future in science or social studies. Collect trade books that could be used in your instructional delivery. Enlist the support of your school and community librarian, your colleagues, students, and their parents. The books could be used for actual instruction and/or as part of a display in a portion of the room that will feature the content being explored. They can be available for guided reading, independent reading, partner reading, and research, as well as for motivation and introduction to the learning.

tivation, and the likelihood that they will have access to materials appropriate for their particular reading ability. In addition, using multiple sources for content area instruction offers various points of view, gives students more ownership of their learning, and provides many opportunities for students to engage in problem solving and decision making (Moore et al., 1998).

Trade Books

In the past, nonfiction was generally associated with textbooks, but today textbooks are being replaced or supplemented by trade books and other quality nonfiction materials. The advantage of using trade books is that there are many titles available on any topic, so teachers can personalize their content area curriculums to match the standards, objectives, and desired activities. In addition, these individual books come in many levels, which can accommodate the wide range of reading abilities in a classroom. Because trade books are less expensive than textbooks, they can be replaced, if need be, more frequently to keep the information current.

Trade books can be classified into the following major categories, all having a place in a nonfiction instructional program:

Concept Books Informational books that generally deal with a single topic or subject, using an expository style of writing:
> *Informania: Sharks* by Christopher Maynard
> *Sugaring Time* by Kathryn Lasky
> *Deserts* by Gail Gibbons

Narrative Information Books Books that can include several types, combining fiction and nonfiction:
> Those that present or embed facts using the context of a story: *Ms. Frizzle's Adventures to Ancient Egypt* by Joanna Cole and Bruce Degen
> Historical fiction: *Lyddie* by Katherine Patterson
> Nonfiction narratives (narrative accounts of actual events): *The Mary Celeste: An Unsolved Mystery from History* by Jane Yolen and Heide Yolen Stemple

Poetry Books that use rhyme and rhythm in their presentation of factual information
> *Spectacular Science: A Book of Poems* by Lee Bennett Hopkins
> *Mammalabilia Poems and Paintings* by Douglas Florian
> *Paul Revere's Ride* by Henry Wadsworth Longfellow

How-to Books Books that provide descriptions of a process and explain how to perform a variety of activities, such as playing a game, making books or jewelry, cooking, being a good friend, how to succeed in school, and so forth.
> *How to Be a Friend: A Guide to Making Friends and Keeping Them* by Laurie Krasny Brown and Marc Brown
> *Art Around the World: Loo-Loo, Boo, and More Art You Can Do* by Denis Roche
> *Earthquake Games: Earthquakes and Volcanoes Explained by 32 Games and Experiments* by Matthys Levy and Mario Salvadori

Biographies, Autobiographies, and Memoirs Books about people who have made contributions to a variety of fields, such as government, entertainment, sports, medicine, and so forth.
> *George Washington* by Cheryl Harness
> *If a Bus Could Talk: The Story of Rosa Parks* by Faith Ringgold
> *Follow the Dream: The Story of Christopher Columbus* by Peter Sis

Figure 2.3 provides a list of some nonfiction authors.

Periodicals

There is a wide variety of reading materials that can be ordered by subscribing to them. Periodicals make excellent instructional materials because they are interesting, timely, and the articles in them are relatively short. The writing found

Figure 2.3	Some Nonfiction Authors

David Adler	Steven Kramer
Aliki	Patricia Lauber
Jim Arnosky	Loreen Leedy
George Ancona	Peter Lourie
Melvin and Gilda Berger	Betsy and Giulio Maestro
Franklyn Branley	Milton Meltzer
Barbara Brenner	Bruce McMillan
Joanna Cole	Jerry Pallotta
Bruce Degen	Andrea Pinkney
Russell Freedman	Rick Reilly
Jean Fritz	Peter and Connie Roop
Gail Gibbons	Seymour Simon
Bobbie Kalman	Diane Stanley

Try This

Creating Author Web Pages

To capitalize on students' interest in technology, students can create home pages for authors they enjoy. To accomplish this, students should be familiar with the authors' works. A home page could include biographical information about an author, a listing of books, reviews (both from the student and from published works), awards, and so on.

Information can be obtained from book jackets, the Web, publishers, and resource books that discuss authors, as well as through e-mails to the author (if available) and the author's Website. Some sources for contacting authors can be found at the back of this book.

in periodicals is understandable and is frequently accompanied by photographs and illustrations, which likewise enhance understanding and motivation. Periodicals can introduce students to new topics, provide additional information on topics, and keep readers up to date on what is happening in the world today. The articles can be used for reading instruction, as sources for research, as models for writing, and for mini-lessons in any aspect of content area literacy. Almost all content areas have at least one periodical, from weekly news magazines such as *Time for Kids* to monthly or periodic publications such as *Cobblestone* and *National Geographic for Kids*. A listing of periodicals that can enhance nonfiction instruction can be found at the back of this book.

Primary Source Documents

A growing trend in the media is the reality-based TV show, in which contestants face daunting tasks under extraordinary circumstances. There is also a growing trend in nonfiction toward using authentic, reality-based materials. These materials, frequently referred to as *primary source documents*, add a dimension of authenticity to nonfiction investigations and explorations. Primary source documents can be any firsthand account, recorded by people taking part in or witnessing events. The formats of the documents include letters, journal entries, government documents, posters, and so forth. They bring the readers' attention to original sources of information and help students take into account the social situation or context in which the event/topic occurred.

Primary source documents can be found in many locations. Some sources for primary source documents include the following:

- Textbooks and trade books
- Newspapers and periodicals
- Government agencies
- Schools and libraries
- Community agencies (e.g., hospitals, police stations, court houses)
- Newspaper archives
- Radio and television stations
- Museums and art galleries
- Local businesses

Try This

Canvassing the Community for Primary Source Documents

Send your students on a primary source document hunt, and see how many examples they can locate. They can look around their own homes, visit the local library or community agency, use the newspaper, and so on. A field trip to a museum or a newspaper could reveal other sources and types of primary source documents.

- Homes (in attics, basements, family records, albums, etc.)
- Flea markets, antique shops, and garage sales
- Recollections of people (e.g., journals, diaries, notes, etc.)
- The Internet
- CD-ROMS

Figure 2.4 provides a listing of types of primary source documents.

Figure 2.4   Primary Source Documents

advertisements	letters
artifacts	library cards
artwork	magazine articles
autobiographies	maps
bank notes	memos
bills	newspaper articles
birth certificates	paintings
birth records	passports
cartoons	patents
Census Reports	photographs
cemeteries	plays
charts	posters
coins	receipts
Congressional Records	records
currency	recipes
diaries	sales slips
deeds	sheet music
documentary films	Social Security Cards
documents (legal, government)	songs
enrollments	stamps
graphs	tapestries
identification cards	telegrams
inventory lists	town meeting records
invoices	wills

Primary source documents introduce the learners to the practices that historians, scientists, and mathematicians utilize when conducting investigations and research—looking for and analyzing original documents and sources. This type of material enlivens the texts by providing images and including the voices of the people and events being studied. Primary source documents are included in textbooks, frequently as charts, diagrams, insets, and so forth; and in trade books when authors include, for example, quotes, diary entries, illustrations, and captions from archival sources. They are also used by themselves to enhance an exploratory study. For example, students might be given the following documents when studying the history of the Erie Canal:

- An excerpt from an account by an observer of the construction of the Canal
- A newspaper account of the construction process
- An editorial or letter to the editor
- A map of the area
- A popular song describing the mules and their trainers

The documents could be accompanied by scaffolding questions, for example, short-answer constructed-response questions that are designed to enhance the understanding of the document. After examining the documents and answering the scaffolding questions, students can be given a prompt or question that allows them to summarize or apply what they have learned using all the provided documents (Figure 2.5).

Technology

A whole new area of learning materials is available to students in the form of technology. Today students have access to computers, videodisks, video players, the World Wide Web, e-mail, and the like, in their classrooms, school libraries, and even in many of their homes. Through technological advances, information is now readily accessible. Students can manipulate their findings through word processing, spread sheets, and graphing programs, and can organize and present their findings and analyses through such multimedia presentations as HyperStudio and PowerPoint. Through multimedia, they can take virtual field trips and experience things far beyond what is provided in books. Technology is an excellent tool for learning, and it widens students' horizons regarding the possibilities of reading and writing nonfiction.

Try This

Guest Speakers Discuss Nonfiction in Their Lives

Invite some school or community members into your classroom to discuss how they use nonfiction materials in their lives. Some possible guest speakers could include the principal, head custodian, director of transportation, police officer, waitress, parents, doctor, and so forth. The students could write up interview questions, which could then be published in the school or local newspaper, or compiled into a book to be placed in the class library or, a nonfiction display.

Figure 2.5   Analysis of a Primary Source Document: Written Document

I.   Type of Document
     ___ letter   ___ newspaper   ___ advertisement
     ___ diary   ___ journal   ___ report
     ___ legal document   ___ patent   ___ Congressional Record
     ___ poster   ___ other _____

II. Creator (Author) of the Document_____
     • Why did the author create the document?
     • Did the person have firsthand knowledge of the event?

III. Date of the Document _____

IV. Purpose of the Document
     _____

V.   Audience for Whom the Document Was Written
     _____

VI. Interesting Features_____
     (e.g., handwritten, seals, stamped, notations, letterhead, etc.)

VI. Document Information
     A. List some things the author stated in the document:
        1. _____
        2. _____
        3. _____

     B. What evidence/statements from the document tell why it was written?
     _____
     _____

     C. Was the document written to inform or persuade others? How do you
        know?
     _____
     _____

VII. Write a question to the creator of the document that is left unanswered.
     _____
     _____

> *Figure 2.6*   Benefits of Using Newspapers in the Classroom
>
> Newspapers are:
>
> - motivational since they are adult-like
> - relevant since the topics are about the students' environment
> - a means to bridge the gap between the real world and the classroom
> - current, as they provide the latest information
> - examples of history in the making
> - adaptable since they can be marked, cut up, colored, glued
> - appealing to everyone since they contain something for everyone, e.g., comics, sports, news, editorials, ads, science features, etc.
> - "textbooks" that students will read for the rest of their lives
> - models for clear, concise writing
> - flexible since they can be used in almost every subject area and instructional situation
> - economical and readily available
> - a way to ensure lifelong learning and reading

Newspapers and News Magazines

Millions of people utilize the newspaper for information and for entertainment in their daily lives, and there are many teachers who use this excellent nonfiction material as an integral part of their instructional programs. The benefits of using newspapers in the classroom are many and can be found in Figure 2.6.

Many newspapers across the United States provide worthwhile Newspapers-in-Education programs free or for nominal fees. Newspapers are often subsidized by local area businesses so that classrooms or students can receive a daily newspaper for free. In addition to newspapers, there are many materials available today, most provided free by Newspapers-in-Education programs, that are designed to assist teachers in using the newspaper. These materials describe how to use the newspaper, discuss the use and purpose of the various sections of the newspaper, and provide a wealth of purposeful activities that can accompany newspaper exploration. An example of a Newspaper-in-Education activity is seen in Figure 2.7.

Because the newspaper contains a wide variety of articles and features, which can be overwhelming, teachers sometimes choose to subscribe to a weekly news magazine instead of a daily newspaper or in addition to a newspaper. These news magazines—*Newsweek, Time,* and *U.S. News & World Report*—serve as a major source of information for many people throughout the world, and are available for classroom use as well. The publishers of these news magazines have prepared materials for teachers to assist them in using their publications effectively in the classrooms. In addition, there are versions written for younger audiences, such as *Time for Kids* and *My Weekly Reader.*

Figure 2.7 Newspaper-in-Education Activity

It's in the Bag: Newspaper Categories

Materials Needed: newspaper, large grocery bag, scissors, glue, markers

A category is chosen and relevant items, articles, and pictures are found in the newspaper to support the category and its subdivisions. For example, if the category *People* is chosen, subcategories could include athletes, politicians, entertainment stars, and regular citizens. Words could be constructed from individual letters found on the newspaper pages or used as they are written. At the end of the activity, a story inspired by the bag's contents could be placed inside the bag for others to read.

Possible categories and their subcategories include:

Categories	*Subcategories*
clothing	men's, women's, children's, seasonal, evening, athletic
transportation	land, sea, air, space, recreational, wheels, work
rooms in a house	furniture, activities, home improvement
foods	junk, nutritional, breakfast, advertisements
sports	equipment, seasonal, local, athletes, indoor
feelings	elated, angry, disappointed, bored, curious
senses	seeing, hearing, tasting, smelling, feeling

As with textbooks and other nonfiction materials, simply having access to newspapers is not enough. Students need to acquire the skills necessary to read, analyze, and interpret the news. Students need to know how events—local through international—affect their daily lives. It is our job, as educators, to model for them and to instruct them.

Franklin D. Roosevelt: Letters from a Mill Town Girl
by Elizabeth Winthrop

Dear Mr. President,
What advice would your students give the president today? Part of the *Dear Mr. President Series*, this book features the letters of a mill town girl to Franklin Delano Roosevelt about the conditions in her town, his New Deal program, and activities in her own family. Through fictionalized letters between a president and a child of his time, our nation's past is explored. Using photos, primary historical documents, and links to the World Wide Web, readers can learn about how cotton is made into cloth in textile factories in the 1930s, and gain insights into the lives and hardships of mill workers. Through this intriguing way of presenting information about what has occurred in the past in our country, history comes alive, and the people who lived in those times are not just words on a page, but actual human beings—people that students can relate to and learn from.

EVALUATING NONFICTION MATERIALS

The publication of nonfiction materials is on the rise, and their availability is greatly increased. This may sound wonderful, but having more may not be the best. There need to be criteria for selecting quality nonfiction materials. Teachers need to make discriminating choices, based on examining the textual aspects of the nonfiction materials, as well as how the materials align with the needs of the students and the purposes and roles these materials will serve in the instructional program (Bamford & Kristo, 2000).

The nonfiction materials used in the classroom must be of high quality, accurate, and visually appealing. Choosing nonfiction is a multilayered process, examining the merits of the book, as well as how the book will work with the students and the curriculum.

First Layer: Examining accuracy, the organizational structure, style, access and visual features, and the formats

Critical Reading of Nonfiction

Obtain a variety of nonfiction titles on one topic or person. Compare them for inaccuracies, inconsistencies, author bias, and so forth. Point out to the students that facts are subject to author interpretation and that authors can interpret them differently, and that they must, therefore, always be critical readers who ask questions about what they read.

Second Layer: Examining the role of the use of the nonfiction in the curriculum, and determining how the book fits the needs of the students

When choosing quality nonfiction, the following should be considered :

- *Accuracy*   Noting and checking the copyright date, the credentials of the author, author bias, inaccuracies, the author's research process, the acknowledgments, avoidance of stereotypes, authenticity of the facts and details, the scope and depth of the information, inclusion of multiple perspectives
- *Organization*   Noting and checking for clarity of presentation, logical development, clear sequencing of information, ways that the author uses to grab and hold the readers' attention, and the means the author utilizes to assist readers in navigating successfully through the information
- *Writing Style*   Noting and checking for the ways that the author combines words, form, and content in presenting the information; the use of vivid, interesting, stimulating language and descriptions; effectiveness of leads and conclusions in enhancing the reading of the text; the use of age-appropriate vocabulary; explanations of complex and technical terms and vocabulary; the tone used in presenting the content
- *Design*   Noting the attractiveness and visual appeal of the text, readability, illustrations that complement the text, appropriateness of placement of the illustrations and the chosen format (McClure, 1998; Routman, 2000; Bamford & Kristo, 2000)

Along with considering accuracy, organization, writing style, and the design of the materials, teachers need to determine the purpose for their use and whether the materials will suit the needs of their students. There is no easy formula for choosing quality nonfiction, but it is necessary that the best materials be available and used, because books and their authors also serve as teachers and models for expository writing.

Now that we have looked at some of the types of materials that are available, it is important to note the organizational patterns that authors use to convey expository text.

TEXT STRUCTURE

Students are expected to learn from content area materials, but many students lack the knowledge about the basic writing patterns that authors use in expository text. Students also may disregard the signal or connective words and phrases that authors utilize to show the relationships among ideas. This is problematic because signal words and phrases call attention to the dominant organizational pattern being used. "Insensitivity to text patterns hinders not only students' comprehension and recall but also their abilities to write well-developed content material" (Richards & Gipe, 1995, 667).

Knowledge of text structure can improve learning from content area texts (Harvey, 1998; Allen, 2000), yet many students are unaware of expository text structures. The structures of expository writing have been defined, and although the terms may vary, lists of text structures generally include description, simple listing, sequence or time order, cause-effect, comparison/contrast, problem-solution, and question and answer (McGee & Richgels, 1985; Piccolo,

Strategy AT A Glance

Knowledge of Expository Text Structures

DESCRIPTION: The basic writing patterns that authors use in expository text. These structures include *description, simple listing, sequence* or *time order, cause and effect, comparison/contrast, problem/solution,* and *question and answer.*

PURPOSE:

Instructional: Aids in understanding, enhances recall and retention of text, and improves the writing of nonfiction. Allows students to identify the major expository structures, glean the important information in the text, and adjust their reading behaviors.

Assessment: Provides information as to whether students have an understanding of the ways that authors structure nonfiction writing.

1987; Harvey, 1998; Robb, 2003). Figure 2.8 describes each of the structures and provides a sample passage, signal words, and a graphic organizer that aids in the representation of each structure.

One of the difficulties with expository texts is that authors do not exclusively use just one of these writing patterns, but often use several patterns interchangeably. For instance, authors may be comparing and contrasting cultures (the comparison/contrast pattern) but may list the comparisons and contrasts (the simple listing pattern). This adds to the complexity of the reading task.

Instruction in the recognition and writing of expository text patterns aids understanding, enhances recall and retention of the material, and improves writing of nonfiction. There are several approaches teachers might use to teach text structure. One approach is to provide instruction on the common structures of expository text. After providing a rationale for the learning of expository text structures, teachers could conduct a series of lessons, which include

Strategy AT A Glance

Signal Words

DESCRIPTION: Words commonly associated with a particular expository structure; similar to traffic lights, which signal meanings to drivers and pedestrians, these words signal or point out the structure that the author is using.

PURPOSE:

Instructional: Triggers the recognition of expository structures and aids in the understanding of text.

Assessment: Assists in determining whether students know how authors structure expository text.

Figure 2.8   Expository Text Structures

QUESTION AND ANSWER

Description: The author introduces a topic by asking a question. The question is followed
by the answer to the question.

Signal Words: what, how, why, if, what would, when, where

Sample Passage:

What is a reptile?
Reptiles are cold-blooded vertebrates with scaly skin, which is good for keeping in
body moisture, allowing them to live in dry places. Their skin is not as successful at
retaining body heat, therefore reptiles depend on their surroundings for warmth.
Most reptiles lay eggs on land, although some give birth to live young. There are 4
groups of reptiles: snakes and lizards; turtles and tortoises; the crocodile family; and
the tuatara.

Graphic Organizer:

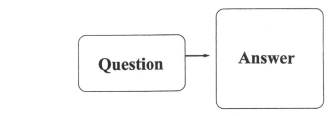

DESCRIPTION

Description: The author presents information about a particular topic or gives
characteristics of the topic or the setting.

Signal Words: the features are, some characteristics are, for example

Sample Passage:

All crocodilians are reptiles with long snouts, long tails, four short legs, tough skin,
and sharp teeth. Members of the crocodilian family include alligators, crocodiles,
caimans, and gavials. Crocodilians live in warm throughout the year and they spend
part of their time in the water and part of their time on land. Almost all crocodilians
grow to be very large, with the largest more than twenty feet long. There are two
kinds of alligators, 14 kinds of crocodiles, eight kinds of caimans, and one kind of
gavial.

Graphic Organizer:

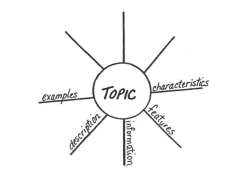

Figure 2.8   Continued

LISTING

Description: The author presents information by listing related ideas, examples, characteristics, or features together. No specific order is required when presenting the information.

Signal Words: and, in addition, besides, as well as, again, also, too, likewise, another, furthermore, other, one, many, various, several

Introductory Phrases: There are several reasons why; Three causes of; There are various

Sample Passage:

Mankind has responded to some members of the crocodile group with repugnance. There are *some* reasons for this distrust and fear of crocodiles. *First*, crocodiles are considered quite powerful. A crocodile can grow up to 20 feet and weigh half a ton. *Another* reason is the crocodile's tusk-like teeth, which are deadly efficient tools for seizing and holding its prey. Now, *finally*, the violence and the crocodile's reputation as a man-eater. Given a choice between a man and another animal such as a buffalo, the crocodile will almost always opt for the buffalo.

Graphic Organizer:

SEQUENCE OR TIME ORDER

Description: The author presents information in a chronological order.

Signal Words: first, second, next, then, after, finally, after, before, on (date), last of all,

Introductory Phrases: The directions for; The events that lead up to; There are several steps to

Sample Passage:

Recently, scientists have gained an understanding of a crocodile's reproductive activity. Crocodiles mate in the water, where the buoyancy keeps them from crushing each other. *Prior* to mating, there are stylized postures, jumping, submerged bubble blowing, and snout contact. *After* mating, hard-shelled eggs are laid in a nest, in a hole scooped in the sand. *When* it is time to hatch, the infant crocodiles begin a loud chirping sounds that lead the female to the nest, which she excavates. *Finally*, when all the babies are accounted for, the mother crocodile transports them to the shallow water where they will remain under adult protection for weeks or months.

Graphic Organizer:

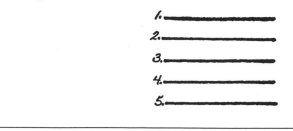

Figure 2.8   Continued

CAUSE AND EFFECT

Description: The author presents ideas grouped in a sequence so that a causal relationship is either stated or implied.

Signal Words: because, as a result, consequently, therefore, reasons why, since

Introductory Phrases: Some of the causes are; Because of; As a result of; The effects are;

Sample Passage:

On the river banks of the Nile River, home to some crocodiles, there are many kinds of birds, sometimes called crocodile birds *because* they are always hopping around crocodiles. The big crocodiles and the birds are useful to each other for *several reasons*. The birds eat flies and leeches that they find on the crocodiles' skin and mouths. In this way, the birds get a good meal and the crocodiles get rid of the leeches and flies. Sometimes an enemy frightens the birds who scream and fly away. *As a result* of the noise, the birds give the crocodiles a warning of danger.

Graphic Organizer:

PROBLEM/SOLUTION

Description: The author presents a problem, question, or remark followed by a solution, answer, or reply

Signal Words: problem, solution, puzzle, dilemma, question, answer

Introductory Statements: The problem is; A solution might be; The answer to the question is

Sample Passage:

In most parts of the world there are not as many crocodiles as there used to be. This is a *problem* because crocodiles are becoming endangered and also crocodiles are necessary to the balance of nature. Many crocodiles have died because people dried up the swamps and marshes where the crocodiles live. An *answer* to this is to set aside land for the crocodiles to live. Poachers have also contributed to the *dilemma* as crocodiles have been desired for their strong, smooth, leathery skins. *In order to* preserve these mighty creatures, people must take care of the crocodiles' environment and help put a stop to the needless shooting of these animals.

Graphic Organizer:

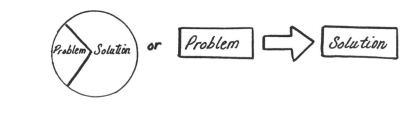

Figure 2.8 Continued

COMPARISON/CONTRAST

Description: The author shows how two or more things or ideas are alike or different.

Signal Words: alike, different, same, but, on the other hand, instead of, however, more-most, likewise, similarly, conversely, unlike, in contrast

Introductory Statements: These are alike; Similarities and differences exist between; There are advantages and disadvantages to

Sample Passage:

Alligators and crocodiles, along with their relatives the caimans and the gavials, are very much *alike*. These crocodilians are reptiles with long snouts, long tails, four short legs, tough skin, and sharp skin. There are some *differences,* however. Gavials have the longest snouts and the most teeth. Some people say that alligators and crocodiles *differ* in the shape of their snouts and the positioning of their teeth. Zookeepers say that crocodiles move faster than alligators and have nastier dispositions.

Graphic Organizer:

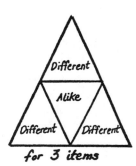

for 2 items

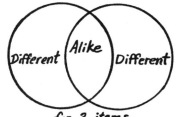

for 3 items

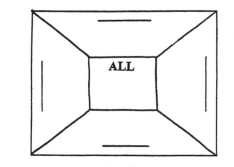

Paragraph Frames

DESCRIPTION: Templates to develop students' ability to write in a variety of forms. Sentence starters that include signal words or phrases, with students having to complete the sentences to form a paragraph that follows one of the expository text structures.

PURPOSE:

Instructional: Teaches the structure of exposition; also used for reviewing and reinforcing content.

Assessment: Assesses what students have learned, as well as their ability to use writing as a tool for learning.

1. defining and labeling the structure being studied,
2. examining model paragraphs and corresponding graphic organizer to locate the important attributes of the pattern,
3. looking for signal words that trigger the recognition of the structure,
4. modeling the writing of a paragraph, using the graphic organizer to help plan and organize the writing, and
5. finding examples of the pattern in other nonfiction writing (Piccolo, 1987).

A variation of this technique is to prepare a graphic organizer for a passage that follows one of the expository structures. The graphic organizer is used to introduce the ideas in the passage to the students, with additional information provided to clarify and expand the content if necessary. The teacher then guides the students in composing their own passages that incorporate the ideas that were presented in the graphic organizer. At this point, the students have not seen the passage, only its organization. Therefore, they naturally focus on the organization of the passage. The students are encouraged to use signal words in order to relate the ideas in their passages. During this process, the teacher draws attention to the kind of structure that is being used, the characteristics of its organization, and the signal words commonly associated with the structure. Once the students have drafted, revised, and edited their own passages, they then compare them to the original text. As a follow-up, other passages with a similar structure can be compared with the original and the student-generated passages (McGee & Richgels, 1992).

The following questions might aid in identifying the patterns:

Description

Is the author telling about something?

Listing

Does the author give a list of things about the topic and tell about each?

Sequence

Does the author give information in a special order or tell how to do or make something?

What is the beginning event?
What other events or steps are included?
What is the final outcome, event, or step?

Cause and Effect

Does the author give reasons why something happened?
What happened as a result of . . . ?

Comparison/Contrast

Does the author show similarities or differences between items discussed in a topic?
What things are being compared?
How are they alike? different?

Problem/Solution

What is the problem? Who had the problem?
Is a problem stated about a topic and some solutions offered?

Question/Answer

What is unknown?
What facts or information does the author provide to answer the question? (adapted from Piccolo, 1987)

These questions might be posted in the classroom, along with the representative graphic organizers. Writing can be used as a tool to help ease the transition from narrative text to content area reading and writing and as a means to teach students about the structure of exposition. Paragraph frames can be used to familiarize students with the ways authors organize their writing in order to inform. Using a cloze procedure, paragraph frames provide students with sentence starters that include specific signal words or phrases. The students' task is to complete the sentences to form a paragraph that follows one of the commonly used organizational patterns in expository writing. Figure 2.9 provides examples of paragraph frames for each of the organizational patterns.

Paragraph frames have an additional benefit as well. They can be used for reviewing and reinforcing specific content. Many at-risk learners have difficulty identifying key information. By using paragraph frames, teachers are able to focus their students' attention on the most relevant material. "Expository paragraph frames provide children with a structured way of using writing as a learning tool. Writing facilitates understanding and retention of material and introduces students to some of the organizational structures authors use to convey information" (Cudd & Roberts, 1989, 403).

By using activities as those just described, teachers can help their students improve their content area learning. Students who are knowledgeable about text structure have better understanding, recall, and retention of what they are learning. So *ask* yourself: What are some *answers* to help students learn from nonfiction? *List* some ways that you can support your students; *describe* them to your students. *Compare and contrast* the activities you might use, *sequence* them in a meaningful way, and note the *effects* on your students' understanding of nonfiction. Therefore, one *solution* to assist your students overcome their *problems* with content area learning is to provide instruction in text structure!

Figure 2.9   Paragraph Frames

Listing
There are several reasons why mankind fears and distrusts crocodiles.
First_____.
Another reason_____.
Also,_____..

Sequence
Scientists have learned a great deal about the reproductive habits of crocodiles.
Before crocodiles mate, _____
_____.
After mating, _____
_____.
Then_____
_____.
Finally_____
_____.

Comparison/Contrast
Alligators and crocodiles are similar in several ways. One similarity is _____
_____.
They are also alike in that _____
_____.
However, there are some differences as well. One way they are not alike is _____
_____.
Another difference is _____.
_____.
Finally, _____.
_____.

Cause and Effect
Crocodile birds are useful to crocodiles for several reasons. One reason is that
_____.
As a result_____
_____.
Therefore, _____.

Problem/Solution
In many parts of the world crocodile numbers are dwindling. This is a problem
because _____.
_____.
Several solutions have been suggested. One answer is _____
_____.
Yet another possible solution is _____
_____.
In order to preserve these mighty creatures, _____
_____.

Fly with Poetry

by Avis Harley

Exposing students to and teaching a variety of poetic forms, some centuries old, some relatively new, is as easy as A-B-C! Author and illustrator Avis Harley has provided a treasure in *Fly with Poetry*, as she introduces many different formats for writing poems, one for each letter of the alphabet (e.g., acrostic, blank verse, and cinquain). Some of the forms are familiar, while others are unique. Want to spice up your writing program by introducing students to rhopalic verse, kyrielles, and utas? Charmingly written and illustrated, the content of each poem is nonfiction and following each poem is a description of the poetic form. Additional poetic forms are provided in the back of the book. Although *Fly with Poetry* is not intended to be a "how-to" book on teaching poetry, it does offer an opportunity to expand children's poetry horizons, especially with nonfiction, and to give them tools to excite their imaginations, express their thoughts creatively, and discover the delight of poetry.

Instructional Activities for the Classroom

1 Chapter-Beginning Activity

Adam Cody, a fourth-grade teacher, read the book *Anno's Mysterious Multiplying Jar* to his students, who then were challenged to produce their own version of the text. Not only were the students able to apply the math concept being featured in the book, but they were able to experience being nonfiction authors.

2 Identifying Text Structures Using the Newspaper or Children's Magazines

Newspaper or magazine headlines, or beginning sentences in articles, can be read to the students, with the students discussing what they might expect the author to say in the article.

3 Using Text Structure as a Writing Activity

Pick any word—for example, *chocolate*, *baseball*, or *lice*—and have the children write some sentences or paragraphs, using a particular organizational pattern, either one of their own choosing or one that you provide. Before undertaking this, it would be beneficial to model this activity, using a topic that is familiar to all of the students. Let's take the word *newspaper* and look at the various prompts that could be provided to encourage writing, using the various text structures.

- What is a newspaper? (Question and Answer Pattern)
- List some of the features and sections found in a newspaper. (Listing)
- Describe one section of the newspaper. (Description)
- Compare and contrast a newspaper and a magazine. (Compare and Contrast)
- Explain how you would place an ad in the Classified Section of the newspaper. (Sequence)
- Although a newspaper is a valuable educational tool, not having enough copies for each student may be a problem. What are some solutions? (Problem and Solution)
- Newspapers are said to have influenced elections. What are some of the effects a newspaper has on elections? (Cause and Effect)

and Beyond
Mathematics

by Irving Adler

If you think mathematics is a boring subject, you are in for a surprise. This book explains mathematics, using lots of great color illustrations by Ron Miller. It also includes fascinating historical background. It covers topics such as the science of numbers and space, polygons, Fibonacci numbers, and much, much more. The important math terms are printed in *italics* so it is easy to identify them. After students enjoy this book, they can create a classroom book with their definitions. Students in Mrs. O'Donnell's fifth grade used fancy scissors to trim the pages of their "Math Talk" book. Each student received a copy for reference.

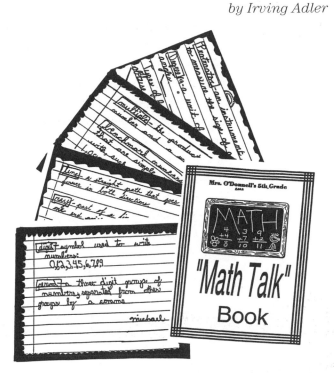

Rescuing Endangered Species

by Jean F. Blashfield

Sometimes we hear or read about how our world, the environment, or certain creatures are in danger. This can cause fear and despair for many children. This book gives a lot of hope because it is filled with interesting information about how some animals have become endangered, and it gives us ideas about how we can help save them from extinction. Every few pages, a feature called "success story" appears. These are true stories about how many species have been saved. Using the Slit book format (directions in Chapter 7), students can research some of the endangered animals in this book and create their own advice book of how humans can help animals.

3

Reading Nonfiction

Before students can effectively read and write nonfiction independently, they must be given ample opportunities to listen to it being read out loud, discuss its unique features, observe demonstrations of strategies that will enhance their success with this genre, and become familiarized with the range of nonfiction materials. Students need to be cognizant of the purposes for reading nonfiction, and how these materials are researched, organized, and written. This portion of

Inspired by Harriet Tubman by Dana Rau

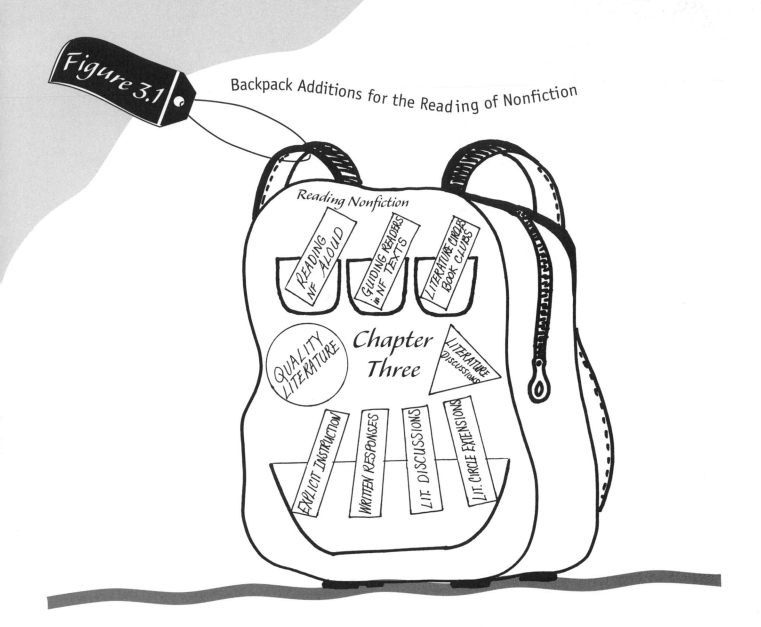

Figure 3.1 Backpack Additions for the Reading of Nonfiction

Reading Nonfiction

READING NF ALOUD

GUIDING READERS in NF TEXTS

LITERATURE CIRCLES/ BOOK CLUBS

QUALITY LITERATURE

Chapter Three

LITERATURE DISCUSSIONS

EXPLICIT INSTRUCTION

WRITTEN RESPONSES

LIT. DISCUSSIONS

LIT. CIRCLE EXTENSIONS

your journey into nonfiction allows you to explore the reading of nonfiction. It provides information on the benefits and tips of reading nonfiction aloud, on browsing through nonfiction texts to discover their attributes, and on using literature circles or book clubs with nonfiction materials. Necessary items for your nonfiction exploration into the reading of nonfiction can be seen in Figure 3.1

READING NONFICTION ALOUD

Reading to children has generally been associated with stories, both in the home and in the classroom, and is beneficial to building background knowledge, familiarity with the structure of narrative text, and expanding vocabulary, as well as being a very pleasurable activity. However, reading aloud should not be relegated to story-like books, because reading nonfiction aloud to students likewise has many benefits. Reading nonfiction aloud introduces students to the variety of nonfiction texts and supports them in thinking about these texts. Some of the benefits of reading nonfiction aloud can be seen in Figure 3.2.

Figure 3.2	Benefits of Reading Nonfiction Aloud

Reading aloud:

- Introduces and exposes students to the variety of types of nonfiction materials.
- Exposes students to topics of learning and builds background knowledge.
- Builds and expands vocabulary.
- Familiarizes students with expository text structures.
- Shows students how nonfiction texts are written and organized.
- Allows teachers to think aloud, e.g., verbalize their thought and reading processes as they read.
- Permits teachers to model strategies.
- Gives all students access to the same information despite reading ability.
- Removes or decreases student anxiety about the content areas, and replaces it with a curiosity about content area topics.
- Allows students to gain valuable social experiences through the ensuing discussions and dialogues in the shared reading of content area texts.
- Provides avenues to tap into undiscovered interests.
- Encourages students to make intertextual connections.
- Can provide innovative introductions to units of study.
- Can act as a bridge to more complicated texts.
- Serves as a source for challenging, provocative discussions.
- Offers a variation for instructional delivery.
- Helps build a literate community in the classroom.

Sources: From Leal, 1996; Routman, 200; Buehl, 2001; Raphael, Kehus, & Damphousse, 2001.

Reading aloud shows students how nonfiction texts are organized and written, and gives teachers opportunities to demonstrate how to successfully read nonfiction texts using *think-alouds*. Teachers can think aloud as they read, pointing out both the access and visual features in the text, and encourage students to discuss what they notice in the reading. By exposing students to nonfiction authors and their styles of writing, students can become familiar with the nature of expository text and with the kinds of thinking nonfiction authors use. "Reading aloud poetry, humorous stories, newspapers, announcements, letters—anything that bridges to everyday life—can stimulate student thinking, provide an overview of the functions of language, and help motivate students to enjoy and learn about new areas of interest" (Leal, 1996, 156).

In addition to giving students insights into the teacher's reading processes and the features that comprise nonfiction texts, teachers can also encourage students to talk about what they heard, wonder about the contents, and raise questions. After some read-alouds, teachers can model their own responses to the text (Figure 3.3) and invite students to share their thoughts. By responding to texts in a variety of ways, teachers are demonstrating that different interpretations, different ways to respond, are not only appropriate but welcome.

Figure 3.3	Sample Teacher Responses to Nonfiction Materials

Title: *The Year with Grandma Moses* by W. Nikola-Lisa
Summary: This stunning picture book celebrates an important American artist. The author's lyrical text is complemented by excepts from Grandma Moses's memoirs, and illustrations by the folk artist herself.
Response: (Personal Connection and Author's Craft) Living in Grandma Moses country in upstate New York makes this book all the more meaningful and relevant, since the landscapes in my own backyard are the very ones that inspired the legendary artist. Not only does this book captivate the reader with its folk art paintings, but the paintings are given a deeper meaning when coupled with the excerpts from Grandma Moses's memoirs. The seasons are described simply, yet elegantly, through the eyes and writing of Grandma Moses, thereby creating a stunning autobiographical picture book.

Title: *A Is for America* by Devin Scillan
Summary: Through delightful verse, accompanied with additional information in expository text, this American alphabet treats readers to a tribute of the United States. The illustrations include replicas of postcards, photographs, maps, artwork, and other artifacts that represent the area being visited.
Response: (Literary Connections) This tribute to America reminds me of another patriotic book - *The Flag We Love* by Pam Munoz Ryan. Both books make the readers proud to be Americans, and give the readers food for thought as to why this country is as beautiful as it is. Both books use poetic language to provide the contents, and both expand upon the primary text with additional factual information provided in the margins or at the bottom of the page. Using both poetry and a more typical expository style of writing, the authors give the readers insights into what makes this country a great place to live and a renewed appreciation of being an American.

Title: *The Mary Celeste: An Unsolved Mystery from History* by Jane Yolen and Heidi Yolen Stemple

Summary: An unsolved mystery from history is chronicled as the captain, crew, and passengers of the *Mary Celeste* vanish. Readers can become detectives as they read this true story, study the clues, and try to solve the fate of this ship.
Response: (I Wonder—Questioning—done in a letter format)

Dear Jane Yolen:
After I read your book, *The Mary Celeste: An Unsolved Mystery from History*, I had lots of questions to ask you. Here they are:

* Where did you first learn about the Mary Celeste and its disappearance at sea?
* Why did you write a book about it?
* In addition to the story, you add a lot of factual information and vocabulary definitions in boxes all over the pages. What made you think of doing this?
* Why did your daughter help you write this book?
* Was there a lot of information about the Mary Celeste?
* Where did you find your information?
* Which theory do you think is the right one to explain how the ship disappeared?

Your book made me do lots of "wonder"ings—just like any good mystery.

Your friend,

Kathy

As with narrative text, nonfiction should be read aloud frequently. An advantage to using nonfiction is that it does not have to be read in its entirety. In addition, there are many types of nonfiction that vary in scope as well as length. As with fiction, there are suggestions that will make the read-aloud time more effective.

Suggestions for Effective Nonfiction Read-Alouds

- Select nonfiction materials that you are interested in and ones that will captivate your students' interest and enthusiasm.
- Utilize a variety of nonfiction materials in your read-aloud sessions.
- Prepare for the read-aloud by reading the selection prior to reading it to the students.
- Provide a meaningful, purposeful introduction to the selection before reading aloud (e.g., discussing the author, style of writing, the content, key vocabulary, organization of the text, etc.).
- Depending on your purpose, decide whether to read the entire text, read only parts of the book, or read the text out of order.
- Read with expression, so that, through your intonation and phrasing, students can get the message of what is being read.
- Point out the relevant access and visual features as you read, and explain their purposes.
- Think aloud as you read; verbalize your reading process and the strategies you are using to make sense of the text.
- Encourage discussions, questions, and comments as you read so that you can spark a dialogue.
- Give students enough time to absorb and process what they are hearing and learning.
- Occasionally, use text sets in your read-alouds, for example, groups or pairs of books on the same topic to allow students to compare or contrast the information, and to note how different authors use and interpret similar information. (Routman, 2000; Buehl, 2001)

Strategy AT A Glance

Interactive Read-Alouds

DESCRIPTION: Involves reading text aloud, along with dialogue, questioning, and discussion with the students. Through this guided technique, students are able to share knowledge with one another.

PURPOSE:

Instructional: Assists students in constructing meaning, provides opportunities for demonstrations of comprehension strategies, and enhances enjoyment of nonfiction.

Assessment: Provides an indication of students' background knowledge, their ability to attend and construct meaning, and their level of understanding.

Strategy AT A Glance

Say Something

DESCRIPTION: An interactive format for listening to nonfiction. Partner-reading with one student reading aloud while the other listens, followed by the listener commenting on what was read. The roles are then switched and the process repeated.

PURPOSE:

Instruction: Stimulates conversation about text, facilitates the making of connections, provides opportunities to resolve confusions, and lets students practice reading complex text orally.

Assessment: Gives insights into students' handling of expository text, noting the kinds of miscues made, along with self-correction abilities, and students' ability to make connections and work through confusions and difficulties in texts.

Teachers may vary how and why they read aloud to their students. They may read straight through the text, focusing on reading for pleasure and entertainment. They may read aloud to provide information, with the teacher doing the oral reading with little or no discussion. There also may be read-aloud sessions in which the students are asked to respond, either orally or in writing. Teachers also could engage in shared readings of the texts, which focus on reading for meaning, as in *interactive read-alouds*.

An interactive read-aloud is an instructional practice that involves reading text aloud, along with dialogue and discussion to assist students in constructing meaning (Barrentine, 1996; Sadler, 2001; Hoyt, 2002). Discussions have been recognized as a way to enhance understanding of text. Through discussion, students can learn to construct meaning from those who are more experienced than they (frequently the teachers), as they are guided through the text. They can also gain from hearing the insights of their classmates, as well as their classmates' different perspectives and viewpoints (Peterson & Eeds,

Strategy AT A Glance

Readers' Theater

DESCRIPTION: A dramatic activity in which readers present and interpret a piece of text primarily using their voices, with minimal body movement.

PURPOSE:

Instructional: Allows students to practice fluent oral reading and interpret nonfiction, enhances motivation, facilitates the learning of content material.

Assessment: Provides insights into students' oral reading behaviors and self-correction abilities, knowledge of subject matter, and ability to interpret what they are reading.

1990; Roser & Martinez, 1995). Conversations about what is being read allow children to construct meanings beyond what they could construct by themselves. In addition to helping students enhance their comprehension of text, interactive read-alouds can

- promote familiarity with a topic in nonfiction,
- enhance the enjoyment of nonfiction,
- facilitate positive social interactions, and
- provide opportunities for demonstrations and practice of comprehension strategies (Barrentine, 1996).

Interactive read-alouds encourage dialogue between teachers and students and among the students themselves. Rather than read the entire text without feedback from the students, the teacher reads the text interactively. Before and during the reading, the teacher encourages the students to make predictions, poses thoughtful questions, and uses the visual and access features of nonfiction text while reading. The students respond to the invitations for dialogue and discussion, and also make spontaneous comments throughout the session. After reading, the students and the teacher summarize their discussions, make connections to prior learning and knowledge, and perhaps make plans for gaining further information about what was learned and discussed.

Teachers are not the only ones who could or should be reading aloud using nonfiction. Students can also share their research, interesting facts, memorable passages, and the like. They can also participate in a strategy, *Say Something*. Students are paired, with one student reading aloud (a paragraph, a passage, etc.) while the other follows along and listens. When the reader has finished, the listener has to *say something* about what was read. He or she could comment on the content, make a prediction, pose questions, identify areas that are confusing, or make connections to their own lives, to other texts, and so on. The partners then switch roles and repeat the process. This strategy also provides an interactive format for listening to nonfiction, and gives students an opportunity to practice oral reading with more complex text. It stimulates conversation about what is being read, encourages students to make connections, and gives them opportunities to work on areas that are confusing or difficult (Buehl, 2001).

Another opportunity to use oral reading in the nonfiction classroom is the use of *Readers' Theater*. Readers' Theater is a dramatic activity in which readers present and interpret a piece of literature primarily using their voices, with minimal body movement. Readers' Theater is a presentation of texts that are dramatically and expressively read aloud by several readers. It is essentially a re-creation of what has been read using vocal expression. When participating in Readers' Theater, students read aloud from scripts, based on literature or other reading materials. Although Readers' Theater is part theater and part oral interpretation, it does not require special training in drama, elaborate props, or costumes. There is a script, but all the information is revealed by the speaking parts of both the narrator and the characters (as would be in the case of historical fiction or biographies) or the students who are presenting key information about the topic being scripted in more factual nonfiction texts.

Readers' Theater has primarily been utilized with narrative texts. However, it can also be an innovative, exciting approach to content area reading and study. By combining nonfiction trade books with Readers' Theater, teachers can incorporate content area instruction with the dynamic and interactive process of Readers' Theater.

Both teachers and students can select nonfiction books or parts of these books to adapt for Readers' Theater. Some books lend themselves more to this activity than do others. Nonfiction books that contain dialogue—for example, *The Magic Schoolbus* series—and nonfiction books dealing with social studies concepts, work wonderfully. Shorter informational books can likewise be effective across the grades due to their simplicity and focus, for example, the science books by Seymour Simon. The process for writing the scripts is similar to that for narrative text, with the students either simply breaking the text into parts or elaborating on the original text to create their own versions. An introduction might be included, as well as a postscript, to bring closure to the activity.

When students participate in developing scripts for Readers' Theater, they become involved in critical reading and revising. When they have completed the process, they frequently are motivated to read the entire text, read other books or articles by the author, or explore the topic even further.

Experiencing nonfiction books through Readers' Theater "gives the words on the page a voice, and the students in the classroom an active role in internalizing and interpreting new knowledge" (Young & Vardell, 1993, 405). Participating in the process and in the performance of Readers' Theater is an effective vehicle for content area learning and also becomes a source of personal pride and accomplishment for the students.

By using such strategies and activities as Say Something and Readers' Theater, students are given opportunities to practice reading orally and fluently with material that may be better understood when heard. Students are also involved in nonthreatening oral reading experiences (Buehl, 2001).

Reading aloud has its rightful place as an essential component to a balanced literacy program, which must include the reading of a variety of genres. Nonfiction materials must be shared, alongside narrative texts, as materials for read-alouds, because students need to be exposed to expository text for information, for familiarity with its format and organizational features, and for pure enjoyment. The more familiar students become with different books and text structures, the more likely they are to use these books confidently and suc-

Strategy AT A *Glance*

Previewing and Overviewing

DESCRIPTION: An orientation and introduction for text that is to be read. A frontloading technique that guides students through text and points out the features of the text that warrant special attention.

PURPOSE:

Instruction: Helps prepare students for the reading and learning of text, assists in determining what's important and not important, and helps students to make and confirm predictions while reading.

Assessment: Assesses students' prior knowledge, knowledge about text structure, and areas that might be problematic.

Try This

Previewing Nonfiction Texts

Prepare a guide to assist students with previewing or overviewing nonfiction materials. Put the students in small groups or in pairs, and give them a designated amount of time (e.g., 5–10 minutes) to look over the materials and fill in the guide. The guide could include such items as these:

- Text/chapter topic
- Main ideas of the headings and subheadings
- Use of access or visual features
- What they already know about the subject or topic
- Questions they might have

cessfully. Teachers need to expand their students' horizons by reading aloud from both narrative and expository texts and provide opportunities for rich, interesting dialogues and discussions (Leal, 1996).

GUIDING READERS THROUGH NONFICTION TEXT: PREVIEWING AND OVERVIEWING

It does not matter whether the nonfiction material is a trade or a text book, it is imperative that students learn how to read nonfiction, and use their time and effort reading nonfiction effectively. This can be accomplished by previewing or overviewing the text or taking the students through chapter tours (Harvey, 1998; Booth, 1998; Harvey & Goudvis, 2000; Routman, 2003; Robb, 2003). A guided tour or orientation to the text gives readers valuable introductions as to what is to be read and learned, gives them insights into what is interesting or important, and provides an overall foundation for understanding. These frontloading techniques guide or talk the students through a text or chapter and point out the features of the text that warrant special attention. They are a form of skimming and scanning the text before reading. These overviews save students time, help them to determine what is important in the text, and condition them to make and confirm predictions while reading.

In conducting previews or overviews, teachers should do the following:

- Activate prior knowledge.
- Call attention to the text features and various visual formats.
- Discuss text structure (e.g., cause/effect, comparison/contrast, etc.).
- Have students scan the material.
- Determine what is important and needs careful attention (the main ideas and themes).
- Decide what can be ignored.
- Point out important words (highlighted, bolded, italicized), sidebars, and insets.
- Peruse chapter questions (if applicable) and bibliographic information.

These overviews can be conducted orally, in their entirety or in part, or can be presented as study/chapter guides to be completed either individually by the students or collaboratively in pairs or small groups. By providing students with

I Wonder, I'm Curious About

After introducing or previewing the nonfiction text to be read or shared, students could respond to such prompts as *I wonder, I'm curious about*. . . . Their wonder statements and questions could be motivational for the learning that is to follow or can serve as inspirations for inquiry and further research.

proper frontloading activities, students can learn to become frontloaders when they are reading. By providing expert guides while reading nonfiction, students are alerted to what is most important in the text and can make effective use of the reading/learning aids that are provided in the text.

There are other introductory activities and strategies that can be undertaken prior to delving into expository materials. These include K-W-L and Anticipation/Reaction Guides. These are discussed in Chapter 4, as effective strategies to use when reading nonfiction texts.

LITERATURE CIRCLES/BOOK CLUBS AND NONFICTION

Classrooms and reading instruction are changing, and many teachers are choosing literature-based reading programs instead of traditional basal reading programs, or they are using the selections in the basal readers as the basis for literature circles. Literature circles, sometimes referred to as literature response groups or book clubs, are a way to structure reading instruction by forming small, temporary groups of students who meet regularly to read, discuss, share, and interpret the reading texts and materials they are reading or have read. These groups are generally determined by book choices, are heterogeneous in nature, and include a wide range of ability levels and interests.

Although there is a distinction among some professionals between literature circles (Schlick Noe & Johnson, 1999; Campbell Hill & Schlick Noe, 2001; Daniels, 2002) and book clubs (Raphael et al., 1997; Raphael, Kehus, & Damphousse, 2001), these terms will be used interchangeably in this resource guide.

Literature Circles/Book Clubs

DESCRIPTION: Small, temporary groups of students who meet to read, discuss, share, and interpret texts.

PURPOSE:

Instructional: Engages students in real conversations about text, facilitates deeper understanding of what is being read, encourages various responses to text, and exposes students to multiple perspectives.

Assessment: Provides information about students' depth of understanding and their ability to write about and talk about text.

A New England Scrapbook: A Journey through Poetry, Prose, and Pictures

by Loretta Krupinski

Here's a book that belongs in a New England Chamber of Commerce! New England is explored through things that make up the unique features of this region (e.g., old stone walls, maple syrup, lobster, cranberries, rocky shores, etc.). The author has combined beautiful and charming paintings, poems, and prose and created a scrapbook of the sights, the sounds, and the sensations found in New England.

Literature circles can take many forms, and have many variations, but all are student-centered with such key elements as student responsibility and personal response to text. Literature circles work best if teachers provide sufficient structure and scaffolding while still giving students enough responsibility and freedom to explore texts.

Why use literature circles? The many benefits of using literature circles include the following:

- They promote a love for books and positive attitudes about reading.
- Students of all ability levels can engage in real conversations about books.
- Students interact with texts on a deeper level as they engage in discussions that lead to inquiry and critical thinking.
- Students interact and collaborate as they construct meaning from text.
- Students respond to texts in a variety of ways.
- Students are exposed to multiple perspectives from the commonly discussed literature.
- Understanding of text is increased when book talk on all levels is encouraged.
- Shared decision making is enhanced as students contribute to the drafting of procedural and managerial aspects of literature circles, including assuming responsibility for the running of the groups.
- Students feel a sense of ownership and empowerment regarding their own literacy development.
- Students learn to set goals, identify ways to achieve these goals, and develop lifelong literacy habits.
- The classroom is transformed into a literate community. (Owens, 1995; Booth, 1998; Raphael, Kehus, & Damphousse, 2001; Daniels, 2002; Campbell Hill & Schlick Noe, 2001)

At the heart of literature circles is the collaboration that takes place among the students as they construct meaning together and reshape and increase their understanding of text. Literature circles help students gain deeper understanding of what they are reading through guided, structured discussions and through their written or artistic responses (Schlick & Johnson, 1999). The community of learners that results from the use of literature circles makes students feel safe and important, giving them a sense of belonging and allowing them to assume ownership of their own learning.

Key Features for Effective Literature Circles or Book Clubs

There are several variations, as mentioned previously, of this model of delivering reading instruction. However, there are commonalities that are essential to all the variations, which include the use of quality reading materials; explicit instruction; small, student-led discussion groups; and whole-class discussions and activities.

Quality Nonfiction Literature and Reading Materials   The success of any literature circle or book club depends on the selection of appropriate reading texts, and this is true for both narrative and expository texts. As was discussed previously, teachers should consider accuracy, clarity, organization, design, and style when selecting nonfiction. Also to be considered are visual appeal, intriguing presentation of the material, and topics that are interesting and relevant to the students. To ensure that literature circles are effective, teachers should make sure that the selected pieces of nonfiction materials promote discussion, facilitate the making of personal or textual connections, and provide opportunities for in-depth learning (Raphael, Kehus, & Damphousse, 2001). Readability of the selections should be considered, or supports need to be in place to assist readers who may have difficulty reading and comprehending the text. It is important that all students have an opportunity to explore issues in nonfiction texts, and this can be accomplished with partner reading, materials placed on tape, explicit instruction of strategies, and so forth.

To locate quality literature and nonfiction materials, teachers can consult book reviews and book lists in professional magazines, review notable award-winning trade books (e.g., Orbis Pictus Award for Outstanding Nonfiction for Children, Robert F. Sibert Informational Book Award, Outstanding Science Tradebooks for Children, etc.), talk with colleagues, obtain suggestions from the school or public librarian, and so forth. In addition, literature circles can utilize such timely materials as articles in the newspaper or magazines and weekly or monthly periodicals. A listing of some suggested nonfiction titles can be found at the back of this book.

Explicit Instruction   For students to succeed with literature circles, teachers must provide explicit instruction in

- procedural and managerial issues,
- the use of reading strategies and skills,
- the use of writing as a means to enhance discussion and higher level thinking, and
- how to participate in discussion groups, both small group and whole class.

This instruction often occurs during mini-lessons that introduce or conclude the workshop session (sometimes referred to as *community share*), in individual conferences with students, or even in the small group discussions when needed. Some mini-lessons and community share activities that may be demonstrated can be seen in Figure 3.4.

It is essential that students be thoroughly aware of and comfortable with the procedures for literature circles and with strategies they can call on if their

Figure 3.4   Mini-Lessons for Literature Circles

Procedural Mini-Lessons
- conducting effective discussions
- choosing books or other nonfiction materials
- ways to respond to nonfiction
- setting up and using reading journals or reading logs
- developing effective conversational skills
- what to do if help is needed with a passage that is confusing
- what to do during literature time (e.g., reading, responding, sharing, discussing), what to do when others are in literature circles
- assessing participation (students' own and their peers') in discussion groups

Strategies/Skills Mini-Lessons
- characteristics of nonfiction
- types of nonfiction materials
- how to read nonfiction
- how to use the visual and access features present in nonfiction
- strategies to use when encountering unknown words
- strategies to use when encountering difficulty in making meaning
- determining what is important
- summarizing
- distinguishing between fact and opinion
- documenting an opinion or position
- determining the author's purpose
- ways to self-monitor while they read (metacognition)

Author's/Illustrator's Craft Mini-Lessons
- formats authors use to present information
- visual and access features
- use of vivid language in nonfiction
- use of illustrations, photographs, etc., and placement to create an effect and to support the text
- various writing styles authors use
- openings and conclusions used in nonfiction texts

Sources: From Redman, 1995; Booth, 1998; Schlick & Johnson, 1999; & Robb, 2000.

reading should break down. The strategies can be introduced, discussed, modeled, and placed on a chart for reference. The time devoted to procedural and strategy lessons should be limited, because it is best to use the majority of the time for reading and responding to texts. However, some mini-lessons, such as procedural ones, may take more time at the beginning of the year when the literature workshop is being introduced.

The other features that compose effective literature circles—student discussions and responding to text—are addressed separately in subsequent sections.

Try This

Getting to Know You

Because the success of literature circles depends on how students interact, teachers might want to spend time at the beginning of the school year having the students get to know one another. A class quilt could be constructed, with each child contributing a quilt block. On each quilt block could be an illustration or photograph of the student, surrounded by information about that student. The quilt block could be partitioned into sections for students to include such information as interests, family, pets, likes, dislikes, goals, things they are good at, favorite books or movies, and so on. An example of a quilt block can be seen in Figure 3.5.

The squares could be "pieced" together on poster board, arranged on a bulletin board with strips of ribbon strategically placed to give a quiltlike effect, or placed in interlocking plastic bags for a plastic bag quilt (directions are provided in Chapter 7).

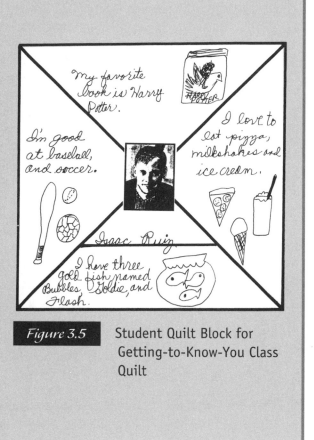

Figure 3.5 Student Quilt Block for Getting-to-Know-You Class Quilt

Establishing Literature Circles Literature workshops typically consist of several components, including community share, independent silent reading, and literature circles, which are the student-led discussion groups. Community share is a whole-class meeting that provides students and teachers with a context for bringing ideas, insights, confusions, and the like, to the attention of the whole class. Community share can occur as an introductory activity or can conclude the session. If used to introduce the session, teachers can use this time to

- provide explicit instruction of comprehension strategies;
- introduce new ideas, skills, and "repair" strategies;
- build background knowledge for the reading that is to occur;
- review what has happened in subsequent lessons;
- draw attention to theme-related issues in the reading;
- instruct students in new ways of responding to literature or discussing their reading; and
- raise questions that might be answered in the next reading of the text (Raphael et al., 1997).

In a community share that follows the book club or literature circle (the time when the students discuss what they have read), students share the issues that arose during their book club discussions. Interesting insights might be shared, as well as unanswered questions. Students might want to discuss interesting vocabulary words, the author's craft, or areas that might have caused confusion. Teachers might want to assist the students in making connections with what they have read with other texts or with their own experiences. Community share helps promote a sense of community in the classroom, allowing students to gain confidence and to get to know one another.

Once the introductory community share has concluded, students engage in independent silent reading. Depending on the teacher's purpose, the entire class or small groups of students might be reading the same text, or they may be reading text sets, books that are related by concept, theme, genre, or author. Student choice is a key element of literature circles when narrative text is used. Teachers give book talks on several book choices, with the students indicating their preferences. The groups are then formed, based on the student choices. This technique of forming groups and using several texts simultaneously can work with nonfiction materials as well, again depending on the purpose and objectives for reading the texts. For example, teachers might offer several choices when studying America the Beautiful, insects, and Ancient Egypt, or when focusing on a particular genre, such as the biography. Examples of these text sets can be seen in Figure 3.6.

Teachers might also want everyone to read the same text occasionally, especially when first establishing literature circles. There might also be a significant piece of text that lends itself to excellent discussions or is particularly relevant to specific instructional objectives. While students are reading their texts, they are taking notes, responding to prompts, and noting key vocabulary, the author's writing style, and so forth, in preparation for the book club discussions that will follow the reading.

When it is time to read the text independently, teachers have traditionally assigned whatever has to be read, but literature workshops encourage student choice whenever possible. First, students were able to choose a book to read (within a range provided by the teacher); now, they can choose how much to read. The students together decide on how many pages or chapters to read by the next literature circle time. If the students are too ambitious and assign themselves an unrealistic goal, the teacher may step in and make a suggestion to reduce the number of pages. Likewise, if the students do not assign enough pages, the teacher can make suggestions. It is important that the students read the assigned pages in preparation for the next meeting.

Once students are engaged in the reading of their texts, they frequently are also writing in response journals in preparation for the literature circle that will follow. At the very heart of the program are the students' small group discussions—the literature circle or book club. Teachers have found that groups comprising four to five children are the most effective (Owens, 1995; Daniels, 2002). Students who are reading the same text gather together in a group to discuss, read, and share responses. Here students have an opportunity to engage in real conversations about books, sharing their personal responses. Because writing and discussion serve such important roles in this model of instructional delivery, these topics are addressed separately later in this chapter.

Literature circles are designed to be used flexibly, allowing teachers to spend as much, or as little, time as they wish on each component. One day, teachers may want to devote more time to community share to develop better

Figure 3.6	Text Sets

America the Beautiful
- *A Flag for Our Country* by Eve Spencer
- *Red, White, Blue, and Uncle Who?: The Story Behind Some of America's Patriotic Symbols* by Teresa Bateman
- *This Land Is Your Land* by Woodie Guthrie
- *Shh! We're Writing the Constitution* by Jean Fritz
- *The United States from A to Z* by Bobbie Kalman

Insects
- *The Icky Bug Alphabet Book* by Jerry Pallotta
- *Butterflies: Pollinators and Nectar Sippers* by Adele Richardson
- *How to Hide a Butterfly and Other Insects* by Ruth Heller
- *It's a Bug's World: A Directory of Awesome Insects* by Paul Wray
- *Flies Taste with Their Feet: Weird Facts About Insects* by Melvin Berger

Ancient Egypt
- *Who Built the Pyramid?* By Meredith Hooper
- *You Wouldn't Want to Be an Egyptian Mummy! Disgusting Things You'd Rather Not Know* by David Stewart
- *Egyptian News* by Scott Steedman
- *Mummies, Bones, & Body Parts* by Charlotte Wilcox
- *Egyptians* by Gillian Chapman

Biographies
- *Martin Luther King, Jr.* by Rosemary Bray
- *Thomas Jefferson: A Picture Book Biography* by James Giblin
- *They Shall Be Heard: Susan B. Anthony and Elizabeth Cady Stanton* by Kate Connell
- *Amelia Earhart: Flying for Adventure* by Mary Wade
- *Harriet Tubman* by Dana Rau

discussion techniques, while on another day, students may be given additional time to engage in extended writing activities. The flexibility that literature circles provide allows teachers to design their reading curriculum according to their objectives or the students' needs or interests.

Introducing Literature Circles   Literature circles need time to become established, especially if students are unfamiliar with the procedures and activities. Introducing, explaining, and demonstrating the concept of literature circles and modeling effective questioning and discussion techniques ensure that students will have successful experiences with this means of instructional delivery.

There are several ways of introducing the concept of literature circles to students. If there are older students in the school who are already familiar with literature circles, they could come into the classroom and demonstrate using a fish bowl technique. In this technique, the experienced students sit in an inner circle and discuss and respond to what they have been reading, just as they typ-

Strategy
AT A *Glance*

Fish Bowl

DESCRIPTION: Technique used for modeling activities or strategies, in which one group of students sits in the inner circle and discusses what they are learning, while other students sit in an outer circle and observe what is occurring.

PURPOSE:

Instructional: To model or provide a demonstration of a strategy.

Assessment: Allows teachers to monitor and determine the depth of understanding of what is being discussed.

ically would in their own literature circles. Those students being introduced to the technique sit in an outer circle (thus, the fish bowl name), watching the students model a way that literature circles can be conducted. After the fish bowl session, questions could be entertained, and charts could be constructed on effective ways to conduct a discussion, giving the observers and the literature circle participants an opportunity to debrief, discuss what occurred, answer questions, and so forth. A *freeze* feature could be added to the fish bowl, which allows anyone to halt the action to ask a question, make a comment, or share an observation.

If possible, videotapes of students engaged in literature circles could be shown and the elements of the procedure discussed. If videotapes are not available during the first year of implementation, it is suggested that once students become familiar with the concept and are adept at conducting discussions, they could be videotaped for use in subsequent years. Students also could visit other classrooms in which literature circles are working and report back to their classmates what they observed and learned.

Picture books or short nonfiction materials, such as articles in the newspaper or in *Time for Kids,* can be used when introducing literature circles, with everyone listening to or reading the same text. Teachers can model various ways to respond to texts during their read-aloud sessions or during mini-lessons. They could demonstrate how they record their responses using Post-its®, reading logs, or worksheets prepared for responding to texts. A collection of prompts or questions can be undertaken and distributed to the students or placed in a prominent place in the classroom. The class can also collaboratively brainstorm what makes for a good discussion (and/or a bad discussion), with their contributions recorded on a chart for reference and for future modification, if need be.

To facilitate the responding to and discussing of texts, students can be assigned certain roles when participating in discussion groups (Daniels, 2002). The roles and accompanying role sheets can be incorporated into the regular literature circle model itself or used temporarily until the discussion groups are performing well. These role sheets, which serve as support devices, help the students construct their own responses, ideas, and questions. There are individual role sheets for each of the assigned roles. Each sheet briefly describes the task and provides prompts for helping the students discover and record the desired information. These roles include the following:

- *Questioner:*　The questioner has the responsibility of constructing good discussion questions, soliciting contributions from other members, and assisting in the analysis of the text. Questioners can seek to clarify or understand the text, or they may challenge or critique the members' contributions.
- *Literary Luminary/Passage Maker:*　The literary luminary highlights memorable, important sections of the text to enjoy, analyze, reread, or share aloud.
- *Connector:*　The connector helps members make real-world connections with the text, helping the readers connect their experiences, thoughts, and feelings to the literature.
- *Illustrator:*　The illustrator invites graphic, nonlinguistic responses to the text. The job of the illustrator is to draw some kind of picture related to the reading, for example, a sketch, diagram, cartoon, or flow chart.

There can be other assigned roles as well, depending on the number of participants in the literature circle and the desired purpose. These include summarizer (who prepares a brief summary of the reading), vocabulary enricher (who is on the lookout for important words), and researcher (who digs up background information on any topic related to the book). All of the task roles are designed to support collaborative learning by offering students clearly defined, interlocking responsibilities. Similar to bicycle training wheels, role sheets are temporary devices, used only as long as they are needed. If used too long, discussion can become too mechanical and rote, stifling the dynamics of effective peer-led discussion groups.

If preferred, teachers can substitute a more inclusive form that invites readers to respond in multiple ways to the reading materials. An example of such a sheet (Nonfiction Discussion Sheet) that helps set reading purposes and encourages readers to notice, visualize, wonder, and make connections can be seen in Figure 3.7 (Daniels, 2002).

Written Responses to Text　Literature circles welcome, celebrate, and build on the students' responses to what they are reading or have read (Daniels, 2002), and this is accomplished through both written response and discussions. In order to utilize writing effectively and to involve students in meaningful literacy experiences, teachers should ensure that the written responses

- develop naturally from the contents of the texts being read,
- encourage the students to revisit and reexamine the text,
- demonstrate what the students have learned from their reading,
- deepen students understanding, and
- foster connections to the students' lives, the outside world, and other texts, (Routman, 2000).

Students should be asked to respond to their reading using open-ended techniques, thereby improving both their writing and critical thinking skills. Used wisely, written responses are a means for students to record their personal reactions and reflections and pose their questions, along with helping them organize their thoughts. In addition, written responses can provide the foundation for

Figure 3.7   Nonfiction Discussion Sheet

Name _____

Title of reading _____   Author _____

While you are reading or after you have finished reading, please prepare for the group meeting by doing the following:

Connections: What personal connections did you make with the text? Did it remind you of past experiences, people, or events in your life? Did it make you think of anything happening in the news, around school, or in other material you have read?

Discussion questions: Jot down a few questions you would like to discuss with your group. They could be questions that came to your mind while reading, questions you'd like to ask the author, questions you'd like to investigate, or any other questions you think the group might like to discuss.

Passages: Mark some lines or sections in the text that caught your attention—sections that somehow "jumped out" at you as you read. These might be passages that seem especially important, puzzling, beautiful, strange, well written, controversial, or striking in some other way. Be ready to read these aloud to the group or to ask someone else to read them.

Illustration: On the back of this sheet, quickly sketch a picture related to your reading. This can be a drawing, cartoon, diagram, flowchart—whatever. You can draw a picture of something that's especially talked about in the text or something from your own experience or feelings, something the reading made you think about. Be ready to show your picture to your group and talk about it.

Source: Reprinted from *Literature Circles: Voice and Choice in Book Clubs and Reading Groups* by Harvey Daniels (2002).

Fabric-Covered Response Logs

Although response logs can be prepared by stapling sheets of paper together and decorating a cover, some teachers prefer to have their students make (if students are old enough; if not, volunteers can make) fabric-covered response logs. All it takes is a marble composition book, some fabric, and fabric glue. Directions for constructing fabric-covered journals can be seen in Figure 3.8.

Figure 3.8 Directions for Making a Fabric-Covered Journal

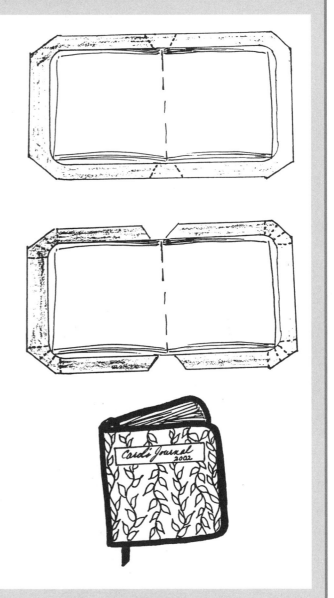

1. Cut two pieces of tag board *slightly smaller* than the inside front and back covers of the composition book. Cut a ribbon twice the length of the spine. Set these aside.

2. Lay the fabric print side down and place the open composition book on it. Cut the fabric 1 1/2" inches larger than the open book on all four sides. Clip off the corners.

3. Cut two diagonal slits, toward the spine, at the top and bottom of the book. Put glue on the two small pieces, *fold them inward,* and run a thin strip of glue along the line where the spine rests.

4. At each corner cut slits at right angles to the book. Then make two more slits between them at each corner. This allows fabric to fold over the curved corners of the composition book smoothly.

5. Put a *small* amount of glue on all corner pieces and fold them over the book. Then put glue on the remaining edges of the fabric and fold them over the book.

6. Next take the piece of ribbon and glue it next to the pages on the *inside* of the back cover. This will be folded over to act as a place marker. Finally, glue the tag board pieces (step 1) to cover the cut edges of the fabric inside the front and back covers.

the "grand conversations" that ensue during book clubs, when students reflect on and discuss what they have been reading (Eeds & Wells, 1989).

When engaging their students in written responses, teachers generally use reading response logs or journals. Because students initially may have difficulty when confronting the blank page in their response journals, teachers must show students how to write effective journal entries. Teachers should first introduce the journals and discuss their purposes, and then model a variety of response options. Students then must be given time to practice writing in their journals, followed by debriefing, reflecting, and assessing the process (Schlick Noe & Johnson, 1999).

When writing in their response journals, students are expected to go beyond summaries and "I like . . ." statements. Emphasis should be on both meaning and content. Responses can be personal, creative, or critical, and can be directed or undirected (Raphael, Kehus, & Damphousse, 2001). To assist students in their responses, teachers can provide prompts, questions, or lists of response possibilities. See Figures 3.9 , 3.10, and 3.11 for some of these options. These response possibilities should be readily accessible to the students; lists of them could be either stapled into their response logs or posted on a chart in a classroom.

The purpose of using response logs is not to provide busywork for the students, but to help students focus on issues in their reading, issues that they then can discuss in their literature circles. During or after reading, students are expected to respond to what they have read. In responding to nonfiction texts, students can discuss their feelings about the topic, raise issues, pose questions,

---

Figure 3.9   Literature Response Prompts

I learned . . .
I agree with . . .
I disagree with . . .
A question I have about . . . is . . .
When I read this text, I felt . . .
I predict . . .
An example of good writing is . . .
I didn't understand . . .
The big idea(s) in this text was . . .
Some important information in the text was . . . because . . .
I think the author wrote this because . . .
The title of the book (chapter) was appropriate (not appropriate) because . . .
What I remember most from my reading is . . .
This was an effective piece of writing because . . .
I don't think this book was accurate because . . .
I think the illustrations (photographs, visuals) were . . .
If I had been the author, I would have . . .
To summarize what I have read . . .
This text helped me to . . .
I wonder . . .

Figure 3.10   Literature Response Questions: Questions to Support
Understanding of Nonfiction

Making Connections (to self and to text)

Informational Texts in General
- What do you know about this topic?
- What does this book (article, etc.) remind you of?
- Does the text provide you with personal information?
- How does what you have read fit in with other information you already know?

Biographies
- What do you know about this person?
- What do you wonder about or want to know about this person?
- Does this person's life resemble yours or anyone you know?
- What do you know about the time that this person lived? How different/ same is it from yours?
- How are this person's problems like problems of people you know or have read about?
- Did anything ever happen to you like it did in this person's life?

Content of the Text

Informational Texts in General
- What are some of the most important facts that you learned about this topic?
- What is the main focus/idea of the text?
- Is the topic covered sufficiently?
- What position does the author take on the topic?
- Are different perspectives or viewpoints presented?
- Does the author explain how he/she got the information?
- What did you learn?
- What more would you like to learn about the topic?

Biographies

- How critical is the setting to the person's life or deeds?
- What details does the author provide to help you get to know the person?
- Does the setting change during the person's life? Does that make a difference?
- At what point in the person's life did the biography begin?
- What were the important events that occurred in the person's life?
- What challenges (opportunities) did the person face (or have)?
- What difference did this person make to . . . ?
- What does this person look like? Act like? Do?
- What kind of person is the subject of the biography?
- Does the person change throughout his/her life?
- What insights does this biography provide about the problems and issues we face today?

Figure 3.10   Continued

Accuracy

Informational Texts in General

- Is the information current?
- Is there enough evidence to justify what the author has presented?
- Are the illustrations accurate and authentic?
- Is any information missing?
- Does the author make a distinction between facts and opinion?
- Is there any misleading information?
- Is the author objective? Biased?

Biographies

- Is the information about the person, setting, events, accurate?
- What does the author do to make the setting (events) accurate?
- Is the information about the person believable and consistent with other sources?
- Does the author discuss the subject objectively?

Author's Craft

Informational Texts in General

- Does the author use interesting, understandable language and examples?
- How has the author made the topic interesting? Not interesting?
- How has the author made the text easy to read? Difficult to read?

Biographies

- How does the author organize the recreation of the person's life, e.g., chronological, headings, etc.?
- Does the author use dialogue, flashbacks, foreshadowing, etc., to describe this person's life?
- What passages, words, etc., do you particularly remember? Why?
- What quotations would you choose that represent the person being written about?

Access and Visual Features

Informational Texts in General

- How does the author present the information?
- Do the headings and subheadings help you understand the topic?
- What information is given in the illustrations, captions, maps, charts, etc.?
- Are the illustrations (charts, maps, diagrams, etc.) easy to understand?
- Are there labels or captions used? Are these helpful?
- Does the author's format help you in understanding and remembering the information?

Figure 3.10   Continued

Biographies
- Does the author use pictures, photographs, etc., in telling about this person's life?
- Is a time line provided?
- Are there any primary sources used?
- Does the author include quotes or examples of the person's writings?

Author

Informational Texts in General
- Is the author qualified to write this text?
- How does the author do his/her research?
- What does the author feel about this topic?
- Do you know other works that the author has written? Are there any patterns in them?
- What questions would you ask the author about this book or about his/her life?

Biographies
- Why did the author choose this person to write about?
- Is the author qualified to write about this person?
- What research did the author use in writing this biography?
- How does the author feel about his/her subject?
- Was there a message that the author was giving in writing this biography?

Evaluation

For both Informational Texts and Biographies
- What did you like best about this material (text, article, book)?
- Was there anything missing from . . . ?
- Was the material challenging for you? Why? How did you handle them?
- Was the book the right length?
- Have you learned anything about yourself after reading . . . ?
- In your discussions, were you able to affect any of your classmates' feelings, opinions, etc?
- How would you evaluate your performance (while reading, during discussions, in responding in your journal, etc.)?

Sources: From Moore et al., 1994; Booth, 1998; and Fountas & Pinnell, 2001.

clarify key points, or provide documentation for their position or arguments. Students can also record words that puzzle them, examples of effective writing from their reading, and questions they would like to ask others in their group. Reading logs are an important means for students to think about their reading, to encourage deeper reading of the texts, and to prepare for sharing their thoughts and ideas. Through these written responses, students share, publish, synthesize, extend, and apply what they have learned (Raphael, Kehus, & Damphousse, 2001). Writing in response logs can solidify the students' thinking, push them to explore different ideas, challenge them to consider multiple perspectives, and prepare them for future reading and discussions.

Figure 3.11   Y-Chart for Response Options for Nonfiction

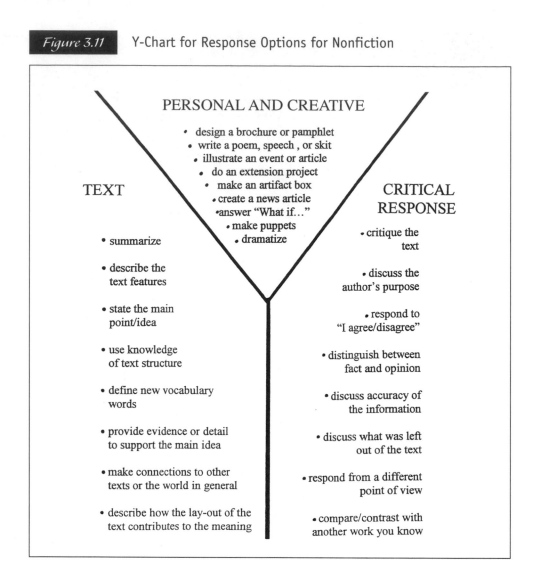

Literature Discussions   One of the most significant benefits of using literature circles is the opportunity that is provided for students to meet and discuss commonly read books or books related to a particular theme or concept. When students talk about their interpretations, pose questions, make connections to their lives or related literature, or wonder about what they are reading, literature assumes a different perspective and a new life. Interpretation of what is being read is limited when readers read alone, but reading texts becomes more meaningful when students listen to one another. Involving students in literature circles is beneficial to all of the students because it acknowledges the insights, ideas, and the experiences of all of the students as they collaboratively increase their understanding of what was read.

Integral to the success of learning from and through nonfiction is the need to discuss and share the literary experiences. All children need an opportunity to converse about books, self-reflect, and analyze. Genuine book conversations are not interrogations or "gentle inquisitions" (Eeds & Wells, 1989) led by teachers who only use questions to engage their students to talk. Rather, they are

Try This

It's Your Turn to Talk

To ensure that each child has an opportunity to discuss in his or her literature circle, some supports may have to be put into place, especially in the initial stages. Talking sticks (similar to what the Native Americans use) can be passed to each participant when it time for his or her oral contribution. Small tokens can also be "traded" in for opportunities to talk. Only students who hold the talking stick or token may speak at that particular time.

lively exchanges that encourage children to explore literature responses and to participate in jointly constructing rich interpretations of literature (McGee, 1995). During these "grand conversations" (Peterson & Eeds; 1990 Raphael et al., 1997; McGee, 1995; Wells, 1995) about books, the students share their own interpretations based on their own experiences, attitudes, and purposes and help their classmates see what they otherwise might have overlooked. Conversations about literature captivate and challenge readers and are powerful tools for expanding children's responses to literature (McGee, 1995).

Whenever a group gets together, several people may dominate the discussion. To assure that this does not occur during book club time, students need to be taught how to converse with their classmates so that everyone participates in building a shared understanding of what is being read. Students should be afforded an opportunity to brainstorm what works and what doesn't work in a good discussion. As a result of this brainstorming, charts such as those seen in Figures 3.12 and 3.13 can be generated. In addition to knowing how to participate in a discussion, students also need to know what to talk about and how to gather information that will be shared (Schlick Noe & Johnson, 1999).

Figure 3.12   Chart for Promoting Effective Discussions

- Be prepared. Make sure you have completed your reading and responding.
- Sit so that everyone can see one another.
- Give the person who is talking your attention.
- Listen attentively to understand what the speaker is saying.
- Ask questions to clarify what you don't understand.
- Speak clearly in an appropriate tone.
- Do not interrupt the speaker.
- Be sure to include everyone in the discussion.
- Build on each other's ideas.
- Respect what every one says.
- Stick to the topic.
- Document what you are saying with facts and evidence.

Figure 3.13   T-Chart for Effective and Ineffective Groups

What Effective Groups Look Like and Sound Like	What Ineffective Groups Look Like and Sound Like
everyone contributes	some people dominate the discussion or do not contribute
everyone participates willingly	some members are unwilling to participate
members are prepared	members not prepared
discussion is focused on a topic	discussion strays, not sticking to the topic
everyone's contributions are respected and valued	put-downs are heard
listeners attend to the speaker	listeners do not pay attention to the speaker
members are polite	members are not kind
evidence provided for comments	little or no documentation is provided
many questions are asked	no or few questions are asked
group responds to the speaker or to other group members	group ignores each other's comments
voices at an acceptable level	loud voices used

Frequently, the written responses that students provide in their response journals are used to assist students with their discussions (i.e., giving them something to talk about), but there are other possibilities that can enhance discussions as well.

- *Highlighted Passages:*   Passages in the text can be marked using stick-on tags (Post-its®) (instead of highlighter markers, which create permanent markings in texts). Not only can the Post-its help the student locate the exact passage or desired information, but students can record their reactions or questions directly on the stick-on tags.
- *Guided Topics:*   Teachers can provide a suggested topic, focusing on important information in the text.
- *Memorable Language:*   Powerful quotes, examples of effective use of language or imagery, can be identified and recorded in the response journals or on stick-on tags. Students can read their selections, discuss the significance of their selections, and the reasons why these particular quotes were chosen.
- *Student-generated Questions:*   A list of open-ended questions can be generated with the class.

- *Bookmarks:* Bookmarks can be provided so that while students are reading, they can record interesting information, puzzling or interesting words, or wonderful quotes. A sample bookmark can be seen in Figure 3.14.
- *Discussion or Think Sheets:* These sheets are designed by teachers to provide a structure for gathering information for the discussion groups. A generic form can be used for all kinds of texts, or teachers can construct one only for the content being explored. An example of a Discussion Think Sheet (3-2-1 Share) can be seen in Figure 3.15.
- *Quote and Question:* As the students read their texts, they locate one (or more, depending on the purpose) quote and one question that puzzled them.
- *Sketching or Drawing:* Students can respond using design, color, shapes, symbols, lines, textures, and images. After reading their selections, students think about and draw what the selection means to them. When the sketches are finished, the artist asks his or her group members what they think is being said in the drawing. Once everyone has interpreted the picture, the student artist offers his or her explanation. (Daniels, 2002; Raphael et al., 1997; Schlick Noe & Johnson, 1999; Raphael, Kehus, & Damphousse, 2001; Hill et al., 2001)

Figure 3.14 Bookmarks for Notetaking

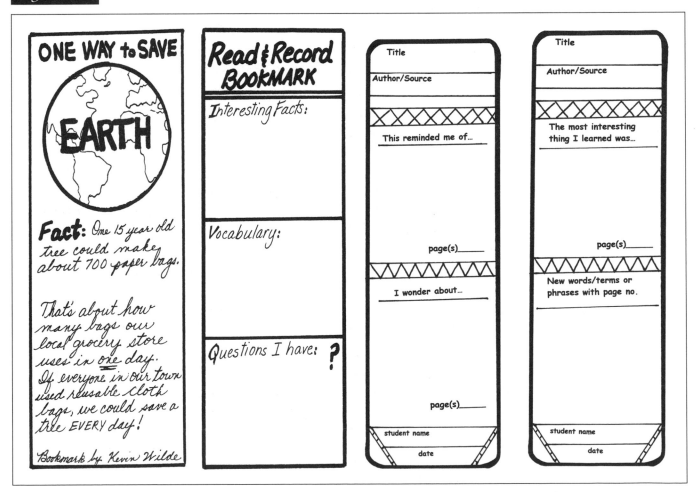

Figure 3.15 Discussion Think Sheet: 3-2-1 Share

3-2-1 Think & Share

Write 3 interesting facts:

1. Rosa Parks was arrested in Montgomery, Alabama for not giving her seat to a white person on a public bus.
2. Rosa was a volunteer secretary for the NAACP.
3. Rosa lost her job because she boycotted the city buses because of segregation.

Write 2 things that are new to you:

1. Rosa Parks was a seamstress.

2. She was 42 years old when arrested on the bus.

Write 1 question you have:

Did Rosa's family approve of her act?

Teachers need to find a balance between providing too many and too few supports when assisting students with choosing discussion topics. Providing students with such scaffolding structures as the prompts, questions, and response options already described is helpful, but can be overdone. These structures can provide initial scaffolding, but can detract from the conversations when they themselves become the focus of the discussion.

Extensions to Literature Circles After finishing the text, students can plan a book-sharing activity. The purpose of the extension projects is to extend and enhance the students' understanding and enjoyment of the text. These projects give students an opportunity to revisit the text, make relevant connections, and

The Fossil Girl

by Catherine Brighton

Children are fascinated by fossils, and should be enthralled with reading about a real-live fossil hunter, Mary Anning, who lived in Dorset, England, in 1810. Through a comic book format, complete with speech bubbles and accompanying historical text, readers can "discover" the Ichthyosaur, the first pterodactyl in England, among other fossil finds credited to Mary Anning.

gain a more complete picture of the theme or concept being explored (Norwick, 1995). There are many activities described in Chapter 7 that can be used as extension projects—biographies in a can, plastic bag books and quilts, graduated pages books—or students can select from other responses—verbal, nonverbal, musical, artistic, dramatic, and written—such as the following:

- *Alphabet Books:* An alphabet book (Figure 3.16) can be created that focuses on key elements, ideas, and information from the topic or reading material that was discussed. This may work best as a group project because of the use of the twenty-six letters of the alphabet. Some alphabet book topics include the ABCs of . . . transportation, the United States, China, creepy-crawly things, famous Americans, and so forth.
- *Flannel Board Story:* A flannel board can display illustrations of nonfiction texts and poems, or it can retell facts from a nonfiction piece. Flannel boards can be used to demonstrate sequence of events and cyclic occurrences, depict scenes in history, or illustrate a science activity. Flannel boards can be constructed by gluing flannel over cardboard or a piece of wood. The figures that will be placed on the flannel board can be made from traditional felt, but they

Figure 3.16   Sample Alphabet Book

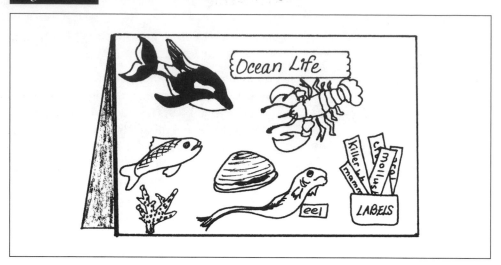

Figure 3.17   Flannel Board Extension Project

can also be made from pellon, an inexpensive material that can be found in stores that sell fabric. Any illustration can be drawn or traced onto the pellon and colored with fabric markers or crayons. The flexibility pellon offers gives students more opportunities to create detailed nonfiction extensions (Figure 3.17).

- *Personality Reports:*   Several quotations from historical figures can be selected that are representative of the personality chosen. The quotations can be accompanied by an explanation as to why the quotes represent this character. A personality cube can also be constructed to represent the historical figure.
- *Lifelines:*   A lifeline can be drawn for a famous figure, showing the important events in his or her life. Rolls of adding machine paper are excellent for this purpose.
- *Letters to (the editor, politicians, the principal) on Important Issues Raised During Book Club:*   Students can write letters to their local newspaper, politician, and school administration on issues they deem significant. Mock letters can also be written—for example, a letter from George Washington to the current president or a letter from an endangered species to the world community.
- *Poetry:*   Students can respond to any topic and to any genre by restating or expressing what they have learned or felt using poetry. An example of this is a sixth grade's reaction to the terrorist destruction of the World Trade Center. After reading numerous articles in the newspapers and in *Time for Kids*, the two sixth grade classes, along with their teachers, constructed a poem, which they shared with other students in the school (Figure 3.18).
- *Drama:*   Drama is both an art form and a powerful tool for learning and teaching. There are various dramatic forms that can be used and easily integrated into the content areas. These include dramatization; Readers' Theater, role-playing, and finger plays. When involving students in extension projects, teachers should consider the following:

The relevancy of the extension project to the texts that were read and discussed. The opportunities for students to revisit the text(s) and to make connections to their personal lives, to other texts, or to other aspects of the curriculum.

Figure 3.18 Poem Written in Reaction to Destruction of World Trade Center

We Watch

We *watch*   in disbelief!
        an explosion with flames and smoke,
        towers crumbling, people running
        panic and fear everywhere.

We *see*   destruction all around,
        streets filled with rubble,
        suffering, tears, loss,
        farewells to loved ones.

We *feel*   afraid!

We *watch*   rescuers risking their lives
        strangers helping strangers,
        everyone giving, sharing, supporting,
        loving.

We *see*   red, white, and blue,
        courage and compassion,
        hands held in prayer,
        a nation uniting.

We *feel*   hope for a better tomorrow!

Written by Jenny Anderson's and Therese Gilbert's sixth-grade classes.

The ability of the extension project to enhance the student's appreciation and comprehension of the text. (Norwick, 1995; Routman, 2000)

Teachers should also ask themselves if the extension is a worthwhile use of the students' time or if would the time be better spent with additional reading (Routman, 2000).

Students need diverse ways to respond to texts through the visual arts, through writing, and through the performing arts. Responding to literature enriches students' minds and imaginations.

Assessment of Literature Circles   Assessment, as is discussed in greater depth in Chapter 8, guides instruction. It provides information about students' strengths and needs in order to determine the most appropriate intervention or next step. There are many opportunities for assessing student learning using literature circles. Meaningful assessment focuses both on the managerial and or-

Figure 3.19 Overview of Assessment Measures for Literature Circles

Assessment Goals	Assessment Measures
Check on the degree of preparation, e.g., reading the assigned material, writing in response log, arriving on time to group session	Teacher observations, student logs, student self-reflection, rubrics
Check on what was learned and the level of understanding	Teacher observations, anecdotal records, retellings, conferences, student self-assessment, student journals, response logs
Determine the quality of responses in the response logs	Rubrics, student self-reflection, group evaluation form
Check on the degree of participation, level, and content of discussions	Teacher observations, student journals, anecdotal records, student self-reflection, group evaluation form, rubrics
Note student self-assessment	Conferences, reflection journals/logs, observation, student discussion, written accounts, class discussions, rubric

ganizational issues of literature circles—for example, coming prepared to the group discussion by having read the material, turntaking during discussions, being courteous—as well as what is being learned (Day et al., 2002). Therefore, it is necessary to evaluate the content of the reading, along with the process of participating in literature circles.

There are many forms of assessment to use in the evaluation of literature circles. These include teacher observation, student conferences, student self-evaluation, and the use of rubrics for literature discussions and journal responses. An overview of these assessment measures can be seen in Figure 3.19.

The ABCs of Reading Nonfiction   Reading nonfiction is essential to student success throughout their lives. Move over, narrative texts—nonfiction is joining you as part of the instructional program (Figure 3.20).

Figure 3.20   ABCs for Readers of Nonfiction

ABCDEFGHIJKLM

ABCs for Readers of Nonfiction

A use the **appendix** to find out more.
B become aware of **bold** print.
C make **connections**.
D **discuss** what they have read.
E **examine** information
F look for **facts**.
G refer to a text's **glossary**.
H read **historical** writings.
I read for **information**.
J make **judgments** as they read.
K use background **knowledge**.
L enjoy **learning**.
M consult **multiple** sources.
N take **notes** to facilitate learning.
O **organize** information.
P make **predictions**.
Q ask **questions** as they read.
R use **research** skills.
S **scan** material before reading.
T take their **time** when reading.
U read for **understanding**.
V select a **variety** of texts.
W create **webs** to organize information.
X **examine** a topic thoroughly.
Y **yearn** to learn about the real world.
Z **zoom** in on main ideas.

NOPQRSTUVWXYZ

Instructional Activities for the Classroom

1 *Chapter-Beginning Activity*

Using a generic body shape (or students can design their own), students turn these shapes into historical figures. Students research a famous person and write a brief summary of that person's life on 3 × 5 cards, which are stapled to an oaktag cutout of the upper torso. These figures can stand up on a shelf or window sill. Displayed beside them, or near them, can be a published biography about that person.

2 *Silhouette Biographies*

Silhouettes can be drawn for famous figures, and form the covers for a report on that person. Key information about that person can be written on blank sheets inside the silhouettes.

3 *T-Shirt/Paper or Plastic Bags Presentations*

To capitalize on the T-shirt craze, students can turn a plain T-shirt into a report on a particular topic in science or social studies. Students can draw representative objects, sayings, and so forth, on the T-shirts themselves with fabric crayons, or they can sew or glue actual objects onto the T-shirts. These shirts can also be constructed from paper bags. A variation of this activity is the designing of "lab coats" to represent a scientist from a particular field. White plastic garbage bags can form the basis of the lab coat, with the students attaching assorted items to represent some scientific field. For example, a budding botanist might decorate her lab coat with pictures of flowers, seed packets, and the like, while a future entomologist might illustrate a variety of insects, designing them from fabric, pom poms, pipe cleaners, and so on. On the back of the bag can be placed some cardboard wings to complete the effect. Figure 3.21 shows an example of a scientific lab coat.

Figure 3.21 Scientific Lab Coat

Book Talk and Beyond

Math Curse

by Jon Scieszka and Lane Smith

One day in math class, Mrs. Fibonacci tells the class in this book that almost EVERYTHING can be a math

problem. That is the beginning of one little girl's journey into math mania. From that moment on, the child sees nearly every object and situation in terms of a math problem. The illustrations are fantastic and full of thought-provoking problems. The story will make any reader see the world differently, and laugh out loud along the journey! Students can do their own take-off using math or any other subject . . . the whole world can be a science lesson, or geography lesson, and so on. One class created a circular book, using two tagboard circles connected at the center with a brad fastener. The top circle is cut slightly smaller, with a section cut out to provide a viewing field for the drawings that illustrate some geometry terms, which are written on the edge of the larger circle.

The Flag We Love

by Pam Munoz Ryan

This patriotic book celebrates a beloved and respected symbol of our country—the United States flag. Facts about the flag are provided through both poetry and boxed information on one page, accompanied by a full-page illustration on the next. Specific topics addressed include the making of the first Stars and Stripes; uses of the flag in ceremonies, in daily school openings, and so on; travels of the flag to unexplored regions as far away as the moon; and the symbolic representation of the flag (e.g., people's rights in a democracy). This book provides readers with an excellent model of how several genres can be used to convey key information, and can spur a thematic study about the flag.

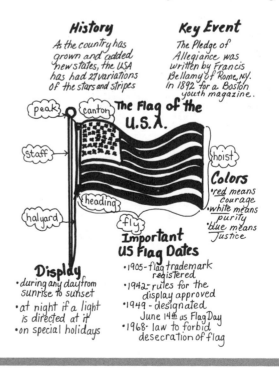

Strategies for Success

Introduction

Prior to discussing strategies that will assist students in comprehending text, there needs to be a general understanding of the reading process, and what constitutes a good reader. Readers primarily use two sources of information

Life's Little Instruction Book for Readers of Nonfiction

inside

- Notice when words are printed in bold type or italics.
- Pay attention to illustrations.
- Study the charts, graphs, or diagrams for understanding.
- Read carefully and slowly.
- Read all captions.
- Jot down words you don't know or understand.

Inspired by Life's Little Instruction Book by H. Jackson Brown

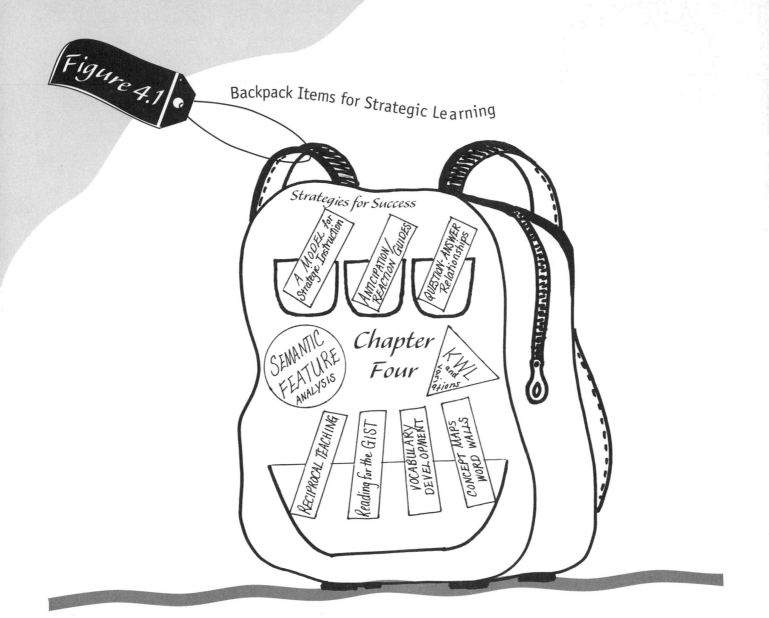

Figure 4.1 Backpack Items for Strategic Learning

Strategies for Success

A MODEL for Strategic Instruction

Anticipation REACTION GUIDES

QUESTION-ANSWER Relationships

SEMANTIC FEATURE ANALYSIS

Chapter Four

KWL and variations

RECIPROCAL TEACHING

Reading for the GIST

VOCABULARY DEVELOPMENT

CONCEPT MAPS WORD WALLS

when constructing meaning: the text and their own background knowledge. Each time students are confronted with the words on a printed page, they use those words along with what they know about the topic and the act of reading in order to figure out the author's message. In addition, social and situational factors affect understanding of what is read. Social factors include the readers' socioeconomic backgrounds, their culturally based expectations about reading, their ages, and their education. What readers interpret from the text is also influenced by the reading situation or the context, because these affect how readers approach the reading act and what they gain from the experience. For example, a novel is read differently from a chapter in a content area textbook because the purpose for reading each of these differs, as does the accountability for reading each of them. Reading, therefore, is an interactive process in which readers use information from the printed text along with what is in their heads to construct meaning in a given situational context

Reading is like a conversation between the reader and the author; some children, being better "conversationalists" than others, become good or proficient readers. This chapter describes what proficient readers look like and the strategies they use in order to gain meaning from text. It also discusses some worthwhile strategies that will give all students the opportunity to become proficient readers. The focus is on helping students become strategic learners—learners who demonstrate control over, and responsibility for, their own learning successes.

Your journey into the realm of nonfiction continues in this chapter with discussions on how teachers can help their students become strategic learners. The additions to your backpack now include several versatile metacognitive strategies, the purposes of which are to help students gain independence while learning, show them the way when they become "lost," and allow them to achieve success in their learning ventures.

STRATEGIES FOR SUCCESS: AN OVERVIEW

Readers use a variety of strategies while reading, the main goal of which is to construct meaning. "Strategies are the thinking, problem-solving mental processes that the learner deliberately initiates, incorporates, and applies to construct meaning" (Routman, 2000, 130). They differ from skills, which are tools that students have traditionally practiced to help improve reading (Robb, 1996). Skills become strategies when learners can use them independently, reflect on and understand how they work, and apply them to a variety of reading materials.

Students must be provided strategic instruction if they are to learn to read with comprehension and independence. However, there is no one program that teachers can follow to teach reading strategically. Strategic instruction requires planning, with teachers being responsive to their students' needs. Teachers first need to become familiar with the strategies that proficient readers use (see Figures 4.2 and 4.3) and the needs and progress of their students. To determine student needs and accomplishments, teachers can use such assessment measures

---

Try This

What Is a Good Reader?

Brainstorm with your class what they think are the qualities of good readers. These qualities can be placed on a chart for students to refer to at any time when they are reading. They can also serve as lead-ins for lessons on helpful strategies that increase understanding of text. During the year, the list can grow or become more detailed, as more strategies are introduced, practiced, and internalized. The following are some of the insights students have provided on what makes a good reader:

- Somebody who enjoys reading and isn't afraid of picking up all different kinds of books (Anna—Grade 3)
- Someone who understands what they're reading (Samantha—Grade 3)
- A person who reads all the time. Someone who enjoys reading. ME! (Caitlin—Grade 3)
- Able to tell what they read back to another person in their own words. A reader makes sense of the words. (Laura—Grade 4)
- Someone who reads a book and tells friends about it (Randy—Grade 5)

Figure 4.2	What Is a Proficient Reader?

Proficient readers have and use a variety of strategies flexibly and independently, including the ability to:

- vary their reading rates for task and text
- visualize and use imagery when reading
- know the purpose of their reading, and can set their own purposes for reading
- predict, confirm and adjust predictions
- self-question
- access what they know about the topic, different text structures, the author
- make connections
- self-monitor—know what and when they are comprehending or not
- comprehending
- be aware of their own thinking processes during learning and problem solving
- use and apply what they have read

as running records or miscue analysis, reading conferences, student interviews, and analysis of the students' reading logs. In-depth information on assessment is provided in Chapter 8.

A MODEL FOR STRATEGIC INSTRUCTION

After becoming aware of their students' strengths and needs, teachers need to think about instructional interventions and activities that will further enhance their students' understanding of text. They need to consider what strategies they can introduce that will be effective for the learning context and the learners. It should be noted that effective strategy instruction is more than just mentioning, describing, or assigning. To be effective, teachers must provide explicit instruction, clearly explaining the purpose of the strategy and why it is beneficial. They then need to model how to use and apply the strategy (Harvey and Goudvis, 2000; Wood, 2001). Initially, teachers assume the responsibility for the learning, as they demonstrate "think aloud," verbally describing the thought processes involved in the task, and as they walk and guide the students through the procedures. Students are eased into the strategy by practicing under the guidance of the teacher, sometimes in small groups or pairs. Meanwhile, the teacher circulates among the students and provides assistance when needed. When the teacher feels the students are ready, they can practice independently and finally apply the strategy to new learning.

This scaffolded model of instruction is known as the *gradual release model of instruction,* with students assuming more and more responsibility as they become more familiar with the strategy and what is expected of them. This can

| *Figure 4.3* | Strategies Good Readers Use before, during, and after Reading |

Good Readers:

Before Reading
- preview the text
- determine and analyze the type of text
- activate or build background knowledge
- set purpose for reading, asking themselves why are they reading this material?; what will they find out?
- make predictions

During Reading
- adjust their rate according to their purpose for reading the material
- use their background/prior knowledge to make sense
- predict and confirm
- visualize the content
- monitor their understanding, and apply fix-up strategies when necessary
- ask themselves questions while reading
- connect the content to something they know
- determine what are the most important ideas
- summarize
- make inferences
- reread
- use the visual and access features of the text
- integrate what they are reading with what they already know

After Reading
- summarize the major ideas
- make connections
- determine if they achieved their goals, e.g., What did I learn? What did I miss?
- evaluate understanding of what they have read, e.g., What does it mean?
- apply what they have learned to new situations

Sources: From Raphael et al., 2000; and Armstrong, 2000.

be likened to scaffolding used in the construction business, which are temporary structures that allow workers to reach areas that are challenging and that are dismantled when no longer needed. Teachers use scaffolds similarly in the form of learning strategies that help their students attain higher understanding, and gradually dismantle them when students no longer need them.

There are many opportunities for teachers to demonstrate strategic learning. Strategies can be taught during minilessons, shared reading, shared writing, read-alouds, and in discussion groups. Teachers can model their thinking and problem-solving behaviors at any time during any curricular area, followed by opportunities for students to discuss these strategies, and then practice and

A Burst of Firsts: Doers, Shakers, and Record Breakers
by J. Patrick Lewis

Move over *Guiness Book of World Records*. You now have a companion in this delightful collection of poems that celebrates many notable "firsts." Read about the first person to make blue jeans, the first American woman in space, the first man to run a four-minute mile, among others. Children have been fascinated by record-breaking events for years, and love perusing *The Guiness Book of World Records*. Now they can create their own versions of other "firsts" (even firsts in their own lives) using the poetic style of this book as a model. It just might be a "first" for your school!

apply them. By engaging students in this process, teachers are encouraging students to think strategically for all reading situations. They are also modeling reading as an inquiry process in which readers self-question, monitor, reflect, and revise while making sense of text (Routman, 2000).

Any type of reading material and context is appropriate for introducing and learning strategies. However, it has been recommended that teachers use a variety of short texts (Harvey & Goudvis, 2000) for strategic learning. Short texts seem less formidable than longer selections, and due to their brevity, do not necessitate devoting long periods of time to the activity.

It is likewise important that students be able to verbalize what they are doing or thinking as they are engaged in strategic learning. Teachers can facilitate their students' learning by asking pertinent questions about reading strategies. In doing so, they are helping the students make their thinking visible. These questions may include the following:

- What did you do when . . . ?
- How did you figure that out?
- What worked for you?
- Is there anything else you can try?
- How did you know that?
- What could you do when your reading doesn't make sense?
- Where in the text does it say that?
- What do you already know that can help you? (Routman, 2000)

Questions to Enhance Strategic Learning

The following questions can be posted in the room to help students grow as strategic learners:

- What do I need to do to make sure that I understand what I am reading?
- Do I understand what I am reading?
- How will I know that I understand what I am reading?
- How will I know that I don't understand what I am reading?
- What can I do if I don't understand?

K-W-L (and Variants)
What I "K"now, "W"ant to Know, What I "L"earned

DESCRIPTION: Technique for activating prior knowledge, promoting thinking, and setting purposes for learning. K-W-L Plus incorporates a writing activity in which learners categorize their information and organize it into a semantic map. K-W-L-H (H = How) gives students an opportunity to discuss ways to locate the desired information.

PURPOSE:
   Instructional: Provides a structure for recording what students know, questions they want to pursue, and what they have learned.
   Assessment: Assesses students' background knowledge and their misconceptions about a topic.

STRATEGIES FOR SUCCESS

Students will not be able to learn all that they need to know during their years of schooling. Therefore, teachers need to continually encourage their students to be lifelong learners who will continue to strive to further their understandings in all their curricular endeavors. By incorporating strategic learning into their instructional repertoires, teachers are encouraging their students to develop into independent, reflective learners. The strategies described in this chapter should assist students in understanding, remembering, and applying what they are reading and learning. However, the strategies described in this chapter should not be the only ones considered. There are many strategies that are valuable, depending on the learning context and the needs of the students. Additional information about other essential ways to promote student independence can be found in the resources at the end of the book.

K-W-L and Variations of K-W-L (K-W-L-H and K-W-L Plus)

One of the most important findings in recent years is how much a learner's background knowledge facilitates understanding of what is to be learned. The importance of prior knowledge in literacy learning has been addressed through the research on schema theory. According to schema theory, people understand what they read as it relates to what they already know. Prior knowledge then becomes crucial to the successful construction of meaning for all learners. There are two aspects of prior knowledge that teachers must consider in their educational programs: overall prior knowledge, and text-specific prior knowledge (Cooper, 2000). Overall prior knowledge is all the knowledge that students possess, whereas text-specific prior knowledge is the specific information needed to understand a particular topic or theme (e.g., key concepts and key terminology). Overall prior knowledge develops from all of a student's accumulated experiences, both at home and at school, such as being read to, reading, being taken on trips, surfing the Web, viewing television, watching movies, and so on.

There are two components of text-specific prior knowledge: knowledge about the type of text and knowledge about the topic. Both play important roles in constructing meaning. Text-specific prior knowledge can likewise be developed through extensive reading, viewing television shows, and going on trips, as well as through demonstrations, exhibits, discussions, and such strategies as K-W-L, Anticipation/Reaction Guides, learning about text structures, and semantic mapping, among others. Several of these strategies and activities are addressed in other areas of this resource guide, and some are discussed in this chapter.

An effective, yet simple, teaching strategy that has proven useful for students across all disciplines is K-W-L (Ogle, 1986, 1989; Buehl, 2001). K-W-L is a procedure for activating prior knowledge, promoting thinking, and setting purposes for learning. It consists of three steps:

1. *K*   To activate prior knowledge, students brainstorm and discuss what they know about the topic. This information is recorded on chart paper or on a worksheet in a column entitled *K—What I Know*. These brainstormed items can be categorized, thereby providing a means to assist students in seeing how the information might be structured and related to information from other sources.

2. *W*   In the second step, the students generate questions about the topic and set purposes for the learning. The questions are recorded in the *W—What I Want to Learn* column. As students read and research the topic, additional questions may be added.

3. *L*   As the students read, they note the new information in the final column *L— What I Learned*.

The K-W-L procedure can be undertaken as a whole class activity, or individually. When recording information in the *K* column, it is important that all the information that the students provide is recorded, even misinformation. Naturally, teachers will ensure that the misinformation is corrected during the course of the study. By welcoming all contributions, teachers do not discourage students from participating, and any misconceptions make excellent opportunities for students to engage in purposeful research. Figure 4.4A is an example of a K-W-L sheet.

There are variations to this procedure. Sometimes a fourth column is added to the K-W-L technique—*H*: *How Can We Find Out* (Figure 4.4B). After the students brainstorm all they know about the topic, they then discuss the various ways they can locate the information—for example, their textbooks, encyclopedias, primary sources, documentaries, and information on the computer.

Another adaptation of the technique is K-W-L Plus, which adds mapping and summarization components to the original strategy (Figure 4.5). Mapping and summarization are added because writing and summarization of text are powerful ways to help students process information. These written components expand "independent learning by helping students to think critically about information as they organize, restructure, and apply what they have learned" (Carr & Ogle, 1987, 628).

Because maps are graphic outlines for organizing and relating text information, they enable students to see associations and relationships in what they

Figure 4.4A   K-W-L Sheet

KWL chart

Canada   *Marianne Ramos*

What I **K**now	What I **W**ant to learn	What I **L**earned
Canada is north of the United States.	How big is the country?	Canada does not have states. It has provinces and territories.
It is colder.	How many states do they have?	It is closer to the Artic Circle so thats why it is cold.
It is a big country.	How do people make a living?	The frozen land is called tundra.
It is friendly to the United States.	What is the weather like?	Inuit (Eskimo) are native to Canada.
	How many people live in Canada?	Canadians speak Inuit, French or English.
	What language do they speak?	Many people work in logging or paper mills.
		About 28,000,000 population
		It is 3,800,000 square miles

have read. In constructing maps, students locate and relate the main ideas and supporting details and display them in an organized whole. Maps can be readily produced from K-W-L worksheets. The first step is to categorize the information that was listed in the *L* column. It is helpful if the students ask themselves what each statement describes. By listing and categorizing the information, the students are selecting and relating the important information that was learned. Once this is completed, the students are ready to construct their map.

Another K-W-L Plus technique is the writing of summaries. Summary writing improves understanding, because it requires students to reflect on what was learned, to write logically and comprehensibly, and to express what was learned in their own words. K-W-L Plus enhances summarization skills because the important information has already been selected, organized, and integrated during the mapping. The students use the map as an outline for their summary. They number the categories on the map according to the sequence they will use in the

Figure 4.4B   Continued

KWHL chart

Insects   Brian Lewitt

What I **K**now	What I **W**ant to learn	**H**ow will I find it	What I **L**earned
Insects are bugs. Insects bite or sting. They can hurt us. They can kill us. Insects are gross.	Where do they come from? What is the biggest insect? How many kinds are there?	Books in our library - Nature Guide- Insects · Bugs encyclopedia under I a b School library ask Mrs. Clemits and look in card catalog Ask my Dad	There are more insects than any living thing on earth. Insects skeletons are on the outside of their body. Some people eat insects. All insects have 6 legs. Some insects live in water. Insects live everywhere. Insects are <u>helpful</u>!

writing of the summary. The core of the map becomes the title of the summary, and each category forms the topic of a new paragraph.

K-W-L Plus clearly demonstrates how to link an instructional strategy to learning tasks. It combines several learning tools into one technique and en-

Try This

"Hand"y Tips for Reading Nonfiction

As students become familiar with a variety of strategies that will enhance their reading (or writing) of nonfiction, they could trace their hands and write these tips on their hand shapes. The hands could be placed on a bulletin board or chart, entitled *Handy Tips for Reading Nonfiction*. See Figure 4.6.

Figure 4.5 K-W-L Plus Sheet

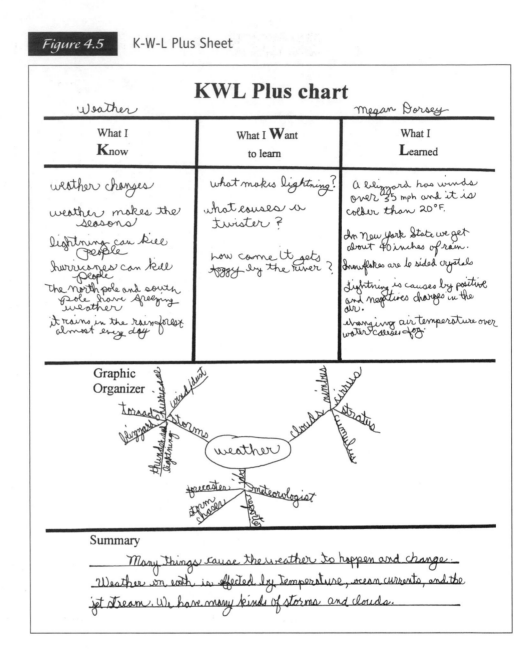

hances students' ability to transfer their learning to a variety of learning situations. Through K-W-L Plus, students can gain control over their learning and understand when and how to use the strategy effectively.

Anticipation/Reaction Guides

The Anticipation/Reaction Guide is a strategy that forecasts the major points in a passage by using a series of statements that activate students' prior knowledge, thoughts, and opinions. It consists of a series of prepared statements that students respond to before and after they read. Prior to reading the text, students agree or disagree with the statements and discuss the reasons for their decisions. The statements also are responded to after reading, with students either

Figure 4.6 Handy Tips for Reading Nonfiction

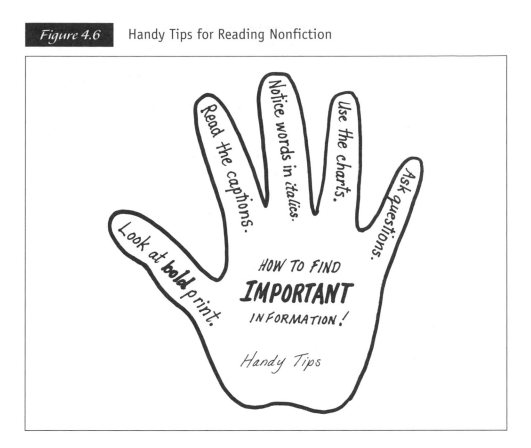

confirming what they had stated initially or changing their answer as a result of the further reading. The Anticipation/Reaction Guide may be used at any grade level and with both print and nonprint materials.

The Anticipation/Reaction Guide serves several purposes. It

- activates students' prior knowledge before reading;
- encourages students to think about what they already know, followed by reading to confirm or adjust their initial reactions;
- motivates students by arousing curiosity for the reading;

Anticipation/Reaction Guides

DESCRIPTION: A series of statements to which students respond prior to and after they read.

PURPOSE:

Instructional: Activate students' prior knowledge, provide a purpose for the reading/learning, and act as guides for postreading discussions.

Assessment: Identify gaps in students' knowledge and their misconceptions about a topic.

- provides a purpose for the reading;
- connects new information with existing knowledge; and
- acts as a guide for post-reading discussions (Tierney & Readence, 2000; Readence, Bean, & Baldwin, 2000; Buehl, 2001).

The Anticipation/Reaction Guide (Figure 4.7) also can serve as an assessment tool. With a before-reading component, teachers can assess the breadth and depth of their students' knowledge about the topic. They therefore have an opportunity to correct misconceptions that may hinder understanding of the key concepts of the text. Once the students have completed their guides after reading, teachers can again assess what the students have learned both through the guides themselves and during the ensuing discussions about the students' responses.

Figure 4.7   Anticipation/Reaction Guide

Anticipation/Reaction Guide
A is for America: An American Alphabet
by Devin Scillian

Mark each statement with Agree (A) or Disagree (D) before and after reading the book.

Before	After	
_____	_____	1. Phoenix, Arizona is the largest capital in the U.S.
_____	_____	2. Henry Ford did not invent the automobile.
_____	_____	3. George Washington Carver invented more than 300 uses for the peanut.
_____	_____	4. Four of the first five presidents were born in Virginia.
_____	_____	5. The name *California* originated from a Spanish story about an island of gold.
_____	_____	6. George Washington introduced the mule to farming.
_____	_____	7. Members of the Navajo tribe helped the United States win WWII with their Navajo language.
_____	_____	8. The zipper was originally designed to replace shoestrings in shoes.

For you readers: The above statements are true, but if this activity is done with students it is advised to mix both true and false statements.

Strategy
AT A *Glance*

Question–Answer Relationships (QARs)

DESCRIPTION: Frameworks or taxonomies for identifying the different sources of information that are available for answering questions.

PURPOSE:
   Instructional: Help students analyze and understand the nature of responding to questions. Assist in the recognition of the kinds of thinking that are needed for responding to questions.
   Assessment: Give teachers a framework for analyzing gaps in their students' understanding and ability to locate information on the literal and inferential levels.

When constructing the Anticipation/Reaction Guide, it is recommended that teachers create three to six statements that relate to the major ideas or concepts of the topic. These statements should be general rather than specific, and challenge students' beliefs. The most effective statements are those about which the students have some knowledge, but yet do not have a complete understanding. After the students have read the text and have confirmed or adjusted their prior predictions, they can mark those passages of the text with sticky notes on which they have discussed the statement, and even rewrite any statement that needs to be changed as a result of their reading.

Anticipation/Reaction Guides promote active involvement on the part of the students as they make predictions and interact with what they are reading to verify or refute their predictions. These guides also enhance the quality of discussions that ensue about the learning. Anticipation/Reaction Guides help develop critical thinking and the understanding of texts.

Question–Answer Relationships

An excellent framework for clarifying the different sources of information available for answering questions is the use of Question–Answer Relationships (QARs). This strategy is useful for helping students locate information, determining when inferential reasoning is necessary, and clarifying how students can approach the reading of their texts and answering questions (Raphael, 1982, 1984, 1986).

Two primary sources of information are used in answering questions: the information provided by the author in the text *(in the book)* and the information that the reader possesses as background knowledge *(in my head)*. Some questions may be answered entirely by reading the text, but others require combining the reader's experiences with information in the text. The two categories, *in the book* and *in my head*, are further divided. The *in the book* category is expanded into 1) *Right There*—answers that are directly stated in the text, generally within one sentence or two closely connected sentences; and 2) *Think and Search or Putting It Together*—answers that are available in the text, but require that the students put together information from different parts of the text. *Right There* (RT) questions are literal questions that are relatively easy to construct and answer, whereas *Think and Search* (TS) questions are inferential questions and involve higher level thinking.

In My Head questions, which require students to use their background knowledge to attain answers, can be divided into *Author and You* (AY) and *On Your Own* (OYO). The key distinction is whether or not the reader actually has to read the text in order to answer the question. Let's say the topic of study was to be World War II and the class was going to be discussing the Holocaust. Prior to initiating the study of the Holocaust, the teacher might ask the students if they had ever experienced being excluded and how it felt. This would be an *On Your Own* question, because the answer would come entirely from the reader's experiences. After the class studies this period of history, the teacher might then ask the students to write some diary entries, pretending to be prisoners who have been rescued by the Allies. The students would then apply what they have learned, and combine this with their own information. This would be an example of an *Author and You* question, because information from the author combined with the reader's background knowledge is necessary. It must be remembered that any time a reader answers a question directly from information from his or her head (i.e., possesses sufficient background knowledge) and does not have to read the text, the question becomes *On Your Own*. This shows the importance of background knowledge. Most prereading questions are *On Your Own* questions that are designed to help students think about what they already know about a topic and how their knowledge relates to what they will be reading. Extension and application activities generally are *On Your Own* or *Author and You* questions, again focusing on the students' background knowledge as it pertains to the text. Figure 4.8 presents a graphic representation of the four types of QARs.

As you may have noted, both *In the Book* and *In My Head* categories contain inferential questions, and these are the questions that frequently present difficulty for students. These are also the types of questions that should dominate instruction because they require integration and application of information. Teachers must alert students to the two basic types of information that are required to answer questions, model the obtaining of answers using these categories, and provide students with opportunities to practice identifying and answering these questions. Figure 4.9 provides an example of QARs.

QARs can serve as both a tool for teachers when conceptualizing and developing questions, and as a strategy for students when locating information or making decisions about using the text and their prior knowledge when answering questions. QAR training and instruction can be quite versatile, enhancing all content areas from science to social studies to mathematics (McIntosh & Draper, 1995). Without QAR instruction, students frequently exhibit a lack of strategic behavior when reading and answering questions. QARs help students realize the necessity of considering both information in the text and information from their own knowledge base. Because this reading strategy does not classify questions in isolation, but considers both the reader and the text, it reflects the current conceptualization of reading as an interactive and constructive process.

Figure 4.8   Question–Answer Relationships

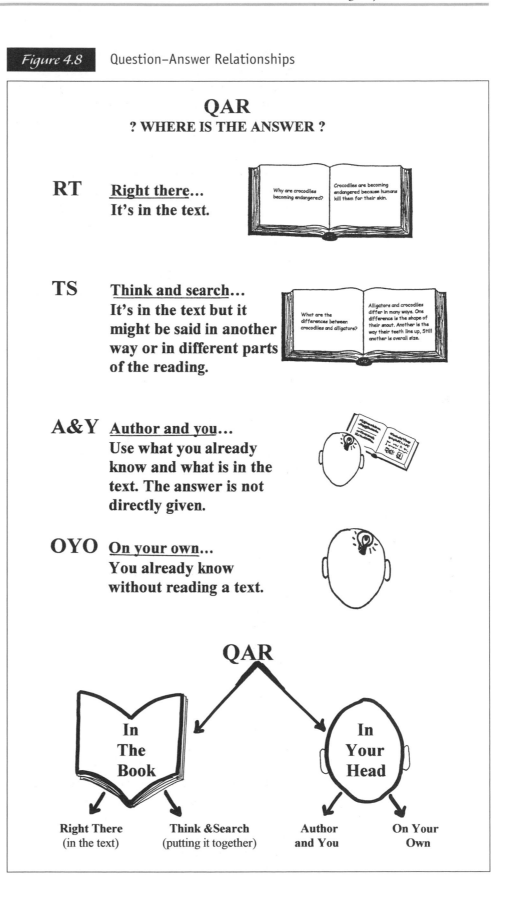

Figure 4.9   Sample Questions for Question–Answer Relationships (QARs)

1. What do you know about crocodiles?
     (OYO—if this question is posed before reading the text, since the response
          would come from the reader's prior knowledge.)
     (A&Y—if the question was posed after reading, and information was given
          that came from both the text and the reader's background
          knowledge.)
     (TS—if the reader used information located in various parts of the text.)
2. Describe a crocodile.
     (TS—if the reader used information throughout the passage to construct a
          response.)
     (A&Y—if the reader used both the text and background knowledge to
          answer the question.)
3. Compare a mother crocodile's care for her young with other reptile parents.
     (A&Y—since the information about crocodiles is provided in the text, but
          information for the care of other newborns is not. This information
          would have to come from the reader's own knowledge base).
4. What uses do people have for the skin and other parts of a crocodile?
     (OYO—since the information is not in the text, and therefore must come
          from the reader's own information.)
5. How does the mother crocodile know when her eggs are about to hatch?
     (RT—since the answer is stated in one sentence in the text and is easy to
          locate.)
6. Compare and contrast alligators and crocodiles.
     (TS—since the reader is able to construct a response based on information
          that is provided throughout the text.)
     (A&Y—if the reader gives additional information from that in the text.)
7. Why do crocodiles kill people?
     (RT—the answer is provided in one sentence in the text.)
8. What else do you know about the eating habits of crocodiles?
     (A&Y—since the question presumes that the reader already knows some
          information about crocodiles from the text, but asks the reader to
          provide additional information from his/her knowledge base.)

Note: Any question can be an "on your own" if the reader is very knowledgeable
about a topic.

Key:
RT = Right There   TS = Think and Search   A&Y = Author and You   OYO = On
Your Own

Semantic Feature Analysis

Semantic Feature Analysis (SFA) is a simple procedure for helping students develop vocabulary, construct meaning, and organize, compare, and contrast information (Anders & Bos, 1986; Buehl, 2001). SFA is also useful for helping students relate the meanings of new words to their prior knowledge and expe-

Strategy **AT A** *Glance*

Semantic Feature Analysis

DESCRIPTION: Word grids that demonstrate how words are related to one another.

PURPOSE:

Instructional: Help students compare features of words, understand word meanings, and remember meanings; enhances vocabulary development.

Assessment: Allows teachers to note their students' ability to perceive relationships among words and ideas.

---

riences, pull together concepts, and review material in preparation for tests or discussion.

SFA provides a meaningful link between the prior knowledge that students possess and new information that is presented. It builds on the concepts stored in students' memory and encourages students to become active learners by retrieving this information and applying it to their reading. By examining the properties and features of words and exploring word relationships, students are helped to organize and categorize the concepts being learned and the words used to name them.

The SFA procedure entails the development of a matrix or grid for the purpose of analyzing similarities and differences among concepts. The procedure for developing a semantic feature analysis grid is as follows:

1. A category or topic is selected (e.g., reptiles, countries, civilizations).
2. Words related to the category are listed in a column on the left side of the grid.
3. Features or characteristics that some of the items have in common are listed across the top of the grid.
4. As each word is analyzed, pluses (+) or minuses (–) are placed in the squares of the grid to indicate the features each word possesses. Question marks (?) are used when the students are unsure as to whether the word possesses the particular characteristic. These make excellent springboards for further research.
5. The discussion continues until the grid is completed. Additional words and features may be added.
6. Students should be encouraged to examine the completed grid, noting the similarities and differences among the words in the category. They should be guided in making generalizations about the words in the category as well as determining what makes each word unique.

After the class has completed the grid, the students should examine the pattern of pluses and minuses to determine how the words are alike and how they differ. Pluses and minuses are generally used in discussing SFA, but other symbols may be used: smiling and sad faces; the letters Y for Yes or N for No; the letters A (almost always), N (almost never), or S (sometimes); or a numeric scale (e.g., 1–5), allowing students to indicate the relative degree of feature possession (Pittleman et al., 1991). Figure 4.10 provides an example of a SFA grid.

Figure 4.10   Semantic Features Analysis Grid

Non-fiction Semantic Feature Analysis CATEGORIES	mixes fiction and nonfiction	primarily factual	includes primary source documents	has characters	includes real people	has a table of contents	has a glossary	uses side bars and/or insets	has an index	includes Timelines	includes maps
articles	−	+	+	−	+	−	−	+	−	+	+
textbooks	−	+	+	−	+	+	+	+	+	+	+
non-fiction tradebooks	−	+	+	−	+	+	+	+	+	+	+
how-to books	−	+	+	−	−	+	+	−	+	−	−
informational story books	+	?	?	+	+	−	−	+	−	+	+
historical fiction	+	−	?	+	+	+	−	−	−	+	+
non-fiction poetry	+	?	−	−	?	−	−	−	−	−	−
biographies	−	+	+	−	+	+	−	+	+	+	+
newspaper	+	+	+	−	+	+	−	+	−	+	+
news magazines	−	+	+	−	+	+	−	+	−	+	+
world wide web	+	+	+	−	+	−	−	+	−	+	+

KEY   **+** generally included   **−** rarely included   **?** NOT SURE – depends on specific book

SFA is one strategy that allows students to conceptualize new knowledge and build relationships among concepts. It is particularly valuable because students are actively involved in the constructing and discussing of the grids. SFA is an excellent means of facilitating collaboration among students and fostering active participation in the learning process. It is easy to implement and is adaptable to a variety of learning activities and subject areas.

Reciprocal Teaching

Reciprocal Teaching is an instructional technique for teaching comprehension systematically (Palinczar & Brown, 1983; Lubliner, 2001; Hoyt, 2002). It takes place in the form of a dialogue between teachers and students regarding segments of text. Reciprocal Teaching was designed to teach students a systematic way of approaching a passage, so that after repeated practice, the students could utilize some effective strategies for increasing their understanding of text. Four strategies are used in structuring the dialogue: summarizing; question generating; clarifying; and predicting. The teacher and the students take turns assuming the role of the teacher in leading the dialogue.

Reciprocal Teaching

DESCRIPTION: A systematic procedure for approaching text, involving four components: summarizing, question generating, clarifying, and predicting.

PURPOSE:
   Instructional: Provides a systematic approach to develop understanding of text.
   Assessment: Allows teachers to note their students' ability to predict, clarify their thinking, generate meaningful questions about what they are reading, and summarize.

1. *Summarizing* (A segment of text is summarized in one or two sentences.) Summarizing provides students with the opportunity to identify and integrate the most important information in the text. The text may be summarized across sentences, paragraphs, or entire passages.

2. *Question Generating* (One or two questions are asked about the segment.)   In order to generate effective questions, the students must first identify the kind of information that is worthwhile for posing questions. Questions may be at any level of comprehension.

3. *Clarifying* (The difficult parts of the text are clarified.)   Clarifying is an activity that is designed to point out to students that there may be many reasons why text is difficult to understand (e.g., vocabulary, pronoun referents, difficult concepts, etc.). Clarification can take the form of explanations, giving examples, making analogies, or providing other clarifying statements. Through clarification, students are taught to become alert to impediments that might present themselves in texts, and measures that might be used to restore meaning, (e.g., reread, read ahead, ask for help). Clarifying is of particular importance to at-risk learners.

4. *Predicting* (A prediction is made regarding what the next segment will be about.)   When students predict, they make hypotheses about what the author will discuss next in the text. In order to accomplish this, students must activate relevant background knowledge. Predictions help students set a purpose for further reading, because readers must confirm or disprove their hypotheses.

When first introducing reciprocal teaching, teachers must discuss with their students the reasons why text may be difficult to understand, the importance of having a strategic approach to reading and learning, and how this procedure will help them understand and monitor their reading. Then students should be given an overall description of the procedure, emphasizing that reciprocal teaching takes the form of a dialogue about text and that everyone will get a turn assuming the role of the teacher.

To ensure that students will be successful with the procedure, it is advised that the students receive practice in each of the four strategies. For example, when teaching about summarization, teachers might explain that to summarize means eliminating extraneous information so that only the main points are retained. They then may introduce some rules that will help in the summarization:

1. Delete trivial information.
2. Delete redundant information.
3. Use a superordinate term for lists of terms.
4. Select a topic sentence.
5. Construct a topic sentence if one does not appear in the text.

When students are familiar with the four strategies, the dialogue may begin. Initially, the teacher assumes responsibility for initiating and sustaining the dialogue. Later, the students can become full partners in the process.

Reciprocal teaching demonstrates to students ways that effective readers approach challenging texts and helps them develop means of dealing with the information in these texts. After a number of practices with Reciprocal Teaching, students may generalize the steps and apply them to other text materials.

Reading for the Gist

When using this strategy, the students must write a summary in twenty words or less. Prior to implementing this strategy, teachers should explain to the students that the gist of something is the main idea, and that it is not always necessary to remember all the details. An analogy to a telegram could be made at this time, in which conciseness and brevity are necessary, while maintaining the essence of the message. Using an overhead projector or the white board, teachers draw twenty-word-long blanks and explain that following their reading, the students must write a sentence in twenty words or less, capturing the gist of the contents. Initially, this should be a collaborative activity, with students telling the teacher what to write, revising if necessary to meet the twenty-word limit. Generally, students are given passages with several paragraphs, and they write a gist statement for each one. However, while writing the statement for the second paragraph, students must incorporate information from both paragraphs in their gist sentence. Using information from both the first and second paragraphs, along with the new information in the new paragraph, is necessary for writing the next gist statement. Using this process, students learn how to ignore

Strategy AT A *Glance*

Reading for the Gist

DESCRIPTION: A structured, collaborative activity for determining the essence of a passage. Involves the identification of key terms and concepts to organize the important information into a summary.

PURPOSE:
  Instructional: Develops students' ability to determine the main idea.
  Assessment: Provides insights into students' ability to generate main ideas and pick out the important ideas in a passage.

superfluous information and get to the core of what they are reading (Moore et al., 1998). A variation of getting the gist can be seen in Figure 4.11. Here, a graphic organizer is used to help students collapse information to a single word that gets the gist of the author's message.

Figure 4.11   Getting the Gist

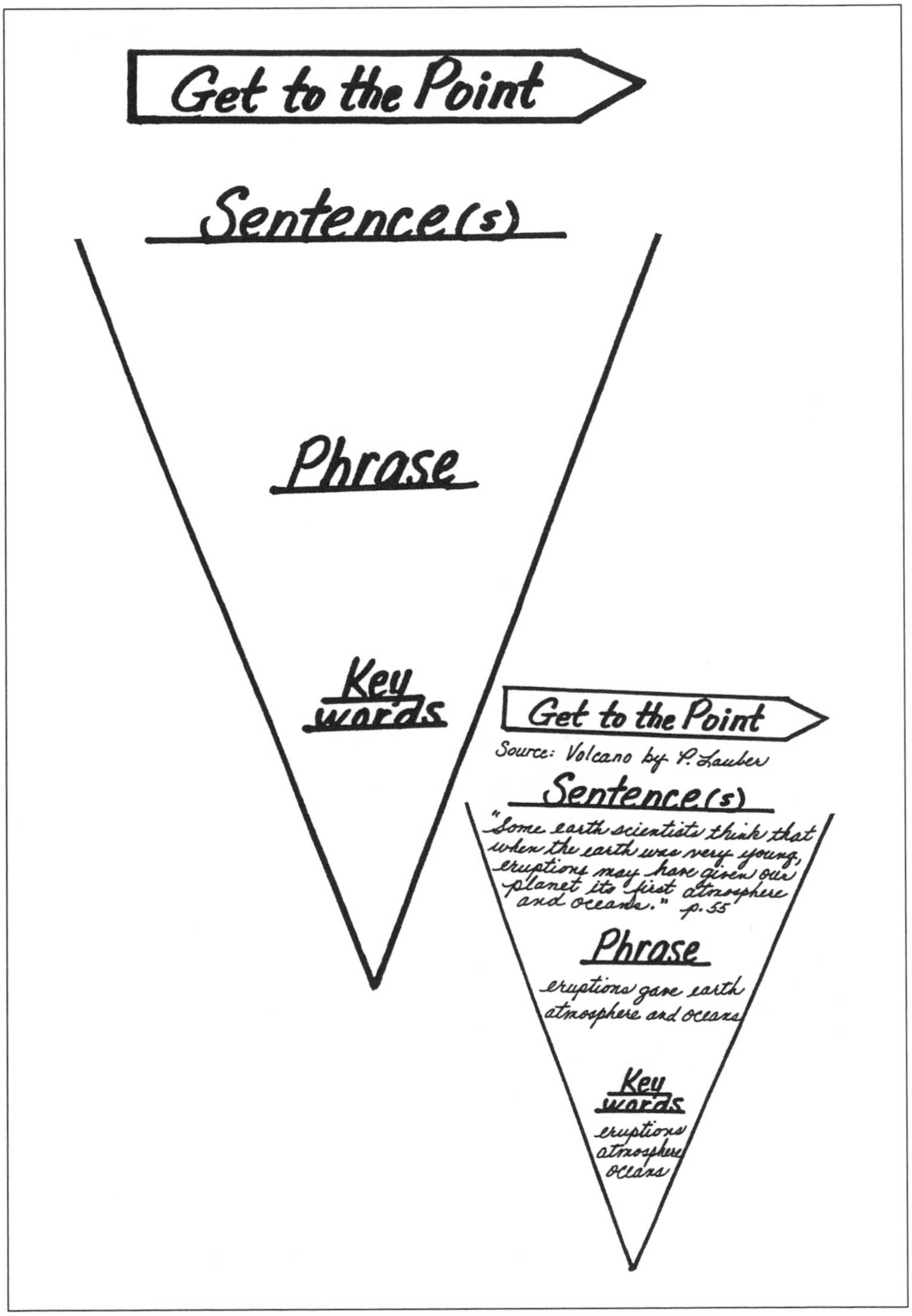

Guess Whose Shadow?

by Stephen R. Swinburne

Do you know what is the biggest shadow on earth? Shadows are a fascinating natural phenomenon, and if the sun is shining at the proper angle, everything in the world has a shadow. Because children are intrigued by shadows, they will enjoy figuring out what shadows are and how they work. With simplistic text and stunning full-color photographs, the author explores the incredible world of shadows. Children are invited to look at and investigate shadows that exist in their own world. This picture book makes an excellent introduction to the topic of shadows, and also shows how effective photographs can be as an art medium for nonfiction texts. By the way, the answer to what is the biggest shadow—*night!*

VOCABULARY DEVELOPMENT

Now for a *word* about vocabulary instruction. Content area teachers have two responsibilities when it comes to vocabulary instruction: 1) instruction in individual meanings and 2) instruction in deriving meaning. It is virtually impossible to teach every new word that students need to learn for the entire school year. Therefore, part of the instructional time has to focus on teaching and reinforcing students' ability to handle unknown words independently. Students must be able to answer the question, "What do you do when you come to a word you don't know?" Students must have at their access a list of strategies they can utilize when they encounter unknown words: for example, reread, read ahead, look for parts of the word that you already know, sound it out, look in a dictionary, ask a friend or the teacher, and so on. An important aspect of the literacy program is to assist students in developing a system of identifying words.

In addition to helping students with their word recognition, teachers are responsible for the teaching of selected vocabulary words in order to remove barriers to comprehension and to boost the understanding of key concepts and ideas that will be encountered in expository text. This can be accomplished through demonstrations, experiments, explanations, the use of concrete objects, discussion, questioning, lecture, and the like. Other techniques to build students' vocabularies in the content areas were discussed previously: semantic mapping, semantic feature analysis, and structured overviews. There are other techniques that may be used: previewing in context, contextual redefinition, word concept definition, word sorts, and word walls. Again, it should be noted that the strategies presented are just the tip of the iceberg when it comes to ways of teaching vocabulary. The resources listed at the end of the book should be consulted for additional techniques.

List-Group-Label-Write

List-Group-Label-Write is a strategy that helps students use their prior knowledge to improve their understanding of text, their vocabulary, and their writing

List-Group-Label-Write

DESCRIPTION: A brainstorming strategy in which students recall as many terms as possible on a given topic, group them according to similarities, and write about one or more of their categories. Can be a pre- or postreading activity.

PURPOSE:
   Instructional: Assists students to use their prior knowledge to improve vocabulary, comprehension, and writing.
   Assessment: Assesses prior knowledge and students' ability to categorize conceptually.

(Wood, 2001). Students first brainstorm as many terms as they can on a given topic and then group these terms according to similarities. Following the categorizing of the terms, the students read the selection and revisit their prior groupings. The categories can be adjusted, if warranted. Students can also provide additional terms to add to their categories or to create additional categories. As a concluding activity, the students can choose one of their categories and write about it.

Previewing in Context

The *Preview in Context* strategy helps students use both their prior knowledge and the context to determine the meaning of preselected words (Readence, Bean, & Baldwin, 2000). The following steps are used in the preview in context strategy:

1. *Preparation.* The teacher selects two or three new words to teach. The passages in the text must contain strong context clues for the terms that are to be taught.
2. *Establishing the Context.* The passage is read aloud, with the students following along in their texts. The passage is reread silently by the students. The

Previewing in Context

DESCRIPTION: Prereading strategy for using the context to determine meanings of words.

PURPOSE:
   Instructional: Enhances vocabulary development.
   Assessment: Assesses students' ability to use the context to figure out the meanings of words.

students have now encountered the term and the context for deriving meaning for the term.

3. *Specifying the Meaning of the Term.*   The teacher now engages the students in discussion to help them discover the definition. The students are encouraged to use their prior knowledge and the clues in the text to derive a meaning.
4. *Expanding the Meaning of the Word.*   After the students have gained an understanding of the word, the teacher then tries to expand their knowledge by discussing synonyms, antonyms, other contexts for the word, and so forth.

After the words have been taught, the students are encouraged to put the words in their learning logs or notes. The preview in context strategy is a pre-reading strategy that only works when the context for the words is strong. The strength in using this strategy is the discussion between the teacher and the students, which contributes to deeper comprehension by the students.

Contextual Redefinition

Unfortunately, texts do not provide enough context for students to determine the meaning of unknown words. The *Contextual Redefinition* strategy helps students to use the context more effectively by presenting them with sufficient context before reading and showing them how to use the clues to make informed guesses about the meanings. A suggested procedure is as follows (Tierney, Readence, & Dishner, 1995; Readence, Bean, & Baldwin, 2000):

1. *Selecting Words.*   Two or three words are selected to be pretaught.
2. *Writing a Sentence.*   A sentence is written with sufficient clues for the word to be taught. The different types of context clues are utilized: direct definition, synonyms, antonyms, comparison/contrast.
3. *Presenting the Words in Isolation.*   The words are presented in isolation and the students are asked to pronounce them. They are also encouraged to guess the meanings of the words.
4. *Presenting the Words in Context.*   The words are then presented in meaningful contexts. During discussion of the meaning of the word, the students are encouraged to come to consensus about its meaning. To help students become more aware of the value of using the context, a discussion may be held on the difference between defining the words in isolation or in context.

Strategy AT A *Glance*

Contextual Redefinition

DESCRIPTION: A strategy for teaching students to make effective use of the context in determining the meaning of words.

PURPOSE:
  Instructional: Provides an effective method for deriving meanings of words.
  Assessment: Assesses students' ability to use clues in text for figuring out vocabulary.

5. *Verifying the Definition.* A dictionary or glossary may be consulted for the definition. This definition is compared with the one given by the students.

There are several benefits derived from this strategy. Students come to realize that focusing on words in isolation is frustrating and generally inaccurate. They then search for more effective methods to derive meaning. They also become more actively involved in the discovery of new vocabulary, as opposed to merely memorizing new terms. Finally, the dictionary is seen as a valuable resource in verifying the most appropriate definition.

Concept/Definition Maps

The *Concept/Definition Map* is an excellent strategy for teaching both key concepts and vocabulary (Buehl, 2001). The Concept Map is a graphic organizer that assists students in understanding the complete definition of a word. This definition includes the category of the word, its characteristics or properties, and examples (or even non-examples). An example of a Concept Map can be seen in Figure 4.12.

By using Concept/Definition Maps, students expand their understanding of vocabulary and concepts beyond mere definitions. By using the graphic organizer format, they construct a visual representation of the definition that assists in remembering and understanding the term.

Word Walls

Word walls are areas in the classroom which are devoted to the displaying of vocabulary words. Word walls can be constructed on bulletin boards or chart paper, or be stuck on walls around the room. Their purposes are to promote an awareness of words and to give students ownership of their learning. All of the words on these walls are derived from the students' reading and writing in the content areas. They are not words that are intended to be studied in isolation. Words from a topic of study are placed on the wall, by both the teacher and the students, and are discussed by the entire class. Word walls promote independence in vocabulary learning and motivate students to want to learn more about words. Figure 4.13 depicts a word wall for the Civil War.

Strategy AT A Glance

Concept/Definition Maps

DESCRIPTION: Graphic structures that focus students' attention on key components of a definition (category, characteristics, and examples).

PURPOSE:
  Instructional: Teach key vocabulary and concepts.
  Assessment: Assess students' knowledge of vocabulary and their ability to categorize and provide relevant, supporting details.

Figure 4.12   Concept Definition for Nonfiction

? ? What is it ? ?

Category
genre

Illustration—
What are examples?

"How To" books
text books
encyclopedia
newspaper
brochure

Concept
nonfiction

Description—
What is it like?

contains factual
information

written text is
accurate

uses expository
writing

Define it: Nonfiction is expository writing to instruct or inform the reader using accurate factual information.

Learning new words is a natural part of content area literacy. The more experiences students have with reading and writing in the content areas, the more they will encounter words that will build up their background knowledge and increase their understanding of the topic being studied. However, vocabulary learning cannot be limited to merely having students read and write in the content areas. Students need to be provided with additional exposure, experiences, and teaching in order to completely understand key content area vocabulary and concepts. Effective vocabulary instruction includes developing students' awareness of words, providing wide reading and writing experiences, teaching students strategies for independently inferring word meanings, and offering students some direct instruction in vocabulary acquisition. It must be remembered that the ultimate objective of all vocabulary instruction is to have students become independent learners.

Strategy **AT A** *Glance*

Word Walls

DESCRIPTION: Areas in a classroom for displaying vocabulary.

PURPOSE:

Instructional: Promote an awareness of words and enhance vocabulary growth.

Figure 4.13 Word Wall for Civil War

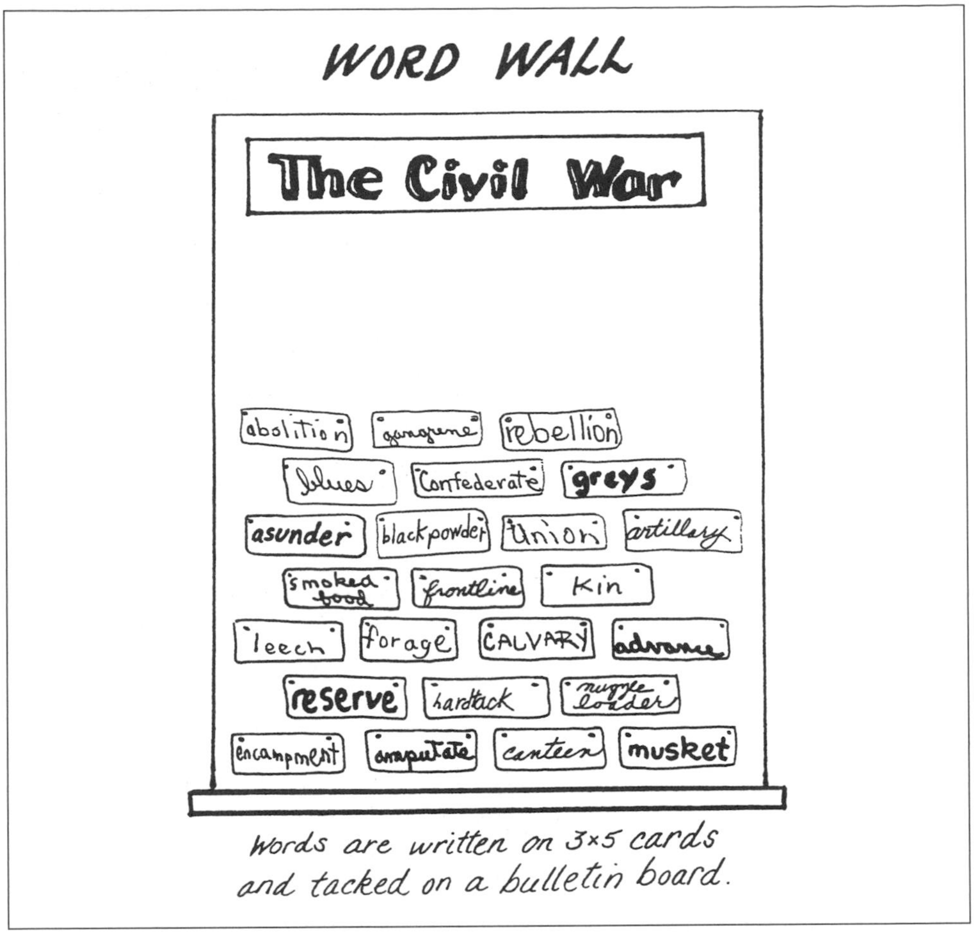

WORD WALL

The Civil War

abolition | gangrene | rebellion
blues | Confederate | greys
asunder | blackpowder | Union | artillary
smoked food | frontline | kin
leech | forage | CALVARY | advance
reserve | hardtack | muzzle loader
encampment | amputate | canteen | musket

*words are written on 3×5 cards
and tacked on a bulletin board.*

Try This

Strategy Interview

After students have been introduced to various strategies, have practiced and seem to understand them, they can reflect on how the strategies support their recall and understanding. They can write their thoughts in their journals, discuss them with their peers in small groups, or conference with the teacher. Some prompts for this purpose include:

■ Which reading strategy did you use?
■ Describe the strategy
■ How did the strategy help you with your (reading, studying, research, project, oral presentation, etc.)?

■ What other strategies did you use, or could you use?

Once students can state how specific strategies, such as those discussed in this chapter, can improve their comprehension and recall, they will see the purpose for using the strategies. Strategy interviews assist students in self-evaluating their learning, as well as give teachers pertinent assessment data.

Instructional Activities for the Classroom

1 Chapter-Beginning Activity

One type of nonfiction text is the how-to or procedural book, and a popular variety can be found on many book store shelves—*Life's Little Instructions*. Students can create their own versions of *Life's Little Instructions*, with the focus being on *Life's Little Instructions on Reading Nonfiction*. The focus would be on the strategies that enhance success with nonfiction texts.

2 Questioning the Author

Students could examine the kinds of questions that the authors of their textbooks use at the end of the chapters. They could determine what kind of thinking is needed to answer these questions, using the QAR taxonomy. They could also examine their own questions that they pose in their logs or in discussions.

3 Picture This

Instead of students writing about the main idea of a topic, they can pretend that they have been hired to photograph the topic or illustrate it for a major magazine, such as *Time for Kids* or *National Geographic World for Kids*. As photographers or illustrators, they have to capture the essence of the topic in their illustrations. A class wall, or the corridor outside the room, can be set up as a gallery to display their "photographs" or illustrations.

Book Talk and Beyond

Animal Homes: A First Look at Animals *by Diane James and Sara Lynn*

Animal Homes: A First Look at Animals is a great introduction to the topic of shelters or animal adaptations. It also is a marvelous model for nonfiction for young readers. The book contains a table of contents, boxed information, and an index. Part of the *Jump Starts* series, this book will interest young readers for its simple, factual, read-along text; amusing illustrations; and superb photographs. Two pages are devoted to such well-known and fascinating animals as prairie dogs, beavers, and grizzly bears. One page provides the facts, broken up with whimsical illustrations, and the following page is a full-page photograph. There's even a quiz at the end to review the contents. This text would be a welcome addition to a thematic study on animals. After reading and learning about animals and their habitats, the children could show what they have learned on a semantic features analysis grid.

Animals	Water habitat	Land habitat	Hatched from eggs	Born Alive	Fur or hair	Scales	Feathers	Raise their young	Survive alone	Can be pets	usually wild
bird	+	+	+	–	–	–	+	+	–	–	+
deer	–	+	–	+	+	–	–	+	o	–	+
fish	+	–	+	o	–	+	–	+	–	o	+
rabbit	–	+	–	+	+	–	–	–	+	o	+
turtle	+	+	+	–	–	+	–	+	–	+	+
cat	–	+	–	+	+	–	–	+	–	o	+
mouse	–	+	–	+	+	–	–	+	–	–	+
fox	–	+	–	+	+	–	–	+	–	–	+
squirrel	–	+	–	+	+	–	–	–	–	+	–
dog	–	+	–	+	+	–	–	+	–	o	+
snake	+	–	+	–	–	–	–	–	+	o	+

+ yes   – no   o sometimes

Amazing Insects: Eyewitness Juniors 26

by Laurence Mound

There are over five million kinds of insects on our planet. Insects have no inside skeleton like most animals, rather the outer covering of the body is their skeleton. This book shows insects up close and enlarged in color photographs. It is filled with fascinating information about how insects defend themselves (have you ever been stung?), what they eat (many eat each other!), where they live (some wasps actually make their paper nests by chewing tree bark), and how they communicate (that's why fireflies light up!). After exploring the amazing insects, a class paper quilt can be created using mural paper, wallpaper, and student drawings, with an interesting, brief, written fact. Glue the drawing, done on a *square*, to a larger *square* of wallpaper; then glue the wallpaper to the mural paper. To simulate stitching, a marker can be used to outline each square. Complete the quilt with a title and date.

Writing Nonfiction

Introduction

Writing instruction in elementary schools has improved significantly over the past few decades, largely as a result of the research on the writing process and the work of such notables as Donald Graves, Lucy Calkins, Nancie Atwell, and

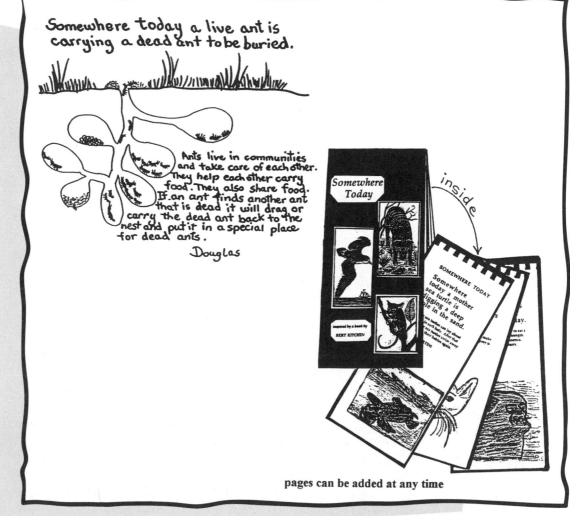

Somewhere today a live ant is carrying a dead ant to be buried.

Ants live in communities and take care of each other. They help each other carry food. They also share food. If an ant finds another ant that is dead it will drag or carry the dead ant back to the nest and put it in a special place for dead ants.

Douglas

Somewhere Today

inspired by a book by
BERT KITCHEN

inside

SOMEWHERE TODAY

Somewhere today a mother sea turtle is digging a deep hole in the sand.

pages can be added at any time

Inspired by Somewhere Today by Bert Kitchen

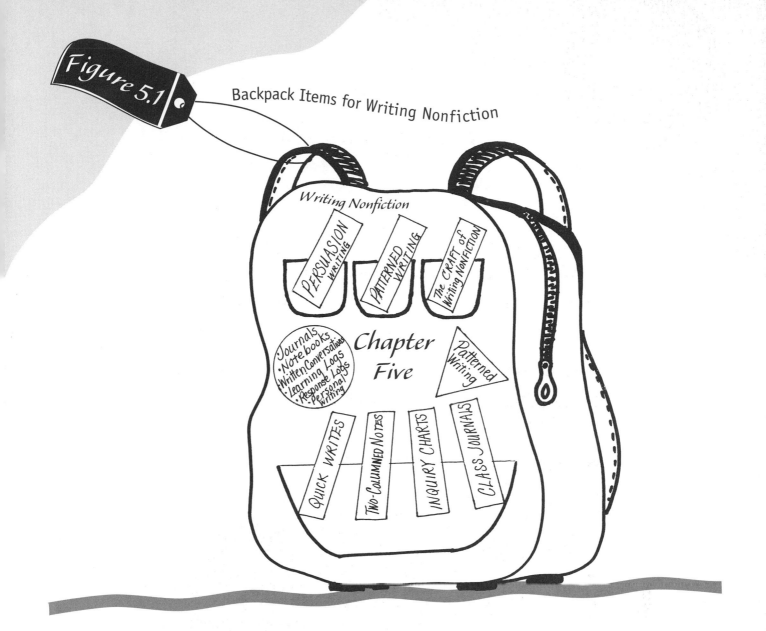

Figure 5.1 Backpack Items for Writing Nonfiction

Donald Murray, among others. This research has influenced the way teachers perceive the teaching of writing. Teachers are now providing their students with more authentic writing experiences and helping them learn how to write for real reasons and real audiences. Teachers are helping students understand that writing is a process, and a craft, and this goes for writing nonfiction, as well as for narrative writing.

The process of writing nonfiction is but one aspect of writing in the content areas. Writing can also play a key role as a means to learn content, because it has been demonstrated that writing can enhance the understanding of text and increases the likelihood that the content will be remembered. This chapter addresses both of these aspects of nonfiction writing: (1) using the writing process and sound instructional practices to teach students how to write quality nonfiction, and (2) using writing as a strategy to increase learning and understanding in the content areas. Figure 5.1 depicts the nonfiction writing tools and information that will be placed in your backpack, so that you will be equipped to assist your students while they are engaged in the writing of nonfiction.

THE CRAFT OF WRITING NONFICTION

Think about the writing you have done in the past week. Have you written a short story, started writing a novel, or responded to a prompt to the book you are reading at home? Probably not. You most likely wrote memos, anecdotal records of your students, information to your students' parents, a grocery list, and so forth. The majority of writing that we do in the real world is expository. We write to inform, persuade, describe, explain, teach, and remind. Students likewise need to write for these purposes, not only for success in school, but for success beyond schooling, at work, and in their personal lives.

Although writing instruction has vastly improved over the years, it is still found that educators do not promote enough nonfiction writing (Stead, 2002), because little nonfiction, beyond personal narrative, is generally written. Many teachers are doing excellent jobs at involving students in narrative writing, demonstrating how to plan, compose, revise, edit, and publish writing pieces. This instruction needs to be extended to nonfiction writing as well. Teachers need to open the doors to the possibilities beyond narrative in their writing programs, both during language arts time and during content area instruction.

Until recently, the focus in writing instruction was on the product, and this was particularly true of any writing in content area classes. Students collected information, primarily using such reference materials as encyclopedias, and wrote a one-shot paper, which was graded by the teacher. This one-draft mentality did nothing to help the students become better writers, nor did it help them master the content that was to be learned.

Realizing that the focus on products was unsuccessful in helping students become better writers or attain content knowledge or literacy, teachers have adopted the process writing approach. See Figure 5.2 for an overview of the writing process. As students move through this process of brainstorming ideas, researching their topic thoroughly, organizing the information, and creating and revising several drafts, they become more effective writers and more knowledgeable about their subject matter.

Along with using the writing process in the content classroom, to be effective, writing programs must address such key elements as audience, purpose, and form. Students need to have wider audiences in addition to their teacher. They need to write for themselves, their classmates, the community, school publications, and commercially produced magazines and newspapers. They also must write for a variety of purposes, which may take many forms. To help

---

Try This

Writing in the Real World

Have your students and their families keep track of the writing they do for a designated period of time (e.g., a school week). Once this information has been collected, it can be categorized into specific writing forms and their purposes, with the results graphed. The students will probably be amazed at how much nonfiction writing they and their families do during the course of one week.

| *Figure 5.2* | Overview of the Writing Process |

Prewriting
(deciding on a topic, identifying an audience and purpose for writing, determining the appropriate form, and gathering ideas and data)
- What should I write about?
- What do I know about the topic?
- Where can I find information?
- Who is my audience?
- What do I want them to know?
- Why am I writing?
- What form is appropriate?

Drafting or Composing
(putting ideas down on paper)
- How do I want to say it?
- How can I write clearly and effectively?
- How should I organize my writing?
- What words should I choose to express what I want to say?

Revising
(clarifying and reshaping the meaning and organization of the writing)
- Does my piece say what I want it to say?
- How can I make my writing clearer and more effective?
- Should I add to, delete, or reorder my writing?
- Does my writing make sense?
- Will my readers understand my writing?
- Am I pleased with my writing?

Editing
(attending to the surface features of writing mechanics, grammar, and spelling)
- How can I get my writing ready for readers?
- Have I identified and corrected my errors in spelling, grammar, and punctuation?

Publishing
(producing a finished product for an audience)
- How should I publish my writing?
- How should I share my writing?

students focus on purpose and audience, teachers may wish to post a reminder to consider these crucial aspects when undertaking writing (Education Department of Western Australia, 1994):

Purpose + Audience = Form

Figure 5.3 outlines some purposes of nonfiction writing and the forms they may take.

Figure 5.3	Nonfiction Purposes and Forms

Purpose	Forms	
To describe	reports	poetry
	letters	labels
	captions	illustrations
	personal recount	retellings
	brochures	pamphlets
To instruct, command, direct, or request	recipes	directions
	warnings	rules
	memos	experiments
	games	lists
	letters	captions
	labels	signs
To persuade	advertisements	commercials
	editorials	graffiti
	signs	arguments
	debates	reviews
	evaluations	letters
	cartoons	posters
	warnings	applications
To explain	textbooks	handbooks
	recipes	captions
	labels	rules
	excuses	brochures
	articles	reports
	letters	personal narrative
	charts	invitations
To retell information about people or events	reports	biographies
	autobiographies	poetry
	journals	diaries
	letters	scripts
To invite reflection	quotations	questions
	learning logs	journals
	diaries	self-assessment forms
To predict or hypothesize	forecasts	predictions
	theories	horoscopes
	graphs	timetables

Figure 5.3   *Continued*

Purpose	Forms	
To inform or advise	announcements	invitations
	pamphlets	surveys
	catalogs	lists
	graphs	broadcasts
	schedules	forecasts
	labels	book jackets
To explore, and maintain, relationships with others	cards	letters
	interviews	poetry
	questionnaires	dialogue journals
	notes	postcards

NOTE: Many forms can be used for several purposes.

Sources: From Education Department of Western Australia, 1994; Lenski & Johns, 2000; and Stead, 2002.

Students can produce quality nonfiction writing if teachers provide the appropriate instruction and allow the students ample time to practice. Teachers must surround their students with examples of high-quality nonfiction, build in time for the students to write nonfiction, and provide *explicit* instruction in writing nonfiction (Harvey, 1998). Following are some guidelines to enhance effective nonfiction writing:

- Give students authentic purposes for writing, with specific audiences in mind.
- Provide students with an awareness as to why authors use and write different nonfiction forms.
- Show students a variety of nonfiction writing models.
- Give students demonstrations on how to write different text forms for different purposes.
- Assure students that there is adequate time to write nonfiction pieces.
- Allow students to assume some responsibility for their learning (e.g., choosing the content or the form).

Try This

A Class Museum or Big Book of Nonfiction Writing Forms

As proposed earlier, examples of nonfiction writing forms could be collected and displayed on a bulletin board, in the writing center, in a display case, and so on. As the year progresses, and the students themselves undertake writing some of these forms, these too could become part of the display or placed in a class book, along with the examples collected from the outside world. This book can then serve as a reference for nonfiction writing, not only for this class, but for future classes as well.

- Help students recognize that writing benefits from the use of voice, proper word choice, and clarity.
- Provide a comfortable, safe environment in which to work. (Harvey, 1998; Stead, 2002)

Unlike those who write narrative, nonfiction authors must convey accurate information; therefore, students have to write nonfiction both accurately and in a compelling way (Harvey, 1998). In writing nonfiction, students need to know how to apply the writing process—for example, plan, compose, revise, and publish nonfiction texts. They have to become familiar with the various formats available and the purposes that drive the writing of nonfiction. They must be aware that when writing nonfiction, writers often have more than one purpose. For example, an article on some environmental concern in a news magazine may describe the issue as well as to persuade the readers to accept a particular viewpoint or stance. Students need to create quality nonfiction pieces, using leads, middles, and conclusions that show, not tell. They must write clearly in their own voices. All of this can be accomplished if students are given *explicit* instruction in writing nonfiction, and are given ample opportunities to write nonfiction. A framework for delivering explicit instruction consists of the following:

- Select a writing purpose and form (one that will be beneficial and appropriate).
- Immerse the students in a content area, to provide a real context for their learning the purpose of writing and its relevant form.
- Assess the students' prior knowledge, skills, and understanding of the selected writing form.
- Implement a whole class exploration of the writing form.
- Allow students to independently explore the form being investigated.
- Assess the students to determine their writing skills and their understanding of the form once the instruction has concluded. (Education Department of Western Australia, 1994; Harvey, 1998; Stead, 2002)

Teachers must explicitly explain the steps in writing each form, model throughout the process, and gradually release responsibility for the learning (Harvey, 1998). Demonstrations of the intended learning are not enough. Simply showing the students *how* without giving them time to practice is not effective. Students need to write the selected form with the teacher providing ongoing demonstrations and support. Finally, they must be given opportunities to engage in independent practice, accompanied by feedback, and then apply what they have learned in real literacy situations. Each of the steps in this explicit teaching framework is essential to the students' success in writing nonfiction forms. An application of this framework to the teaching of *persuasion* follows.

A FRAMEWORK FOR TEACHING NONFICTION WRITING— PERSUASION

The general purposes of persuasive writing are to convince, put forward a particular point of view, or justify a position. Persuasive writing also can be writing that encourages people to buy something, participate in some sort of activity, or think in a certain way. The forms used in persuasive writing include advertisements, expositions, debates, arguments, signs, posters, poems, letters, editorials, reviews, and pamphlets. For the purposes of this demonstration, one of these forms—exposition—is used.

The primary purpose of an exposition is to present a basic position and develop the ideas logically from a particular viewpoint. In expositions, authors provide a statement of the basic position that is taken, sometimes referred to as the thesis statement, followed by a series of reasons or arguments to support the stance. Generally, the exposition ends with a conclusion or summary statement. Figure 5.4 provides an overview of the organizational pattern used in writing expositions. Both facts and opinions are used in proposing the arguments, along with the use of such transition words as *because, although, but, in contrast, nevertheless, on the other hand, therefore, so,* and *the reason why.* Visuals and sound effects—diagrams, labels, pictures, illustrations, graphs, charts, and the like—might also be included—to help persuade the reader.

To introduce the selected writing form, teachers should immerse students in examples of the form, sharing the forms while reading aloud, during shared and guided reading, as the focus of minilessons, and so on. If available, big books make excellent models for this purpose (Freeman, 2001), because the enlarged text permits the entire class to see and hear the example simultaneously.

| Figure 5.4 | Organizational Pattern for Exposition |

Subject and Thesis
(overview of the topic stating the basic position)
- What position will be taken?
- What information is needed?

Reasons and Arguments
(the evidence that is provided to support the chosen stance)
- What points will be made to support the position?
- What transition words can be used to deliver the argument?
- What examples can be included to strengthen the argument or case?
- What visuals/sounds can be used?

Summary and Conclusion
(restates the subject of the paper, summarizes how the reasons support the point of view, and concludes with a summary of the position)
- How can the points be restated to redefine the position that was taken?
- What concluding words can be used to convincingly state the position to persuade the readers?

Sources: From Education Department of Western Australia, 1994; and Lenski & Johns, 2000.

The purpose of this phase of explicit teaching is to develop an awareness of the form that is being taught, along with pointing out the specific features of the particular form. Teachers also should assess what the students already know about the form, perhaps placing the information that the students relay onto chart paper. A K-W-L format can be used for this purpose.

Unfortunately, there are few trade books available to teach persuasive writing, but teachers can use such nonfiction materials as articles, editorials, and even advertisements to address the teaching of this form. As students hear, read, and discuss these examples, characteristics of the form can be noted and recorded on chart paper. The students could brainstorm and look for examples of what makes a good persuasive argument (see Figure 5.5 for an example of such a chart). This information can later be developed into a rubric for assessing the persuasive writing piece that the students undertake independently.

After students are familiar with the purpose and format of persuasive writing, teachers can model writing a piece, using a decision tree graphic organizer (Figure 5.6) to help formulate and develop their position and arguments. The topic of the piece can be related to some aspect of classroom management— "Should sixth graders be allowed to walk to specials on their own?"—or to some aspect of the curriculum, "Should trees in the rain forest be cut down?" While writing, teachers can demonstrate the following:

- Choosing a topic
- Beginning pieces with interesting leads
- Organizing the information logically
- Using persuasive language (e.g., transition words)
- Incorporating visuals or sound
- Differentiating between fact and opinion

Figure 5.5   Chart for What Makes a Good Argument in Persuasive Writing

- Pick a topic, and choose a position, or state your opinion.
- Research your topic.
- Use books, magazines, the computer, and other resources.
- Provide strong reasons to justify your position.
- Include facts to support what you are trying to say.
- Avoid personal bias and emotional words.
- Use transitional words in your writing.
- Use visuals, e.g., illustrations, charts, graphs, etc., to convince others.
- Stick to the topic—maintain your point of view.
- Organize and present your information logically.
- Summarize your position and key points.
- Have an interesting lead and a powerful conclusion.

NOTE: This chart can be modified depending on the experiential level of the students.

Figure 5.6 Decision Tree Model for Expositions

- Providing reasons that support the point of view
- Writing an effective conclusion (Stead, 2002)

Next, teachers and students can collaboratively write a piece, choosing a relevant topic to explore. Young children can choose a favorite animal, school activity, video, or book, and provide justification for their choice. Older students can address topics in any curricular area.

English Language Arts   the banning of books like the *Harry Potter* series
Social Studies   continuation of bombing in Afghanistan to help end terrorism
Science   genetic altering of food (or cloning)
Music   allowing rap music to be played on the school bus

During the teaching, examples of exposition can continually be analyzed, placing the writing piece on an overhead projector for this purpose. Teachers can use articles in news magazines, student examples (it's beneficial to collect samples over the years), or examples of student writing in some professional resources, such as *The Writing Resource Book*, developed by the Education Department of Western Australia.

When it is time for students to write independently, the class should review the qualities of effective persuasive writing, as well as the steps in the writing process. The rubric that will be used for assessment could be developed at this time (see Figure 5.7 for an example). Students may now have a good idea of a topic to explore, but some students still may need assistance. Although there are not many elementary-school level books that use persuasive writing, trade books can become springboards for topic selection (e.g., *So You Want to Be President?*).

Incorporating writing process instruction into content area classes and using an explicit model of teaching are effective practices to promote the writing of nonfiction. Replacing the one-shot report or essay of the past with process writing causes students to think and act like authors in search of ques-

Figure 5.7   Rubric for Persuasive Writing

Assessment Rubric

Persuasive Writing	3 strongly included	2 some evidence	1 beginning use-minimal	0 not shown
Student Name: _____ Title: _____ Date: _____				
PURPOSE				
• shows an understanding of persuasive writing				
RESEARCH ABILITY				
• able to locate information				
• used multiple sources				
• used information to support an argument				
WRITING CRAFT				
• has an opening statement				
• cites supporting material				
• organization is clear				
• includes persuasive language				
• uses facts				
• use opinions				
MECHANICS				
• presentation is neat				
• spelling is correct				
• grammar is correct				
• punctuation is correct				
FINAL GRADE:	Comments: _____			

A Mountain Alphabet

by Margriet Ruurs

If you enjoy taking walks and being outdoors in natural surroundings, you'll love this book. The text and illustrations provide the beauty and majesty of the Rocky Mountains. You can watch a fly fisherman, sit around a campfire, climb the canyon walls, and ski down a slope. The illustrations also provide a challenge to identify many objects for each letter of the alphabet hidden on every page. The book is filled with the wonders of nature and interesting information.

tions, information, and answers. Instead of merely assigning reports, explicit teaching helps produce writers who are knowledgeable about the craft of writing, who now can put their thoughts together and write!

Patterned Writing

Before we leave the topic of the craft of writing, another aspect of a writing program that should be addressed is *patterned writing* (Allen, 2000). Patterned writing is possible when students use the writing style or formats of particular pieces of literature or expository texts. Teachers need to locate pieces of literature or other forms of nonfiction writing that can be replicated. Poetry can be used—cinquains, haikus, bio-poems, I Am poems, and so on—as can such literature selections that use a predictable format throughout the text. Alphabet books also can provide models for students to use when presenting what they have learned. Patterned writing sometimes can be the first successful writing pieces for some students, because it provides a safety net when students run out of ideas for their writing. Although not limited to struggling learners, patterned writing especially helps these students generate text in depth and breadth. Figure 5.8 lists some examples of nonfiction that can be adapted by students. Student examples of patterned writing can be seen in the introductory activities in many of the chapters, as well as in Figure 5.9.

WRITING TO LEARN

Writing is a powerful vehicle to guide student learning. Writing can be used to explore and integrate ideas in the content areas, as a means of reflection, and as a way to deepen understanding of nonfiction texts. Therefore, the remainder of this chapter focuses on writing strategies that enhance students' success with nonfiction texts. This discussion is only the tip of the iceberg, because space limitations preclude a more expansive discussion of this topic. Rather, our discussion highlights some very effective, useful, and practical strategies and activities, devoted to strategic learning, so that additional information and support in this area can be obtained.

| *Figure 5.8* | A Sampling of Nonfiction Texts for Patterned Writing |

Selected Pieces of Literature
- *If I Were in Charge of the World* by Judy Viorst
- *Somewhere Today* by Bert Kitchen
- *And So They Build* by Bert Kitchen
- *Imagine* by Alison Lester
- *When I Was Little* by Jamie Lee Curtis
- *Anno's Mysterious Multiplying Jar* by Anno

Books Using Letters and Postcards to Tell Story or Provide Information
- *Kate Heads West* by Pat Brisson
- *Dear Laura: Letters from Children to Laura Ingalls Wilder* from HarperCollins
- *Letters from Rifka* by Karen Hesse
- *Dear Dr. King: Letters from Today's Children to Dr. Martin Luther King, Jr.,* from Hyperion Books
- *Postcards from Pluto: A Tour of the Solar System* by Laureen Leedy
- *Beethoven Lives Upstairs* by Barbara Nicol
- *A Dialogue With Today's Youth* by Rosa Parks
- *Nettie's Trip South* by Ann Turner
- *Stringbean's Trip to the Shining Sea* by Vera Williams
- *Dear Children of the Earth* by Shim Schimmel

Selected Series
- *Alphabet Book* Series by Jerry Pallotta
- *Questions and Answers About* Series by Melvin & Gilda Berger
- *Postcards From...* varied authors, published by Steck Vaughn
- *Look What Came From...* published by Franklin Watts
- *If You Were There...* published by Scholastic
- *Fascinating Facts About...* published by Millbrook Press

Journal Writing

"Dear Diary." How many of you kept diaries at one time in your life? How many of you have read diaries, journals, or excerpts from logs written by other people? In the school setting, journals are documents of academic and personal growth, records of developing insights, and tools used to gain those insights. Using journals presents an opportunity to use writing on a regular, if not daily, basis. Journals serve a variety of purposes—self-expression, thinking through issues, and solving problems in content areas.

Journals have been around since the invention of paper and were even found among the ruins of Pompeii and in Egyptian tombs. Many famous people have kept diaries or journals, including Leonardo da Vinci, Fyodor Dostoyevski, Louisa May Alcott, and Anne Frank. People have used journals to express their thoughts, share their experiences, and try out ideas. Now teachers are incorporating *journal writing* into their instructional programs as they recognize the benefits of journal writing. Journals serve the following purposes:

Figure 5.9 Student Example of Patterned Writing

San Francisco Earthquake
by Kelli Kanrin and Alana Schultz

Earthquake	Earthquake
Earthquake cracks open	
	Shaking violently
chairs and tables	chairs and tables
fly all over	
	just missing you
As they pass by	As they pass by.
The first thought	
	Is death
As you sit	
	waiting for it
To end.	to end.

Inspired by *Joyful Noise: Poems for Two Voices* by Paul Fleischman, and *Earthquakes* by Seymour Simon.

- Provide a forum for students to reflect, learn, and gain an understanding of the content areas.
- Help students make personal connections to the subject matter being studied.
- Clarify thoughts and promote thinking.
- Help students prepare for class discussions, study for tests, and understand reading assignments.
- Provide a vehicle for evaluation (both self-reflection and a means for teachers to note student growth and progress).
- Assist students in becoming independent learners (Harvey, 1998; Lenski & Johns, 2000; Readence, Bean, & Baldwin, 2000).

Strategy AT A Glance

Personal Journals

DESCRIPTION: Notebooks for students to record events in their own lives and write about self-chosen topics.

PURPOSE:
  Instructional: Activate prior knowledge, encourage self-reflection, increase involvement and motivation.
  Assessment: Provide insights into student feelings and interests.

Without much difficulty, journals can become an integral part of the curriculum. The possibilities for incorporating journal writing into the school day and throughout the day are many. Journals can take many forms: personal journals or diaries, dialogue journals, nonfiction notebooks, reading response logs, simulated journals, and class journals.

Personal Journals   The purpose of personal journals is for students to record or recount events in their own lives and write about self-chosen topics. To help students who may have difficulty deciding what to write, a list of possible topics for journal writing can be brainstormed and placed on a chart or sheet, to be inserted into a writing folder (see Figure 5.10). The topics listed here pertain to nonfiction, and are not meant to be exhaustive.

Figure 5.10   Topics for Journals

- things I like to do
- personal events
- movie or sports stars
- travels
- Today I did . . .
- early memories
- I feel . . .
- I used to think (believe) . . .
- What I like best (least) about . . .
- The best (worst) thing that happened to me . . .
- looking back
- looking ahead
- The way I would change my (life, school, country, etc.) . . .
- People place too much importance on . . .
- I'm different from everyone else because . . .
- Let me tell you about (how to) . . .
- If I could trade places with . . . I . . .

Nonfiction Notebooks/Wonder Books

DESCRIPTION:　Writing tools for students to explore their passions, interests, reflections, thoughts, and questions.

PURPOSE:
　Instructional:　Activate prior knowledge, encourage student reflections, self-questioning, and wonderings.
　Assessment:　Offer information on student metacognitive behaviors, student concerns, interests, and questions.

Nonfiction Notebooks/Wonder Books　Many writers keep notebooks to record their daily thinking. This practice can be implemented in the classroom and can become an important tool for students to use to explore their passions, interests, reflections, thoughts, and questions (Harvey, 1998). Used daily, Wonder Books can help students discover valuable insights, as well as lead them to explore more meaningful, thought-provoking research questions. Teachers can introduce nonfiction notebooks and journals to students by reading books in which the authors or characters in the books record or reflect on their thinking in a notebook, journal, or diary (see Figure 5.11).

Wonder Books may contain information such as the following:

- Questions students may have
- Wonderings
- Lists for writing or research topics
- Interests or passions
- Background knowledge statements
- Notes from research, observations, experiments
- Models of effective writing
- Quotes or memorable language
- Interview questions or notes
- Drawings, diagrams
- Ideas for projects
- Bibliographic information

Dialogue Journals

DESCRIPTION:　Written conversations between two or more individuals.

PURPOSE:
　Instructional:　Present opportunities for interactions and communication between students and/or the teacher.
　Assessment:　Give insights into student interests, questions, and concerns.

Figure 5.11   Journal, Notebook, or Diary Writing in Trade Books

Journals and Notebooks
- *Stranded on Plimoth Plantation* by Gary Bowen
- *I, Columbus: My Journal* by Christopher Columbus
- *Antarctica Journal* by Meredith Hooper
- *Tschaikovsky Discovers America* by Esther Kalman
- *Trial by Jury/Journal* by Kate Klise
- *Wish You Were Here: Emily's Guide to the United States* by Kathleen Krull
- *Learning to Swim in Swaziland: A Child's-Eye View of a Southern African Country* by Nila Leigh
- *The Ledgerbook of Thomas Blue Eagle* by Gay Matthaei and Jewel Grutman
- *How We Crossed the West: The Adventures of Lewis and Clark* from National Geographic Society
- *The Year with Grandma Moses* by W. Nikola-Lisa

Diaries
- *Louisa May Alcott : Her Girlhood Diary* by Louisa May Alcott
- *So Far from Home: The Diary of Mary Driscoll, an Irish Mill Girl* by B. Denenberg
- *Zlata's Diary: A Child's Life in Sarajevo* by Zlata Filipovic
- *Only Opal: The Diary of a Young Girl* by Barbara Cooney
- *Diary of a Young Girl: The Definitive Edition* by Anne Frank
- *Diary of a Drummer Boy* by Marlene Targ Brill
- *My Prairie Year* by B. Harvey
- *An Owl in the House: A Naturalist's Diary* by B. Heinrich
- *Antarctic Diary* by T. Hart
- *A Journey to the New World: The Diary of Remember Patience Whipple, Mayflower 1620* by Kathryn Lasky

Dialogue Journals   Dialogue journals are defined as written conversations between two or more individuals. Here students and teachers (or students and other students) converse with one another through writing on a meaningful, continued basis. Dialogue journals present opportunities for true interactions and communication between teachers and students and between students and their peers. Dialogue journals involve purposeful, personalized communication that can enhance literacy. See Figure 5.12 for a sample of a dialogue journal.

Written Conversations   Written conversations are similar to dialogue journals in that two or more individuals are involved in writing or responding to one another. Written conversations may take on a more instructional focus because they are frequently used in conversing about a curricular area. For example, students may discuss the content they are learning about in a thematic study, a world crisis in current events, or a topic in science or social studies. They may go beyond writing about the content and may reflect on their learning, note difficulties, or make connections to their own lives.

Figure 5.12   Sample from a Dialogue Journal

Entry

I didn't know weather was so awesome. For my unit assignment I read Seymour Simon's <u>Volcanos</u>. I learned so much. Magma is melted rock inside the volcano. When it escapes it is called lava. When a volcano explotes the ash can travel thousands of miles. Volcanos are found all over the earth. Some are actin and some are extinct.

I watched watched storm chasers on the weather channel. I was wondering if there are people who travel around to watch and study volcanos. That is something I'd like to do because it would be so interesting. Someone took the pictures for the book and that would be a great job. This weather unit is pretty cool.

Response

Jason,
Simon is one of my favorite NF writers — his books are great. He came to our school, with his wife, for Authors Day seven years ago. You weren't in school yet! Our librarian has his address. You can write to him.

Strategy
AT A *Glance*

Written Conversations

DESCRIPTION: Written conversations between two or more individuals with an instructional focus.

PURPOSE:
   Instructional: Allow participants to discuss issues and content through writing.
   Assessment: Identify gaps in learning, confusions, knowledge, and concepts learned.

Strategy
AT A *Glance*

Learning Logs

DESCRIPTION: Places where students can record and react to what they are learning.

PURPOSE:

Instructional: Provide a vehicle for students to reflect on their learning, explore relationships, explain how to do something, and clarify their thinking.

Assessment: Assist in noting gaps in learning, misconceptions, and reactions to subject areas.

Learning Logs   Learning logs are places where students can record and react to what they are learning in subject areas. Writing is used to reflect on the learning, to note gaps in students' knowledge, and to explore relationships between what is being learned and students' prior experiences and knowledge. Learning logs can be used in all subject areas. Students can explain how to do a math problem or science experiment, record observations, or react to a word or slogan before beginning a social studies topic. The purpose is to help students clarify their own thinking about what they are learning. Figure 5.13 is a listing of some prompts that could be used in the mathematics program.

Figure 5.13   Prompts for Math Journals/Learning Logs

- I think the answer is . . . because . . .
- I figured out the answer by . . .
- During math time, I . . .
- Today I learned . . .
- Write a math problem. Show how you solved the problem.
- What I know about . . .
- Draw a picture or diagram to explain . . .
- Explain how . . .
- Why is it important to learn . . .
- My goals for math this quarter are . . .
- My feelings about . . .
- I don't understand . . .
- I wonder . . .
- I think math is (hard, interesting, easy) because . . .
- The trouble with math is . . .
- Write a problem for your math test.
- What confused you today? What did you (or can you) do to understand?
- To study for a math test, I . . .
- Describe some strategies you can use when . . .
- What questions do you have?
- What is . . .
- Describe a . . .

Strategy
AT A *Glance*

Reading Response Logs

DESCRIPTION: Tools for students to react to books or respond to open-ended prompts or questions.

PURPOSE:
   Instructional: Provide opportunities for students to gain insights into what they are reading.
   Assessment: Give opportunities for teachers to note depth of understanding and level of comprehension.

Reading Response Logs   Reading response logs are an integral part of book clubs or literature circles, as discussed previously. Students react to books or respond to open-ended questions. Although frequently used with narrative texts, responding to what has been read is appropriate for nonfiction as well.

Simulated Journals   In simulated journals, students assume the roles of other persons, writing from that person's point of view. For instance, they may pretend that they are Christopher Columbus on his first voyage to the Americas or write log entries as if they were astronauts. Written conversations between historical figures can also be included in simulated journals.

Class Journals   Class journals present opportunities for the entire class to write and reflect on a topic or issue. These journals are kept in a central location and are circulated when students are ready to record their own entries. Students can react to a recent class event, respond to an article that was read and discussed, contribute to project planning, or record observations about field trips, guest speakers, or experiments. The idea is that the class write on a common topic that is of interest or concern to all. Class journals also can become memory books for the year.

Strategy
AT A *Glance*

Simulated Journals

DESCRIPTION: Receptacles for students to be able to assume the role of another person, writing from that person's point of view.

PURPOSE:
   Instructional: Encourage students to extend their learning and apply it creatively and give an opportunity to empathize with another's circumstances.
   Assessment: Afford teachers opportunities to see how their students apply what they have learned in another context.

Strategy AT A Glance

Class Journals

DESCRIPTION: Journals in which an entire class writes and reflects on a topic or issue.

PURPOSE:
   Instructional: Encourage class reactions, the recording of observations, and responses to topics and issues of interest.
   Assessment: Assess class interest, knowledge, confusions, and insights.

To introduce any of these forms of journal writing, teachers must explain the purpose of the activity and model a sample entry. Teachers can read interesting excerpts from published diaries and journals, read entries from characters who use journal writing in literature, and share actual student entries (with permission). It is essential that teachers prepare students by taking the time to talk about possible topics, demonstrate the process of journal writing, and show the value of journal writing activities (Routman, 1991).

Quick Writes

Quick Writes are brief, focused writings in response to specific prompts. They are an informal means to engage students in thinking about a content topic at the pre- or postreading stages. Prior to reading, Quick Writes are used to get an idea of students' prior knowledge, and after reading, they assist students in synthesizing ideas. They serve as bridges to the new concepts or ideas that will be learned, because they help students perceive the connections between prior learning and their current learning experiences. This flexible activity, which lasts about five to ten minutes, engages students in additional thinking about a topic (Readence, Bean, & Baldwin, 2000; Stevens & Brown, 2000).

Strategy AT A Glance

Quick Writes

DESCRIPTION: Brief, focused writings in response to prompts.

PURPOSE:
   Instructional: Informal means to engage students in thinking about a topic.
   Assessment: Provide insights into students' background knowledge prior to the learning and what they have learned after the learning.

Possible Sentences

DESCRIPTION: A writing-to-learn strategy whereby students generate sentences from a given listing of vocabulary.

PURPOSE:

Instructional: Acquaints students with key vocabulary, involves them in higher order thinking and reasoning.

Assessment: Assesses student knowledge of vocabulary and ability to determine meanings from context.

Possible Sentences

Another writing-to-learn strategy that reinforces the understanding and recall of technical vocabulary and related concepts in the content areas is a strategy known as *Possible Sentences*. This strategy helps students process the most important vocabulary terms before they begin reading. Students play an active role in predicting an author's use of language in a text and evaluating their written predictions against the actual passage or article. Therefore, when students actually begin reading the text, they have previewed the major ideas that are presented.

To implement this strategy, a list of terms (approximately ten to fifteen) that are well defined by the context is given to the students. Some of the terms may be familiar, but others might pose some difficulty in the reading. Students are to select two words and dictate or write them in a sentence. The teacher writes the sentence on the board, exactly as dictated, even if the information is incorrect. After a number of sentences have been generated, students search through the passage to check the accuracy of their predictions. After evaluating their possible sentences, a discussion is held on how to revise those sentences that differ in intent from the text to make them consistent with the author's message. New sentences could also be generated. Through Possible Sentences, students become acquainted with key vocabulary terms prior to reading, are actively engaged in their learning, and are involved in higher order thinking and reasoning as they are asked to identify examples in the text that support or refute their pre-reading sentences (Readence, Bean, & Baldwin, 2000; Buehl, 2001; Wood, 2001).

Two-Column Notes

This activity, also referred to as a *Double-Entry Journal*, is designed to help students process and reflect on information that is being learned. Useful for both narrative and expository text, *Two-Column Notes* is a system for note taking in which the students engage in a discussion with the author, responding to, questioning, or reflecting on information in the text. To undertake this activity, a piece of paper is divided into two sections (T-charts can be also be used for this

Two-Column Notes

DESCRIPTION: A system of note taking in which learners engage in a discussion with the author, reflecting about and questioning specific information. Notes about the text are written in the left-hand column, and notes on the notes and the learners' personal responses are written in the right-hand column.

PURPOSE:
   Instructional: Helps students reflect on and process new information.
   Assessment: Assesses students' understanding, reactions, insights, and misconceptions about what is being learned.

purpose). On the left-hand side of the paper is a column in which information from the text is recorded. Students' comments on these notes are recorded in the right column. There are variations of this technique, in which the headings can differ, thereby eliciting other types of student reactions and responses to the reading material. See Figure 5.14 for a Two-Column Note format with sample headings that could be used for this writing activity (Harvey, 1998; Tovani, 2000; Wood, 2001).

Inquiry Charts or I-Charts

Have you ever read a student report that mirrors an encyclopedia article? Unfortunately, many student reports are merely collections of bits of information, taken from a single source, usually the encyclopedia. To help students generate

Figure 5.14   Two-Column Notes and Sample Headings

What the Text Said	. . . .	My Response to the Text
What I Know	. . . .	What I Would Like to Know
What I Know	. . . .	What I Learned
What Is Important	. . . .	What Is Interesting
Facts from the Text	. . . .	Questions I Have
Opinion	. . . .	Evidence or Facts
Quotes from the Text	. . . .	My Response to the Quote
Topic	. . . .	Supporting Details

Inquiry Charts or I-Charts

DESCRIPTION: A matrix for helping students generate meaningful questions for their investigations, using multiple sources.

PURPOSE:
   Instructional: Assists students in researching pertinent questions and organizing information using multiple sources.
   Assessment: Provides information about students' research abilities, from inquiry to choosing relevant sources.

meaningful questions to investigate and write about, a useful strategy, known as *Inquiry Charts,* can be introduced (Figure 5.15). Inquiry charts, or I-charts, assist teachers and students in organizing information from multiple sources. Designed to foster critical thinking by having students examine multiple sources of information, they encourage students to collect information and data from a variety of sources and organize it in preparation for analysis, evaluation, comparison, and summarization. A matrix is used for this purpose, with the topic and key questions listed in the top row of boxes. Along the side of the chart are listed sources from which students can obtain information (textbook, Internet, trade book, news magazine, newspaper, etc.), along with such categories as *What We Already Know* and *Summary.* Once students have collected the information, they synthesize the data from the questions into a summary, which provides a transition from the inquiry to the actual writing. By using the I-chart strategy, students obtain essential practice in synthesizing and summarizing key data, and their writing is more likely to center on significant questions (Buehl, 2001; Wood, 2001).

TECHNOLOGY IN THE WRITING CLASSROOM

Multimedia is a perfect tool to utilize to establish a positive learning environment and enhance and motivate student writing (Offutt & Offutt, 1997). Students can use multimedia to locate resources, develop projects, and present their findings creatively. Multimedia develops writing skills, improves word-processing abilities, develops skills in researching and interviewing, and facilitates student-centered learning. Some examples of multimedia that can be incorporated into a writing program include the following:

- *E-mail:*   E-mail creates live responsive audiences who answer relatively quickly. E-mail can be used to send messages or documents back and forth. Some uses for e-mail include corresponding to others throughout the world; interviewing key people for needed information; preparing electronic book reports; communicating with others through on-line dialogue journals; sharing projects; and so forth. When using e-mail, students can keep e-mail logs addressing such pertinent questions as

  What kinds of information did you seek?
  What kind of help did you get?

Figure 5.15　Example of an Inquiry Chart, or I-Chart

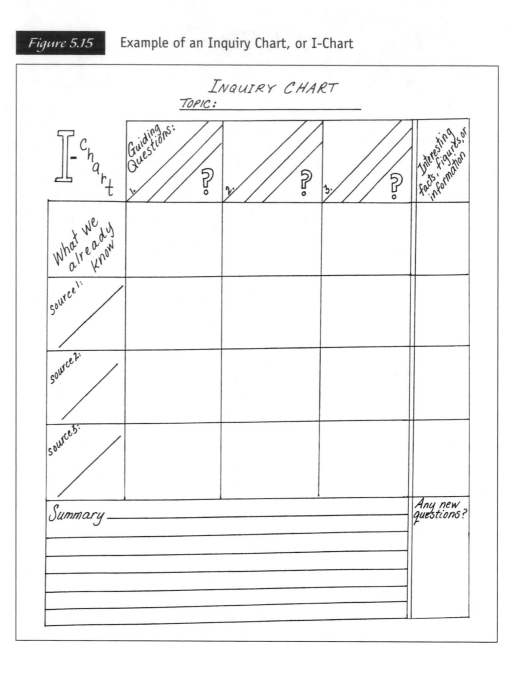

How useful was the information or help?

What benefits did you get from your e-mail correspondence?

Was this an effective use of your time? Why/Why not?

- *Reports/Presentations:*　Students enjoy opportunities to develop their own multimedia projects. Using word-processing or other authoring programs, students can prepare various audiovisual reports. Students can enhance their text, using visuals, charts, sounds, video clips, and the like. Some excellent software programs for this purpose include Claris Works, Kid Pix, Microsoft PowerPoint, and HyperStudio.

- *Web Pages:*　Web pages can be designed, and can serve several purposes. They provide a location for publishing student work and showcasing student pro-

| Figure 5.15 | Continued |

INQUIRY CHART

TOPIC: _____

I-Chart	Guiding Questions: 1. How did mathematics get started?	2. Who made up our system of mathematics?	3. How has math affected the world?	Interesting facts, figures, or information
What we already know	math uses numbers and symbols	Einstein was famous for math equations	We use math every day. It's the way we organize money and time.	
Source 1: Mathematics by Irving Adler	Base 10 (0-9) system of counting	Euclid - geometry; Newton - calculus and gravity	architecture, geometry, time, temperature measurement	time is determined by lines of latitude. Internat'l Date Line
Source 2: Computer	Ancient Greece Roman Numerals		games flowcharts	computers use only 2 basic symbols (0 and 1)
Source 3: Math textbook	Place value odd/even	Fibonacci (the golden ratio and triples)	cooking units computers calculat	
Summary _____				Any new questions? What is the difference between Math + Arithmetic

jects. They are places where students can publish a newspaper of classroom events. They can also help organize Internet resources for classroom instruction and research. Moreover, designing Web pages allows students who have some technology expertise to help teachers and their fellow students. Prior to undertaking Web page design, a purpose should be set for the page: It should be a purposeful merger between the content to be written on the page and what the students will learn through the use of technology. Students can design class Web pages that reflect learning emphases in their classrooms, and they can design Author Web Pages, which showcase what they have learned about a particular author, for example—background information about authors, excerpts from their books, reviews of their work, and so on.

A Street Called Home
by Aminah Brenda Lynn Robinson

Lift the flaps in this accordion book and gain an insight into the tumultuous life of Mount Vernon Avenue in Columbus, Ohio—a street called home. Inside each flap is information about the iceman, the ragman, the medicine man, the chicken foot woman, and others who lived and worked on this street in the 1940s. The author, an artist since her childhood, when she joyfully walked on Mount Vernon Avenue, created this outstandingly illustrated book as part of her ongoing, multimedia work *Symphonic Poem*, which incorporates poetry, music, dance, paintings, and dialogue. The format—an accordion book that can be closed by tying together the ribbons that are attached to the front and back covers—is particularly unique, giving children an example of how nonfiction content can be presented in many interesting ways. Does history have to be learned solely in a textbook? Take your students to "a street called home" and show them a moving depiction of a piece of history—perhaps inspiring them to use accordion and flap books when writing nonfiction.

THE ABCs OF EFFECTIVE NONFICTION WRITING

Students are more successful in school when they become strategic readers, writers, and thinkers. By learning and using strategies, students can grow from being dependent to independent learners and writers. However, students need

Writing to Other Schools or Communities

To learn about other parts of your state or other states, you might try a multimedia project with your students. After deciding on which community or state you would like to learn more about, it would be beneficial to prepare a letter describing your project and include such key information as the correct address, e-mail address, telephone number, and FAX number of your school. Using the Internet, locate the schools in the area that is to be studied. If available, note and record their addresses, e-mail addresses, phone numbers, and FAX numbers. It is advisable to call ahead or write to each school to see if they are interested in working on this project. Make a list of suggested materials that could be exchanged—pictures, postcards, souvenirs, brochures, newspaper clippings, newsletters, student publications and artwork, video clips, slide shows, and the like. Interactive Web pages could be constructed incorporating the materials that were exchanged from the various participating schools (Offutt & Offutt, 1997).

Figure 5.16   The ABCs of Writing Nonfiction

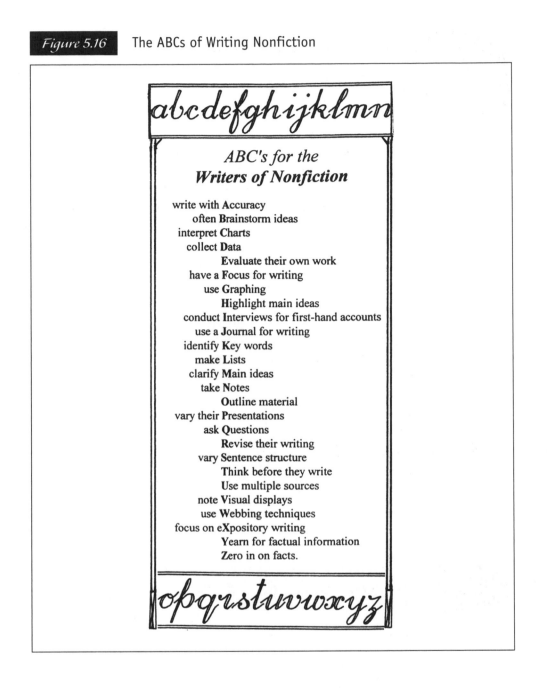

to discover what strategies work best for them, and when to apply them. Strategies are not magical cure-alls, and just going through the motions of using them won't necessarily guarantee success. It is the thinking that matters—not the strategy itself. "Classroom strategies that guide students in assessing the learning situation, setting their own purposes, choosing the most effective actions, and evaluating their success lead to more self-sufficient individuals capable of becoming lifelong learners" (Buehl, 2001, 7). Students can grow into competent writers of nonfiction—It's as easy as ABC.

Instructional Activities for the Classroom

1 Chapter-Beginning Activity

After reading *Somewhere Today* by Bert Kitchen, students can create their own versions, using the format presented in the book. Their entries can be related to a specific content area (e.g., in science), the students can discuss the various types of weather that are occurring "somewhere today," or they can describe a current event taking place "somewhere today."

2 Walk Your Way into Writing

Take your students for a walk, either around the school or during a field trip. Give the students clipboards on which to record their observations and reactions to what they witness. On returning to the school, or even while on the walk, have the students brainstorm—and write—about their observations, using as many writing forms as they can, such as an article for the school newspaper, a poem, a persuasive piece to clean up the area, a report, and so on.

3 Memorable Language in Nonfiction Texts

As students come across some interesting quotes, memorable language, and excellent examples of leads and conclusions, have them record them on index cards, adding machine paper, or the like, and place them in an accessible place for all students to refer to and view, such as on a bulletin board, on the walls, or in a file in the writing center.

Book Talk and Beyond

Wooden Teeth and Jelly Beans
by Ray Nelson, Douglas Kelly, Ben Adams, and Mike McLane

ADVICE TO THE PRESIDENT

Mrs. Mumper's fifth grade class at the Ostrander School in Wallkill, N.Y. spent some time this fall investigating the process of electing a President in our political system in the United States of America.

At the conclusion of our unit the students brainstormed advice we would like to share with our President.

This advice, given from the heart, is sent from children living in rural New York State.

Older drivers should have to take a road test each year. MELISSA

We need more public trash cans. CRAIG

Our country needs more police to help lower crime. MISTIE

Airbags injure people. They need to be redesigned. DANA

Teenagers drive too fast. The age to drive should be older. LAURA

Ban cigarette machines. MONIQUE

Help people who grow tobacco find different jobs. ROBERT

Kids should have a curfew. DANNY

Prisoners in jail should have to do jobs in community service. JUSTINE

Our country needs more shelters for the homeless and hungry people. KAYLEIGH

Cars should not be made to travel so fast. SIOBHAN

Curvy roads should be made straight. ASHLEY

School should go all year long and families should choose which two months to take off. LAURA

It's a good idea to change the people in political jobs to get new ideas. SEAN

Keep more land public. KARA

We need more playgrounds. DOMONIQUE

Schools should be air-conditioned in the summer. BEN

Families should be allowed to only have one car to cut down on pollution. NICHOLAS DOMENECH

It would be a good law if everyone HAD to recycle. CHRISTINA

Doctor bills cost so much that some people can't get better. JOHN

Do you know who the first president to live in the White House was, or who liked to dress in overalls, or who threw the first ceremonial pitch at a baseball game? If these bits of trivia might be of interest to you, this is a book you'll enjoy! It tells all the important information about our nation's presidents plus a lot of trivia that are amusing to read about. The illustrations are especially funny. They are in exaggerated caricature cartoon style. The book includes information about presidents' personal lives, their interests, the "firsts" they accomplished, and their families and pets. After a unit of study about the political system and the election process, a fifth-grade class wrote some advice to the president. The advice was their attempt to solve some of the problems they identified.

Postcards from Pluto: A Tour of the Solar System

by Loreen Leedy

Wouldn't it be great to be able to take a trip to outer space and visit the planets in our solar system? In this imaginative book, Dr. Quasar gives a group of children a tour of the planets, with a description of each one. After doing independent research, each child in Mrs. Mumper's class wrote postcards "back to earth" using 5×7 index cards. The cards were addressed to the class. In their messages they included interesting facts and information. They then illustrated the blank side with a colorful drawing.

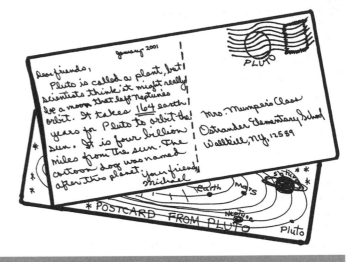

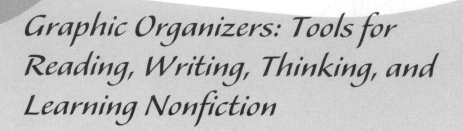

Graphic Organizers: Tools for Reading, Writing, Thinking, and Learning Nonfiction

Introduction

If we reach into our backpacks for a tool that has multiple uses, we will pull out the very versatile graphic organizer. Graphic organizers can be used with every genre in every subject area for a variety of purposes. They can be found, for example, in textbooks, on standardized tests, on overheads in classrooms, in

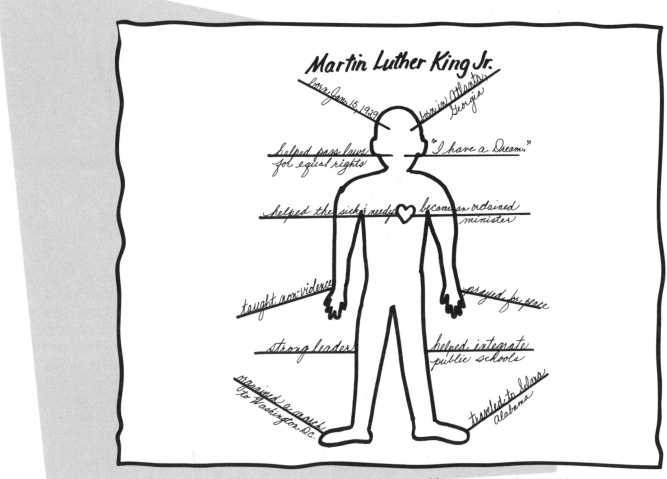

Inspired by <u>Martin Luther King</u> by Rosemary Bray

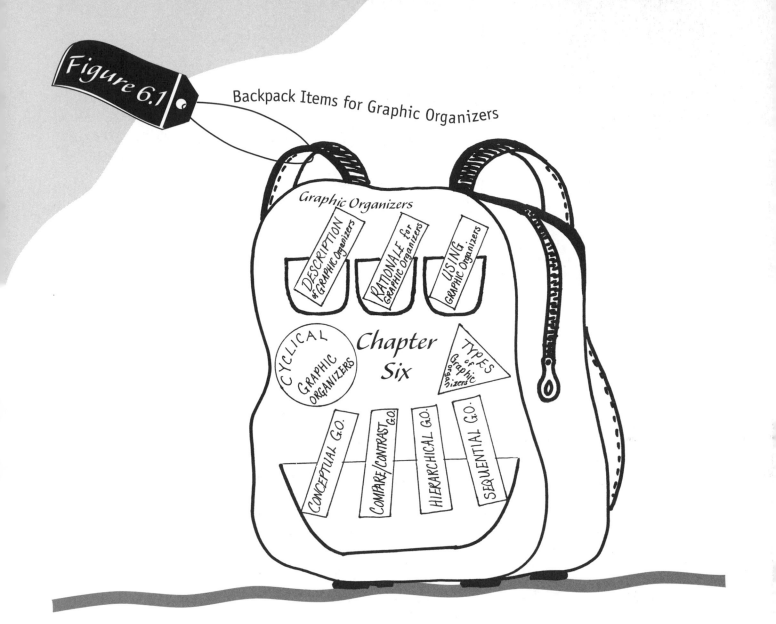

Figure 6.1 Backpack Items for Graphic Organizers

Graphic Organizers

DESCRIPTION of Graphic Organizers

RATIONALE for Graphic Organizers

USING Graphic Organizers

CYCLICAL GRAPHIC ORGANIZERS

Chapter Six

TYPES of Graphic Organizers

CONCEPTUAL G.O.

COMPARE/CONTRAST G.O.

HIERARCHICAL G.O.

SEQUENTIAL G.O.

students' journals or reading logs, on charts, and in workbooks. They are used for brainstorming, gathering information, summarizing, organizing, self-evaluating, and so forth. They are valuable tools for reading, writing, thinking, and learning. Because they use both visual images and words, they are useful with all kinds of learners—regular education students, gifted students, special needs students, and English Language Learners (formerly referred to as English as a Second Language).

This chapter describes graphic organizers, outlines their uses, and gives some examples of how they can be used. Because graphic organizers have so many uses, and are themselves the subject of entire teacher resource books, this chapter is not able to offer an in-depth exploration of the topic, but does provide a useful and practical overview of graphic organizers. Figure 6.1 depicts the contents of this chapter, using the unifying graphic organizer that has been chosen for this resource guide—a backpack.

DESCRIPTION OF GRAPHIC ORGANIZERS

Graphic organizers display information that enables readers to see the relationships among the ideas and concepts being explored. They are visual representations of information, with the key concepts and ideas arranged into patterns that are labeled (Bromley, DeVitis, & Modlo, 1999). Graphic organizers are known by a variety of terms: semantic maps, webs, structured overviews, and mind maps. There are many kinds of graphic organizers, which can be, and are, created by commercial publishers, teachers, and students.

RATIONALE FOR USING GRAPHIC ORGANIZERS

There are many reasons for teachers and students to incorporate graphic organizers in their instructional delivery across the curriculum. Some of the benefits of using graphic organizers include the following:

- Serve as a means for teachers to plan instruction and for students to plan and organize their reading, writing, projects, reports, oral presentations, and so on.
- Provide teachers with the opportunity and structures to teach effective learning strategies (e.g., K-W-L, semantic feature analysis, main idea, and supporting details).
- Encourage teachers and students to focus on process-oriented, strategic learning.
- Help teachers and students focus on what is important.
- Serve as mental tools, helping the students remember the presented information.
- Help students comprehend, summarize, and synthesize complex ideas.
- Require students to be actively involved in the process.
- Improve the social skills of the students.
- Encourage students to work collaboratively and cooperatively.
- Facilitate more positive attitudes toward learning.
- Enable teachers to assess student understanding at a glance.
- Provide a means for students to assess their own learning (Drapeau, 1998; Bromley, DeVitis, & Modlo, 1999).

Graphic organizers are visual representations of knowledge, which provide a structure for information by arranging the critical aspects of topics or concepts into a pattern, design, or illustration. Graphic organizers depict the major ideas and relationships among word meanings, concepts, or topics, and highlight the relationships and organization of ideas.

Try This

Graphic Organizers beyond the Classroom

Invite some professionals from the community—business leaders, school board members, or technology coordinator, for example—and have them show how they use graphic organizers in their work. They might bring along computer slide shows, brainstorming webs, or graphic organizers that might appear in brochures or reports that were used in their businesses.

USES OF GRAPHIC ORGANIZERS

Graphic organizers can be used at any stage of the learning process. They can be used to record brainstorming sessions when teachers are activating the students' prior knowledge about a subject, as well as in the recording of what was learned as a result of a unit of study. They can be utilized to help students structure their literature responses, to guide students in determining the significant information in their text books, and to assist students in preparing extension projects or in reviewing for a quiz or test. Graphic organizers are also effective tools for teachers in their planning, instruction, and assessment practices. See Figure 6.2 for how graphic organizers can be used.

TYPES OF GRAPHIC ORGANIZERS

There are a variety of graphic organizers, with many names and purposes. Several types are discussed, with examples of their use and a brief description of the roles they can play in enhancing the reading, writing, and learning of nonfiction. It should be noted that graphic organizers are used as tools throughout

| *Figure 6.2* | Uses of Graphic Organizers |

Graphic organizers can be used to:

- display and explain the relationships between ideas
- help learners note the key concepts and information
- organize and clarify information
- help students see patterns among ideas
- assist students to integrate prior knowledge with new information
- review material
- represent complex ideas
- assess student learning
- help students self-evaluate projects, processes, products, reading and writing abilities, progress, etc.
- help teachers plan instructional units, activities, and assessment possibilities

Figure 6.3 Conceptual Graphic Organizers

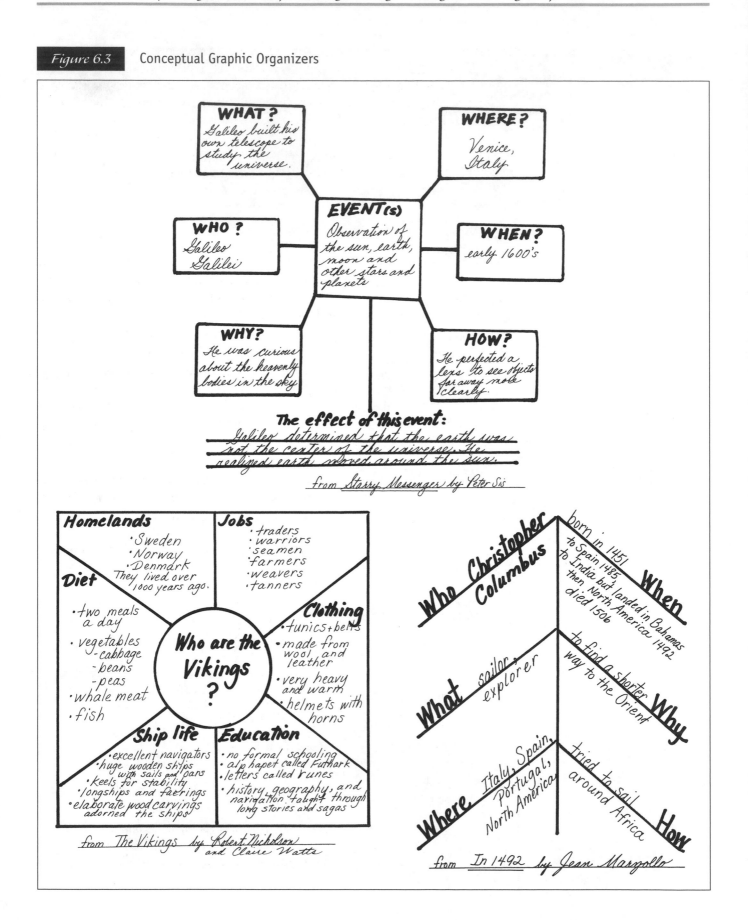

this resource guide on nonfiction—for example, as a preview for the learning in each chapter (the backpacks); as organizational features designed to clarify concepts and to help students learn these concepts (e.g., the frames and graphic organizers used in the discussion on text structure); and as integral parts of instructional strategies (K-W-L and semantic feature analysis).

Although there are many variations and possibilities for combining graphic organizers, most of them can be placed in five categories: conceptual, comparison/contrast, hierarchical, cyclical, and sequential (Bromley, DeVitis, & Modlo, 1999).

Conceptual Graphic Organizers

Conceptual organizers include a main or central idea with supporting details, facts, evidence, or characteristics. They are used for activating prior knowledge; organizing what was known; recording additional information on the topic after further study, research, and exploration; assessing growth of knowledge about a topic; and as a prewriting tool.

There are several types of conceptual graphic organizers:

- *Topical Graphic Organizers or Semantic Webs* This type of graphic organizer breaks a topic down into subtopics. An example of this is a fourth-grade brainstorming session on the topic of the genre nonfiction. After the students brainstormed what they knew about nonfiction and listed their responses on a chart, a semantic map was created. See Figure 6.3 for examples of conceptual graphic organizers.
- *Concept/Definition Maps* Concept/definition maps are used to help students gain an understanding of a concept or a vocabulary word. A concept/definition map can be seen in Figure 6.4.

Figure 6.4   Example of Concept/Definition Map on Poetry

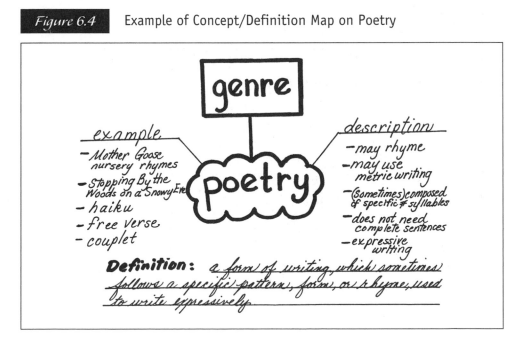

Figure 6.5	Biographical Profile Chart

NAME *Thomas Jefferson*

Known for *being President of the United States and author of the Declaration of Independence.*

Birthplace *Shadwell Farm, Albemarle County, VA in 1743*

Early life *As a boy he loved to read and write. He went to boarding school at 9 years of age to study Latin, Greek, and French.*

Education *At 17 yrs: College of William and Mary, VA Studied Law*

Major life events
① While in law school (1764) he heard a speaker attack the policies of Great Britain.
② Married Martha Wayles in Jan. 1772
③ Elected to the House of Burgesses, VA
④ Boston Tea Party in 1773
⑤ Attended Second Continental Congress in 1776
⑥ Wrote the document to free Americans

Other information *Served as Secretary of State and Vice President of U.S.*

Quote *"He who permits himself to tell a lie once, finds it much easier to do it a second and third time, till at length it becomes habitual."*

• *Profile Charts* Profile charts are used to help students locate and organize information about political and historical figures, family members, and their own city, state, country, animals, and so on. Once a topic is chosen to research, essential categories are brainstormed or provided; these are listed in the left-hand column of the profile chart. Students record their findings in the matching space in the right-hand column. An example of a biographical profile chart can be seen in Figure 6.5.

Comparison/Contrast Graphic Organizers

Comparison/contrast graphic organizers are used to represent information that is being compared or contrasted. They focus on similarities and differences. Examples of these types of organizers can be seen in Figure 6.6.

| Figure 6.6 | Comparison/Contrast Graphic Organizers |

Leopards

- have spots
- may be all black
- drag kill up a tree to keep it safe while eating it
- hunts in the daytime
- average weight is 100 pounds

BOTH

- groom themselves with their tongue
- have whiskers
- warm-blooded mammals
- communicate by hissing, growling, snarling, and purring
- have double-layered fur
- are felines

Tigers

- have black stripes on a tan body
- may have black stripes on white fur
- eats its prey on the ground
- hunts at night
- can weigh up to 600 pounds

from *Eyes On Nature: Cats* by Jane P. Resnick

Fact	Fable
Bats can see, but they use their hearing more than sight!	Bats are blind.
Bees can often sting many times!	Bees can sting only once.
Goats do eat many things, but they only chew on cans because they like the taste of the glue for the labels.	Goats eat anything — even cans.

from *Animal Fact/Animal Fable* by Seymour Simon

Figure 6.6   Continued

Who

Leonardo
DaVinci

When

Born in 1452
Died in 1519

**Biographical
Notes**

artist
architect
inventor
engineer
astronomer

What

Born in Italy
Died in France

Where

from *Lives of the Artists* by Kathleen Krull

Coral
is made of
living
ocean-dwelling
animals attached
to dead skeletons.

**Coral
Facts**

Coral gets its
color from
algae that
live inside
it.

Corals live in
reefs. They look
like tree branches,
fingers, or
brains.

from *The Magic School Bus on the Ocean Floor* by Joanna Cole

Hierarchical Graphic Organizers

Hierarchical graphic organizers depict a topic or concept, accompanied by ranks or levels below the topic. A key characteristic of hierarchical organizers is that they proceed from top to bottom or vice versa. An example can be seen in Figure 6.7.

Figure 6.7   Hierarchical Graphic Organizer

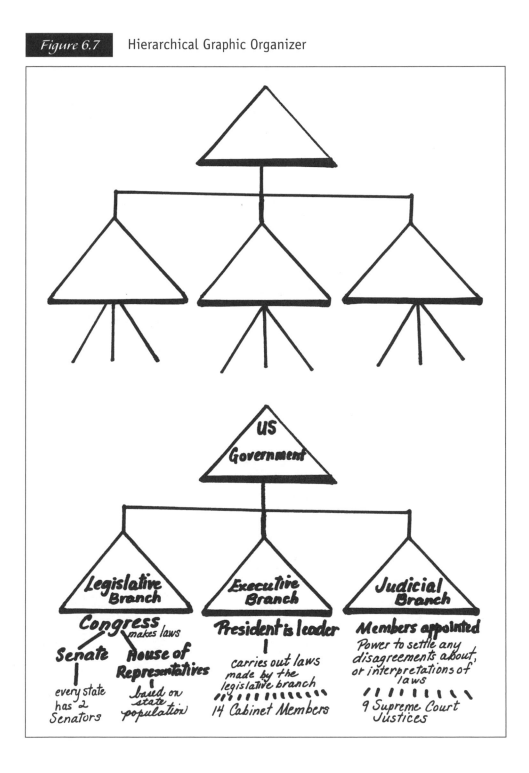

Cyclical Graphic Organizers

Cyclical graphic organizers depict a series of events without a beginning or an end. These organizers are circular and continuous. Examples can be seen in Figure 6.8.

Figure 6.8 Cyclical Graphic Organizers

CIRCULAR EVENTS MAP

As many events as needed can be placed around the circle. Shapes or drawings can be added to enhance the visual image.

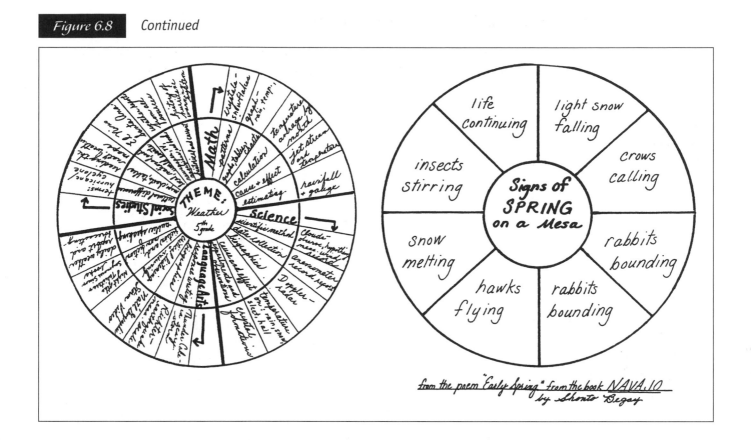

Figure 6.8 Continued

Sequential Graphic Organizers

Sequential graphic organizers arrange the depicted information in sequential or chronological order. Events tend to have specific beginnings and endings. These organizers are also used for cause-and-effect, process-and-product, and problem–solution texts. A linear pattern is characteristic, as in a time line. Examples of a sequential graphic organizer can be seen in Figure 6.9.

These categories of graphic organizers can serve as the base for many variations and combinations. Designing graphic organizers is limited only by the creator's imagination and ingenuity, along with such constraints and considerations as time, purpose, and availability of materials.

The purpose of the lesson, the content, and the organization of the material should be considered when choosing the type of graphic organizer to use. Teachers can construct their own, as can students, once they are familiar with the variety of organizers available and they have enough information about the topics and ideas being investigated. Students can initially fill in already-prepared graphic organizers, then be given partially constructed organizers before they are asked to create them independently. The goal is to move from direct instruction, and complete teacher control, to student independence.

Graphic organizers can be constructed on standard-sized paper, on chart paper, on overhead transparencies, on the white or chalk board, or on flannel boards. Colored markers, crayons, or pencils can be used for highlighting different aspects of a topic, or to note individual contributions. In addition, there

Figure 6.9 Sequential Graphic Organizers

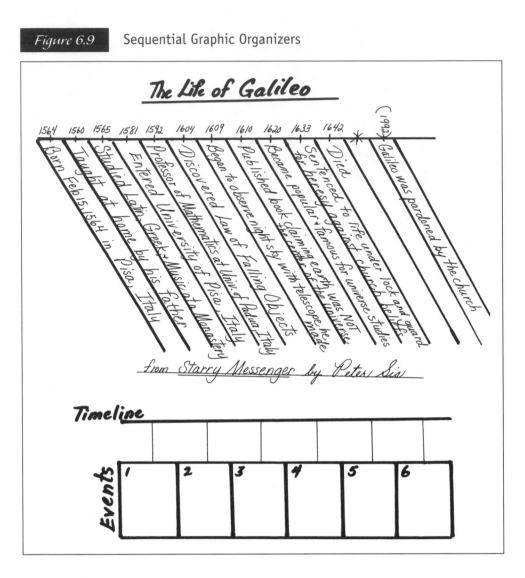

Apples, Bubbles, and Crystals: Your Science ABCs
by Andrea Bennett and James Kessler

Book Talk

Here's a double treat for readers! Each letter of the alphabet is represented by a poem and a science experiment or activity that is related to the content of the poem. This unique and imaginative book combines reading, rhyming, and simple science activities. It is designed for children who ask questions and wonder. The experiments extend the understanding of the poem and can be the basis of some wonderful family activities together. At the back of the book are clear explanations of the science principles behind the enjoyable poems and activities. For the budding scientist, for the curious, for the alphabet book collector—you're in for a real treat!

is computer software available that allows students to produce professional products using their graphics: *Inspiration*, *Kidspiration*, and *Graph Maker*, among others.

A FINAL WORD: EFFECTIVE USE OF GRAPHIC ORGANIZERS

A variety of graphic organizer possibilities have been presented. However, it should be noted that information and instructional delivery should be represented and delivered in many ways. There is no one right way, and graphic organizers, as effective as they can be, are not always the best use of the students' time. Following are some suggestions that should be considered before choosing to use graphic organizers:

- Be sure that there is a match between the purpose and content of the lesson and the type of graphic organizer chosen.
- Because one visual does not meet all instructional purposes, a variety of graphic organizers should be used.
- Students must have enough knowledge and familiarity with the type of organizer in order to be successful.
- To gain the most from graphic organizers, students should construct or work on them collaboratively.
- Discussion of the ideas and relationships should be an integral part of the process.
- Students should also be involved in the construction of graphic organizers.

Graphic organizers have an important place in classrooms today. They are fundamental to the development of critical thinking because they provide information and the opportunities for analyzing the learning that otherwise might not occur. Graphic organizers are wonderful teaching tools that appeal to all students for all the reasons and purposes discussed previously. Graphic orga-

Mapping Penny's World

by Loreen Leedy

"Lost" for a good idea to teach map skills? Put aside those work sheets and workbooks and share *Mapping Penny's World* with your class. Instead of conventionally mapping her own environment for a school project, Lisa decides to map her Boston terrier's world— from her favorite places, her hide-outs, her bike trip in a basket with Lisa, to faraway places that Penny could visit. Map symbols, map keys, longitude, latitude, and scale are all addressed creatively. So map out some fun for your kids, and think of interesting ways to apply map skills. While you're at it, you might want to check out *Measuring Penny*, a delightful, award-winning math concept book about measurement. Both books are great introductions to their subjects and provide a "measure" of enjoyment while learning crucial concepts.

nizers also can save teachers time, along with fulfilling the specific needs of instructional programs. The examples provided in this chapter are intended to serve merely as springboards for teachers and students to design, create, and use their own versions of graphic organizers. So, as you unpack the backpack in this chapter and prepare for your own journey, repack the backpack with ideas and modifications that suit your own classrooms and curricular needs. Happy exploring!

Instructional Activities for the Classroom

1 Chapter-Beginning Activity

Students choose an historical figure to showcase, using a character/historical figure analysis graphic organizer. Students may already be familiar with this process of using a character from a book, or they may have to be guided into thinking about the depicted categories. The graphic organizer could merely ask for the information, using separate blocks to record the particulars about the person being researched, or an outline of a figure can be provided, similar to the one depicted at the beginning of this chapter.

2 Student-Created Graphic Organizers

After students have had an opportunity to see a variety of graphic organizer models, from simplistic to cleverly designed ones, have them create their own. For example, if they are studying volcanoes, their graphic organizer can incorporate the volcano shape into the design, or if they are comparing two historical figures, the circles on which the information is written could

become the bodies of the two people. Heads, arms, and feet, representing the historical period of the figures, could be added.

3 Graphic Organizer Showcase

Just as there are author teas, science and social studies fairs, and all-about-me museums, there can be a time toward the end of the year when parents, students in other classes, and other school community members can come and view the variety of graphic organizers that were created or used during the school year. Textbooks could be opened to pages where graphic organizers were used to explain a concept, accompanied by student-written captions about their relevance and importance. Graphic organizer charts and individual student-created graphic organizers could be displayed around the room. In addition, a PowerPoint presentation could be shown, featuring the graphic organizers that were created using one of the computer programs available.

Book Talk and Beyond

Ben Franklin and the Magic Squares

by Frank Murphy

We all know that Ben Franklin was a creative genius, and are indebted to him for *Poor Richard's Almanac*, The Franklin stove, the establishment of the first library, the first fire station, and the first hospital, but did you know that he was a "magician," too? Among his proud accomplishments was the creation of the Magic Squares. Part of the *Step into Reading + Math Series*, this book combines an age-appropriate math activity with an enjoyable, humorous reading experience. It demonstrates that math can be pleasurable and shows yet another contribution of this amazing American, which he allegedly created while bored during meetings of the Pennsylvania Colonial Assembly! This book is a good mix of history and math, complete with directions

1706   1790

Ben Franklin

Report by Johanna Cruz

The Statesman, and Writer
Ben Franklin was a very important person in the history of the United States. He wrote and published a newspaper and almanac. He set up a subscription library and helped found the University of PA. He is the signer of four important documents in American history: The Declaration of Independence, the Treaty of Alliance with France, the Treaty of Peace with Great Britian and the US Constitution.

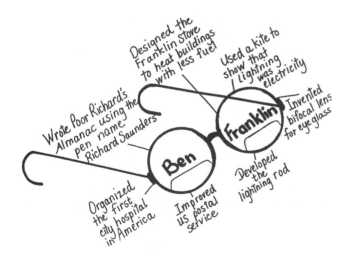

Designed the Franklin stove to heat buildings with less fuel

Used a kite to show that lightning was electricity

Wrote Poor Richard's Almanac using the pen name Richard Saunders

Invented bifocal lens for eyeglass

Ben Franklin

Organized the first city hospital in America

Improved US postal service

Developed the lightning rod

on how to create magic squares. Students can get "hung up" on such historical figures and inventors as Ben Franklin, prepare biographical sketches and portraits, and display them on ordinary hangers. They could also prepare graphic organizers, using a symbolic representation of the person (e.g., Franklin's eyeglasses or kit) as the focal point of the graphic organizer.

7

Showcasing Student Learning of Nonfiction, Using Creative Projects and Bookmaking

Introduction

By responding to literature in a variety of ways, students deepen and extend their interpretations of what they have read. Involving learners in response

Why We Honor Our Flag

It flutters proudly in the now peaceful breezes throughout the United States of America. However, it has not always been so peaceful. Everyone recognizes the "Stars and Stripes" as a symbol of our country, but do they really know what it represents? Some people mix fact with fiction, so that we are not sure if some things are necessarily true. One of these things is whether Betsy Ross or Francis Hopkinson was the first to make the flag for the 13 colonies. We do know that on June 14, 1777, the Continental Congress passed this resolution: "Resolved: That the flag of the United States be 13 stars, white in a blue field, representing a new constellation." The red symbolizes courage, zeal, and fervency. Blue is for loyalty, devotion, friendship, justice, and truth. The white is for purity, cleanness of life, and positive behavior.

When I look at the flag, I think of all the people who shed their blood and died fighting in wars for our freedom. When I think about these people, it overwhelms me with mixed feelings. It makes me proud to be an American where I always know I'm free and that fellow Americans died to make it that way. However, it makes me feel like crying to think about the fact that innocent people had to die to give all Americans this freedom. We must honor the flag at every time, in every place, by what we say, think, and how we act. It's that with which we keep the flag alive.

By Nikki Thompson
Grade 6
Cambridge Central School

Inspired by The Flag We Love by Pam Munoz Ryan

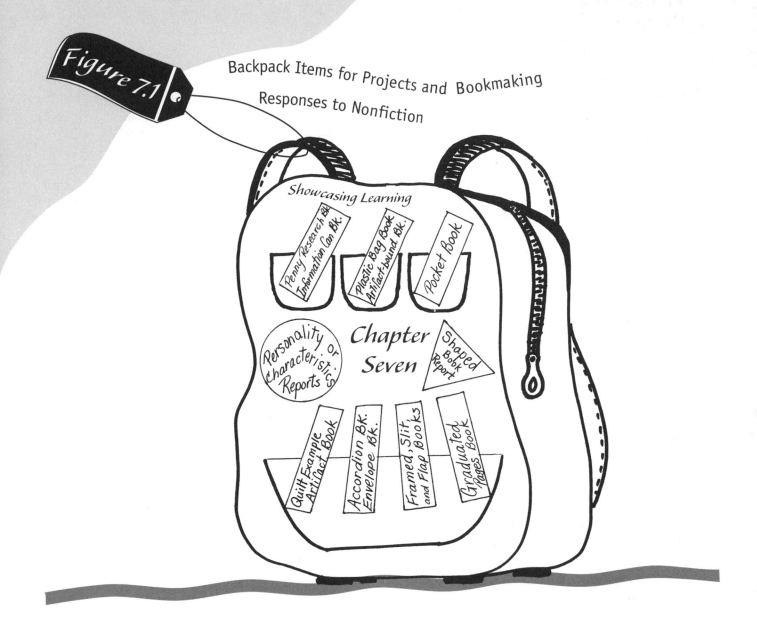

Figure 7.1 Backpack Items for Projects and Bookmaking Responses to Nonfiction

Showcasing Learning

Penny Research Bk. Information Can Bk.
Plastic Bag Book Artifact-bound Bk.
Pocket Book

Personality or Characteristics Reports

Chapter Seven

Shaped Book Report

Quilt Example Artifact Book
Accordion Bk. Envelope Bk.
Framed, Slit and Flap Books
Graduated Pages Book

activities permits readers to savor literature and gives them time for application and reflection. Responding to literature should involve both verbal and nonverbal activities. This chapter explores the many possibilities for showcasing student learning of nonfiction, using projects and bookmaking. Your backpack for this phase of your journey will now contain such items as those depicted in Figure 7.1.

LITERATURE RESPONSE ACTIVITIES

Responding to literature is an integral part of a balanced reading program, and is a way that writing can be used purposefully as well. Although at times teachers and students may wish to share books and other nonfiction materials only through discussion and dialogue, frequently they may want to pursue additional activities. Extending nonfiction reading through writing, art, drama, and bookmaking allows students to return to the text many times for enjoyment, as well as for additional information. Reinspection of the text reveals additional insights and appreciation of the author's craft. Through literature extensions, students are given additional time to enjoy nonfiction, to reflect on the author's message, or to make personal connections to the text. Students need time and opportunities to respond to nonfiction in a variety of ways throughout the year.

Response activities should not be undertaken just for the sake of doing projects or art activities; rather these activities should foster students' imaginations and creativity, as well as promote understanding. Responses to literature may take many forms; some are described in this chapter. However, it is important to remember that the possibilities that are presented are not recipes to be followed verbatim. The type of literary response utilized should be appealing to children, be a natural outgrowth of the reading material, and be open-ended enough to permit and encourage individual exploration and interpretation.

SHARING LITERATURE THROUGH WRITING

Writing to share nonfiction materials has been addressed throughout this resource guide—literature response, patterned writing, simulated journals, and so forth. There are other activities as well that incorporate writing to share or publish what has been learned in the content areas. These activities are highly motivating and should complement and enrich any content literacy program.

Letter Writing

Students can take virtual field trips (through literature or on the Internet) and write letters to family, and classmates about their trip. When studying periods of history, they can take on the identities of historical figures, and have these figures correspond to one another, for example, John Adams writing to his wife Abigail Adams, or the children writing to their presidents in the *Dear President . . .* series.

Newspaper Reporting

Using a newspaper format is an interesting way to showcase student learning. Books such as *The Egyptian Newspaper* can be shared and analyzed to see how the various types of writing found in newspapers can be used to present information in the content areas, as was done in this book. Students can create newspapers describing historical events (e.g., the Revolutionary War or the Suffragette Movement), geographical areas (e.g., China, California), science topics (e.g., the weather, the rain forest, creepy crawly creatures), and so forth.

Alphabetical Book Reports

Alphabetical book reports can be written about historical events, famous people, geographic areas, science, and other topics. There are numerous alphabet books to serve as models (e.g., *A is for America*). Moreover, there are authors such as Jerry Pallotta and Bobbie Kalman, whose primary means of presenting information is through the alphabet.

Figure 7.2   Alphabetical Nonfiction Personality or Characteristics Reports

Ax swinger
Beaver skin hat
Reserved
Assertive
Honest
Arbitrator
Muttonchops

Log Cabin
Illinois
New Salem
Coonskin cap
Orator
Lawyer
National hero

Personality or Characteristics Reports

This is a version of the alphabetical book report (Figure 7.2), with the letters from an historical figure's name, a scientific phenomenon, or other item, being used to describe the figure or topic. There are poetry books available that use this technique—for example, *Fly with Poetry*—that can serve as models.

Silhouette Biographies

Silhouettes can be drawn for historical figures or characters in historical fiction. Two silhouettes can serve as the covers for a biography, with key information about the person and his or her life described in the pages inside.

Famous Quotes Report

Several quotations from an historical figure can be selected that are representative of the personality, deeds, or motives of the person. The quotations can be accompanied by an explanation as to why these quotes were chosen.

Try This   Building a Quotations Collection

Just as you might collect examples of mini-lessons or specific materials to accompany a unit of study, you might also want to collect quotes from famous people around the world. These quotes can be written on adding machine paper and hung around the room. They can serve as introductions to units of study or as inspirations for reflection and analysis.

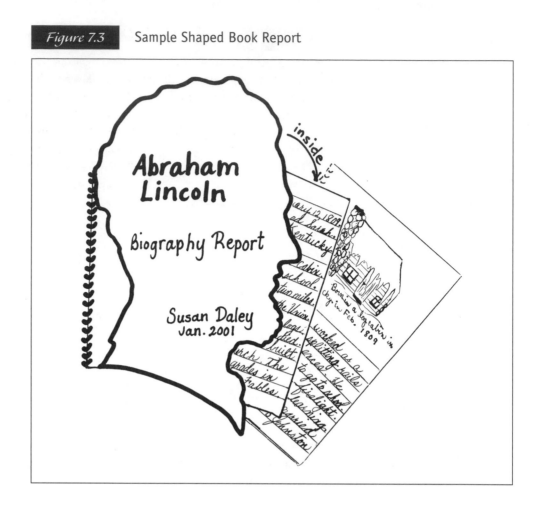

Figure 7.3   Sample Shaped Book Report

Shaped Book Reports

Information obtained from nonfiction materials can be written on shapes that are representative of the topic being studied. For example, a mountain-shaped book can house information about volcanoes or an outline of a country can serve as the covers of book or report about that country. See Figure 7.3 for an example of a shaped book.

SHARING NONFICTION THROUGH ART

Art activities for responding to literature can be as extensive as the teachers' and students' creativity and creative energy permit. Having a well-stocked art center can lead to many innovative projects and literature response activities. Materials that are useful include construction paper, poster board, paints, crayons, markers, fabric and wallpaper samples, cardboard tubes, egg cartons, pipe cleaners, toothpicks, dowels, plastic meat trays, small boxes of various sizes, buttons, socks, paper plates, and yarn. Following are some possible art activities.

Hung Up on Nonfiction

Sharing books using ordinary hangers can be an unusual and motivating way to respond to nonfiction. Historical figures or characters in informational storybooks can be represented using hangers, with a paper-covered hanger serving as the body of the character. A head can be pasted on the neck of the hanger, and hands placed on the two ends of the hanger. On the body of the hanger (which can be dressed in an outfit that the person might have worn) can be descriptions of the person or character or a significant event in the person's life.

Costume Designing

For historical figures, people from other cultures or lands, or characters in historical fiction, costumes can be designed and constructed from fabric, yarn, fur, beads, lace, wallpaper, and fringe. Actual dolls, paper dolls, pipe cleaner characters, or clothespin dolls may be used to represent the person or character.

T-Shirts, Quilts, and Tapestries

T-shirts, quilts (Figure 7.4), or tapestries can be created that depict natural phenomena, historical events, slogans, and so on. Fabric crayons or liquid embroidery can be used, as well as actual stitchery.

Time Lines or Lifelines

A lifeline or time line can be drawn or constructed, showing important events in history or a person's life. Both can be created from construction paper or adding machine paper, as well as from ribbons or other materials to which the key events are pinned or stapled. Accordion books can also be used for sequential events such as time lines or any other information depicted chronologically. Figure 7.5 is an example of an accordion book that was used to present penny research findings. Students researched key events that occurred during the year the penny was minted.

SHARING NONFICTION THROUGH DRAMA

Drama is a powerful tool for helping children learn. Through drama, children work cooperatively, develop their self-expression and thinking abilities, and foster their creative imaginations. Drama can be a springboard for many language experiences, because it provides opportunities for children to talk as they assume roles, and also to read, write, and reflect both individually and collaboratively as they think about the problems posed by the drama. There are many roles within drama that provide meaningful contexts in which children can share, extend, and apply what they have learned and enjoyed in their reading materials. Some dramatic activities that lend themselves to extending nonfiction, historical fiction, or informational storybooks include the following:

Figure 7.4   Example of a Paper Quilt

A bulletin board paper quilt display of research information about the state of Wisconsin. Students found an interesting item or fact to correspond with each letter of the alphabet.

Living Books

Living books, books that come alive through pantomime and improvisation, can be used as a means to share what was learned in a topic of study. Students can dress up as historical figures or characters and act out events. A variation of this activity is to have pictures or portraits in an art gallery come "alive" and talk to the audience about the subjects or activities in the pictures. The pictures or portraits can be illustrated by the students, or can be reproductions of those found in trade books, text books, museums, and the like.

| Figure 7.5 | Penny Research Accordion Book |

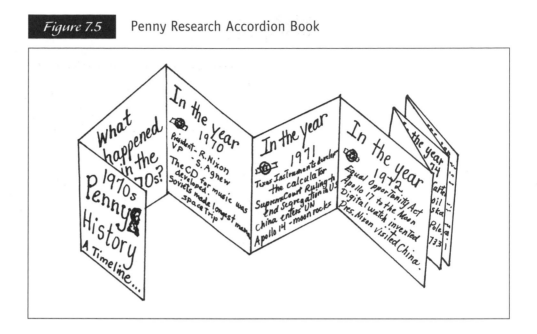

How-to Demonstrations

If a procedural or how-to book has been read that teaches its audience how to do or make something, a demonstration showing others how to do it can be given.

Role-Playing

Students can role-play historical figures or characters in informational story-books. Scripts, adapted from texts that were read, could be written to accompany the role-playing, or the students may improvise the dialogue as they perform.

Mock Trials

A mock trial may be held after reading about such events as the Salem Witch Trials or the Holocaust, or about such historical figures as Benedict Arnold or Robert E. Lee. People written about in today's current events can be subjects for trials, with students creating the roles of the defendants, prosecutors,

Try This

Featuring How-to Books

As a class, collect a variety of how-to or procedural books and display them in a prominent place in the classroom or class library. Analyze the variety of devices that authors use in writing how-to books, from lengthy lists of steps to cartoon depictions.

Yankee Doodle

by Steven Kellogg

Most students know the song "Yankee Doodle," but may not know the historical background that laid the foundation. This award-winning artist takes the patriotic song and illustrates each verse. Readers are taken on an adventure through the battlefields of the American Revolution. In an afternote, Kellogg defines many of the terms used in the song and explains the significance of much of the text. This book won an ALA Notable Book Award.

defense lawyers, the judge, witnesses, and the jury. Student reporters can also be on the scene to record the information for the class newspaper.

Other activities that incorporate drama in the instructional program are puppetry, Readers' Theater, and storytelling.

SHARING NONFICTION THROUGH BOOKMAKING

When responding to nonfiction, students may choose one of the many bookmaking formats available, which make use of a variety of materials, from those typically used in making books (e.g., paper, paints, markers), to such unique materials such as interlocking plastic bags, cardboard cylinders, boxes, and so on. Some relatively easy, yet different, bookmaking activities follow.

Information in Cans

Students will be fascinated when they learn that they can present their research and informational reports in a can (Figure 7.6), as opposed to a plastic-coated binder. Any kind of information in any content area that is descriptive, sequential, cumulative, procedural, or biographical in nature can be represented in cylindrical containers. After preparing the information on scroll-like paper, students can roll their reports and place them in soft-sided containers that have slits through which the reports are pulled prior to reading. You <u>CAN</u>'t beat that!

Interlocking Plastic Bag Books

Using see-through plastic bags, available in various sizes in grocery stores, this type of book provides a protective cover for photos, illustrations, or small artifacts. Students place their drawing, photograph, or material inside the bag. Individual bags serve as single pages, which can be bound with tape to create a book (Figure 7.7). A variation can be created by placing the bags side by side in a quiltlike pattern and binding them with clear or colored plastic tape. A generic "plastic bag quilt" can be constructed at the beginning of the year, changing the contents to suit curricular needs. This quilt is easily maintained, because it can be folded up and stored until needed.

Figure 7.6   Information in Cans Books

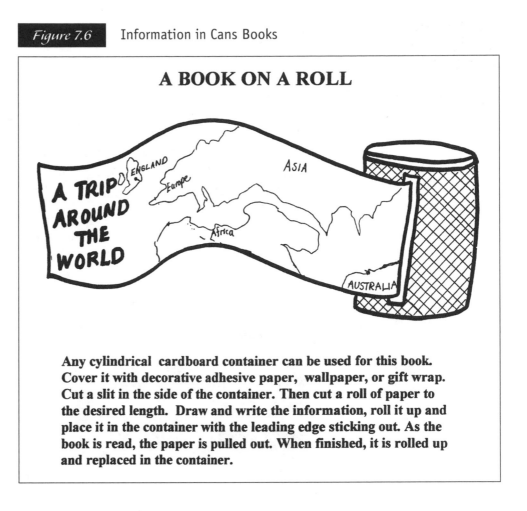

A BOOK ON A ROLL

Any cylindrical cardboard container can be used for this book. Cover it with decorative adhesive paper, wallpaper, or gift wrap. Cut a slit in the side of the container. Then cut a roll of paper to the desired length. Draw and write the information, roll it up and place it in the container with the leading edge sticking out. As the book is read, the paper is pulled out. When finished, it is rolled up and replaced in the container.

Figure 7.7   Locking Plastic Bag Book

Artifact-Bound Books

You can give your stapler a rest when students bind their books using artifacts. Once student books are completed, holes are punched either along the top of the book or along the side. Elastic bands, ribbons, or string hold "artifacts" or objects related to the contents and concept of the book to produce a unique binding (Figure 7.8). A twig can bind a book about trees, a spoon used for a recipe book, a small ruler for a math book, and a paintbrush for an art book.

Artifact Books

This bookmaking technique is not truly a "book." Rather, it is a collection of objects and writings that are placed in a decorated bag, box, or container. The contents are pieces related to a specific topic or theme. The outside of the container is decorated and includes the information generally placed on the title page of a book (Figure 7.9).

Accordion Books

Accordion books are created from paper folded like a fan. Pieces of cardboard can be attached to the front and back pages to serve as covers for the book.

Figure 7.8   Artifact-Bound Book

Leaves
of
Deciduous
Trees

Science Research
by Mrs. Mumper's
5th Grade

Artifact Bound Book

Figure 7.9 Artifact Book

Prior to attaching the cardboard to the pages, ribbon can be inserted so that when the book is closed, it can be tied, resembling a gift package (Figure 7.10).

Graduated Pages Books

Similar to a tabbed address book, this book contains pages that are folded in such a way, leaving the edges of each page showing when the book is closed (Figure 7.11). Graduated-pages books are perfect for displaying key words, specific topics, colors, and so forth. By having this information readily visible, the specific information is easy to find.

Framed Books

Many professionals, families, and students, for example, are so proud of some accomplishments that they frame them and place them in conspicuous places. So, why not give students an opportunity to "frame" their nonfiction projects? Although flat paper frames can be used for this purpose, paper can be folded in such a way that the paper frames resemble more conventional wooden or metal ones (Figure 7.12).

Envelope Books

Students may think of the mail, rather than books, when they think about envelopes, but envelopes of varying sizes can be used to create unique books. Information about different aspects of a topic is placed in separate envelopes, which are then attached and bound to create a book (Figure 7.13). The envelope can be decorated and a title or heading added to indicate the contents. This book is flexible in that information can be added or deleted at any time.

Figure 7.10   Accordion Book

ACCORDION GIFT BOOK

This is a simple variation of an accordion folded book. A long strip of heavy paper is best for this book. The strip is folded alternately left, right, left, and so on, to the end. On the final page a ribbon is glued to the back. When the book is closed the ribbon, tied in a bow, secures the pages and makes an attractive cover.

Figure 7.11   Graduated Pages Book

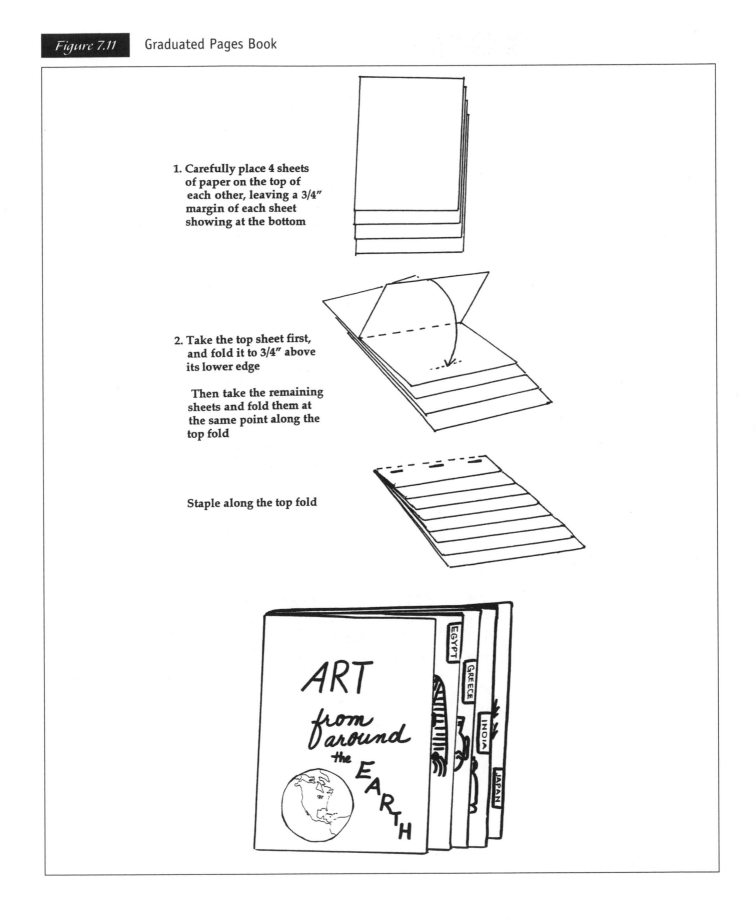

1. Carefully place 4 sheets of paper on the top of each other, leaving a 3/4″ margin of each sheet showing at the bottom

2. Take the top sheet first, and fold it to 3/4″ above its lower edge

   Then take the remaining sheets and fold them at the same point along the top fold

   Staple along the top fold

Figure 7.12   Framed Book

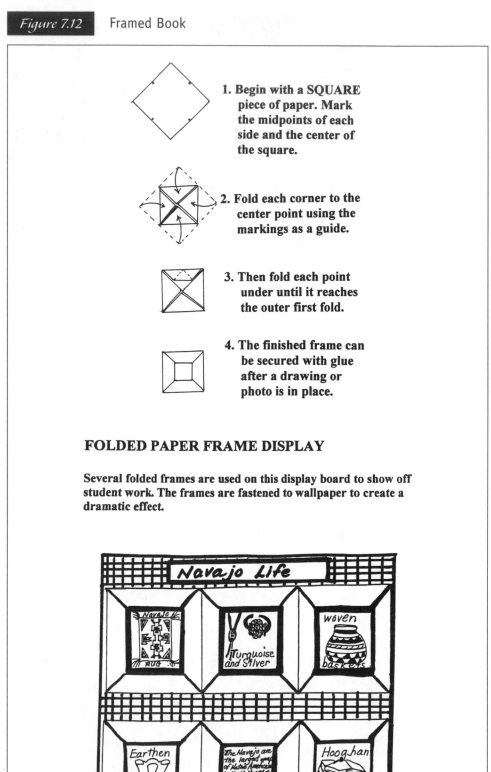

1. Begin with a SQUARE piece of paper. Mark the midpoints of each side and the center of the square.

2. Fold each corner to the center point using the markings as a guide.

3. Then fold each point under until it reaches the outer first fold.

4. The finished frame can be secured with glue after a drawing or photo is in place.

FOLDED PAPER FRAME DISPLAY

Several folded frames are used on this display board to show off student work. The frames are fastened to wallpaper to create a dramatic effect.

Figure 7.13 Envelope Book

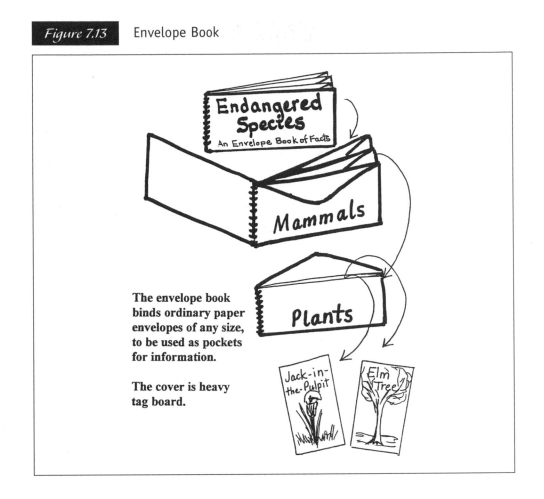

The envelope book binds ordinary paper envelopes of any size, to be used as pockets for information.

The cover is heavy tag board.

Slit Books

When materials are limited, a slit book is the perfect book! It requires only paper. The way the paper is cut along the spine, when folded, allows the sheets to slip into place and remain together as a book (Figure 7.14). This simple book is a favorite of the students.

Flap Books

No turning of pages for this book—just lift the flaps! Created from paper folded into sections and cut in such a way that allows separate parts to be lifted to reveal the written text or illustrations beneath (Figure 7.15), flap books are ideal for how-tos, descriptions, and sequential or cyclical information.

Pocket Folder Books

Are you looking for a way to hold larger materials to accompany a unit of study? Pocket folder books may be the perfect solution! They can accommodate vari-

Figure 7.14 Slit Book

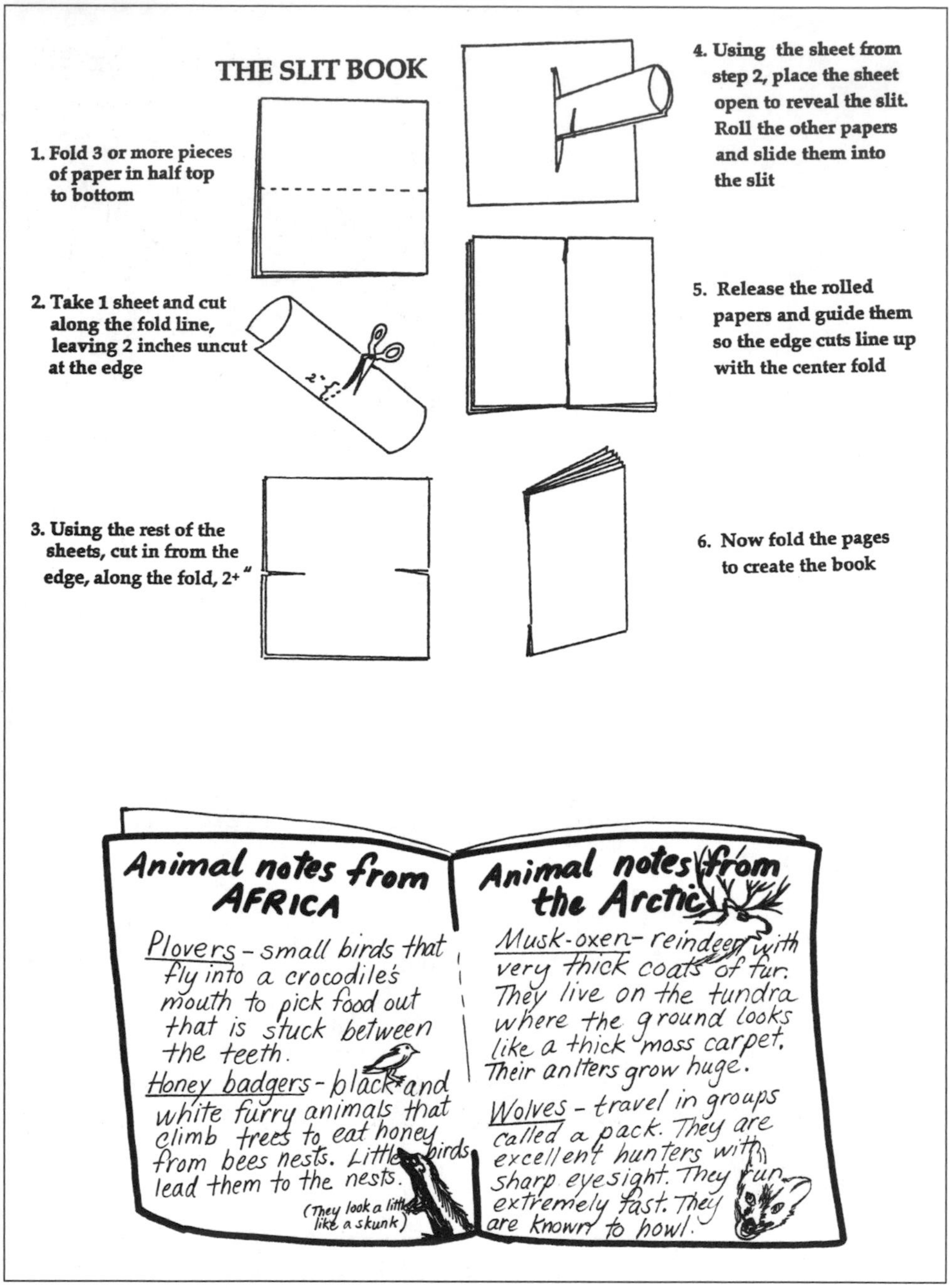

THE SLIT BOOK

1. Fold 3 or more pieces of paper in half top to bottom

2. Take 1 sheet and cut along the fold line, leaving 2 inches uncut at the edge

3. Using the rest of the sheets, cut in from the edge, along the fold, 2+ "

4. Using the sheet from step 2, place the sheet open to reveal the slit. Roll the other papers and slide them into the slit

5. Release the rolled papers and guide them so the edge cuts line up with the center fold

6. Now fold the pages to create the book

Animal notes from AFRICA

<u>Plovers</u> – small birds that fly into a crocodile's mouth to pick food out that is stuck between the teeth.

<u>Honey badgers</u> – black and white furry animals that climb trees to eat honey from bees nests. Little birds lead them to the nests.

(They look a little like a skunk)

Animal notes from the Arctic

<u>Musk-oxen</u> – reindeer with very thick coats of fur. They live on the tundra where the ground looks like a thick moss carpet. Their antlers grow huge.

<u>Wolves</u> – travel in groups called a pack. They are excellent hunters with sharp eyesight. They run extremely fast. They are known to howl.

ous sized materials—brochures, booklets, maps, notes, cards—which can be easily removed from the folders. Several pocket folders can be bound together to create a pocket folder book (Figure 7.16). Not only can students write on standard-sized paper or on oaktag, which can comprise the pages, but the pages of the "book" can be a compilation of various formatted materials, for example a postcard, travelogue, and photo essay.

Figure 7.15 Flap Book

A FOLDED SECTIONED BOOK

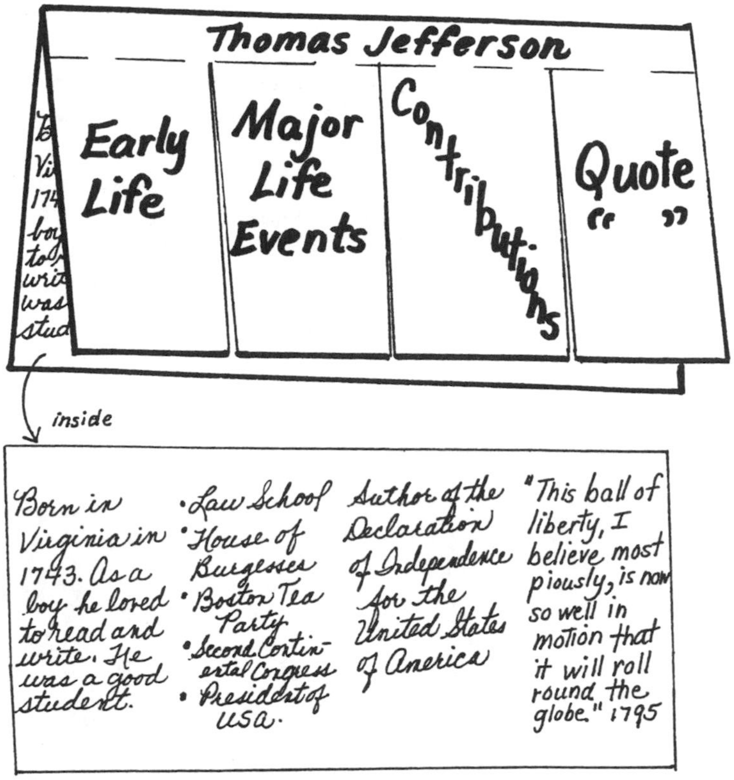

Thomas Jefferson

| Early Life | Major Life Events | Contributions | Quote " " |

inside

Born in Virginia in 1743. As a boy he loved to read and write. He was a good student.

- Law School
- House of Burgesses
- Boston Tea Party
- Second Continental Congress
- President of USA.

Author of the Declaration of Independence for the United States of America

"This ball of liberty, I believe most piously, is now so well in motion that it will roll round the globe." 1795

A piece of copy paper is folded in half, top to bottom. The top half is cut into sections for specific categories, topics, or facts. Under each flap, the information is written.

ASSESSMENT OF BOOKMAKING AND OTHER CREATIVE PROJECTS

As is discussed in greater detail in Chapter 8, there are a variety of assessment options for teachers to use for project-based learning. Teachers will want to gain insights into what was learned during the process, both content-specific knowledge as well as the use and effectiveness of strategies and research processes used in creating the project. Some of the assessment possibilities include the following:

- Learning logs
- Conferences with the teacher
- Teacher observations
- Student self-evaluation
- Rubrics (Figure 7.17)

Figure 7.16   Pocket Folder Book

Pocket Folder Book

Pre-made pocket folders are readily available in bright colors. They are durable and inexpensive.

To create a pocket folder book, use tag board folded and stapled at each edge. Pre-made or school-made folders can be bound with spiral bindings or punched with holes to be placed in a regular 3-ring binder

Information can be added to this book throughout the year. It can hold research cards, photos, maps, etc.

 ## CONCLUSION

The extensions described in this chapter can be very worthwhile activities for students. However, the activities are meant to have students gain a deeper understanding of the texts they read, not be the primary focus. These extensions should be used judiciously and occasionally, and not be a permanent replacement for purposeful discussion and dialogue.

Figure 7.17 Rubric for Project-Based Learning

Project Assessment Rubric

	④ Exemplary	③ Proficient	② Developing	① Poor
Accuracy of Information	many accurate facts / most important information included	some accurate facts / missing some major pieces of information	few accurate facts / minimal information (or wrong)	facts are inaccurate / lacking basic information (or wrong)
Organization of Ideas	well organized / clear information / excellent examples	fair organization / somewhat unclear / some interesting examples	poor organization / difficult to understand / few examples	shows no attempt at organization
Use of Materials	Wide variety with creative and interesting use of materials	Some variety and creativity in use of materials	Marginal use of materials with little interest	Materials are not adequately used
Project Appearance	Visually appealing / neat, colorful, varied images / Well planned	Somewhat appealing / some images included / attempt at planning	Little visual appeal / few or poor images / poorly planned	Messy / project not complete / little sign of planning
Presentation *(if applicable)*	Clear delivery, eye contact and voice / Incorporated use of visuals and materials	some hesitation eye contact, clear voice / some use of visuals and materials	Delivery not consistent; poor eye contact; did not speak clearly, no material use	Not prepared / No audience contact / Poor delivery

Comments: _____

_____

The History of Counting
by Denise Schmandt-Besserat

Did you ever think of numbers and counting as an invention? Denise Schmandt-Besserat turns counting into a fascinating, true story. Accompanied by beautiful illustrations, the text provides an account of how different cultures developed a counting and recording system. Many fundamental mathematical ideas are presented, along with an explanation as to how counting has changed the world. Here's a book you can "count" on!

Instructional Activities for the Classroom

1 Chapter-Beginning Activity

Books, holidays, and celebrations can serve as springboards for students' personal responses. In this chapter-beginning activity, sixth graders were asked to describe what the American flag meant to them. The students researched the flag, read trade books about the flag, and then composed their pieces. The products were shared both at the school for Flag Day and at a local veterans' organization.

2 Bookmaking Library

There are many resources available on bookmaking techniques for both teachers and students. Collect an assortment of these books for your own professional library, as well as for your class library. By having them readily available, they can enhance the publishing possibilities of your students. A few excellent titles are *Making Books Across the Curriculum* (Natalie Walsh); *Books Don't Have to Be Flat* (Kathy Pike & Jean Mumper); *Making Books* (Paul Johnson); and *Making*

Books That Fly, Fold, Wrap, Hide, Pop Up, Twist, and Turn (Gwen Diehn).

3 Bookmaking Models

Check out your school or public library, bookstores, and personal collections for examples of uniquely published or illustrated books. These would make a wonderful display for your classroom or school showcase, and can be tied into such national celebrations and recognitions as the awarding of the Caldecott Medal (January), *Read Across America* (March 2, Dr. Seuss's birthday), National Poetry Month (April), or PARP (Parents as Reading Partners). Some wonderful examples include *A Place Called Home* (an accordion and flap book); *Pieces: A Year in Poems and Quilts* (patchwork illustrations); *The Christmas Alphabet* (pop-up and flaps); *Whales* (overlays and cut-aways); and *Exploring Space* (movable parts, cut-aways, graduated pages). Student-made examples could also be included.

Book Talk and Beyond

Richard Orr's Nature Cross-Sections

by Richard Orr

I have always been fascinated by animals and how they live. As a child I was lucky to be able to watch a group of beavers build their lodge one summer. When I saw this book, I was able to see what the inside of the beaver lodge probably looked like. The colorful illustrations take you inside beehives, rain forest habitats, ocean dwellings, and homes in nature we rarely ever get to see. Read this book to explore incredible places. As a follow-up activity, students created an interactive book about animal homes by taping tagboard flaps to the pages of an accordion book and adding information under each flap.

Bees Dance and Whales Sing: The Mysteries of Animal Communication

by Margery Facklam

If you have ever wondered how ants know where a picnic is, or how whales make their haunting songs, you will enjoy this book as you explore the world of animal communications. At the conclusion of a unit of study on communication—body language, signing, Braille, and hieroglyphics—a fifth-grade class enjoyed this book about the marvels and mysteries of animal communication. It discusses various creatures, from elephants who rumble infrasonically, to bats who use echolocation, to ants who leave a path of chemicals only other ants can follow— that's how they find your picnic! After enjoying this book, the students created an interactive, informational book to summarize the material. The left of each page asks a

question and has a drawing. A folded flap covers the answer on the right of each page.

8 Assessment of Nonfiction Learning

Introduction

It is now basketball season, and it is time to select the members of the school's basketball team. Eagerly, the team hopefuls suit up and are given an opportunity to prove that they have the talent and abilities to play on the team. However, instead of demonstrating their capabilities by running, shooting, and dribbling, these players are given a standardized test. Anyone not getting a particular score will be cut from the team.

When I was little, I pretended to read.
Now I can really read.

When I was little, I didn't have a job.
Now I do. It's called school.

When I was little, I did my "business" in my diaper.
Now I use the toilet.

By Clare O'Grady

Inspired by <u>When I Was Little</u> by Jamie Lee Curtis

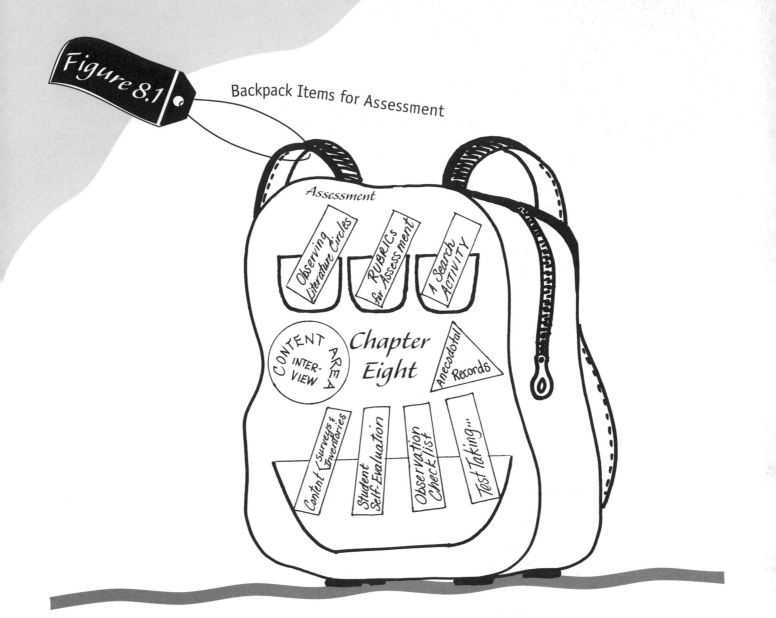

Figure 8.1 Backpack Items for Assessment

Sound ridiculous? No coach would choose a team based on a solitary test score. If this were true, basketball players would be studying *How to Pass the Basketball Entrance Exam* instead of learning how to shoot, dribble, pass, and work cooperatively and effectively as a team. Although the analogy used may not be directly applicable to literacy acquisition, because language learning is far more complicated than an athletic event, it does give the reader some cause for thought. A sole test score can influence a teacher's decision about a child's literacy and learning abilities. To address this, informed educators are reexamining their assessment practices to include more ongoing assessments that provide feedback that will enhance instruction and guide student learning. Teachers are now using assessment that provides information for guiding student improvement throughout the entire learning process, instead of waiting to give feedback once the instruction has ended.

In past years, assessment was something that was done *to* students after the learning was considered completed. Today, with an emphasis on a constructive interactive perspective of the reading and writing processes, assessment and evaluation have become integral components of the instructional process. Although often used synonymously, there is a distinction between the terms *assessment* and *evaluation*. Assessment involves collecting data about the progress of learners through such measures as oral reading analysis, observation, looking at work samples, conferences, interviews, and so on. Evaluation is the analysis and interpretation of this information in order to determine whether teaching modifications or interventions are necessary (Cooper, 2000; Orb, 2000).

No longer is it a valid notion that assessment is a one-time activity; rather, assessment is an integral part of instruction that helps guide teachers' planning and delivery of instruction. Being aware of what children have learned, knowing how to help them learn and develop as learners, and knowing how to plan for instruction are important aspects of the educational process. This chapter offers a framework for looking at assessment measures that draws on current data and research about literacy growth and effective instructional practices using nonfiction. As we near the end of our journey with nonfiction, the assessment items that are packed into our backpack are integral to helping students become successful with this genre (Figure 8.1). It is critical that the needs and strengths of the students be known, so that interventions may be planned, instructional delivery may be modified, and proper strategies may be introduced and practiced.

PURPOSES OF ASSESSMENT

Assessment has a variety of purposes, incorporating both the types of informal assessment that occur in classrooms daily (the focus of this chapter) and the more formal reporting assessments that are required by districts, legislators, and state education departments (Fountas & Pinnell, 2001). All learning events are opportunities for assessment. Effective teaching commences with knowing students and their strengths and needs. The real power of continuous assessment is that it informs teaching and helps teachers decide what to do next. Data gleaned from assessment measures help teachers know *how*, *what*, and *when* to teach.

Assessment goes hand in hand with instruction (Bridges, 1995; Daniels, 2001). Linking assessment and instruction enhances both teaching and student learning (Meisels, 1996/1997). Effective assessment also helps students take ownership of their literacy development, allowing them to see what they know and to plan ways to foster their own academic growth. Moreover, effective assessment provides information to the community as to whether schools are doing a good job educating students. In sum, to be effective, assessment

- is an integral part of instruction;
- continually informs instructional decisions;
- utilizes multiple measures;
- systematically determines students' strengths and knowledge;
- discovers what the students are able to do, independently and with teacher guidance;
- documents progress for the students, the parents, and the community; and

Book Talk

Erie Canal: Canoeing America's Great Waterway
by Peter Lourie

Ready for a canoe trip from one end of the Erie Canal to the other? Well, join author/photographer Peter Lourie as he takes a three-week adventure exploring the entire Erie Canal—its sites and its history. The author's enthusiastic narrative, accompanied by his photographs and archival black and white photos, illustrations, and excerpts from songs about the Erie Canal, help the reader appreciate the size and history of the Erie Canal.

Readers can experience going through the locks in the canal as they paddle on this photographic adventure. Not only does history become alive in this book, but the author uses journal writing to record his trip and a wide variety of primary sources in his retelling, which can serve as models for students' own exploration into writing nonfiction.

- summarizes achievement and learning over time, including how students are faring on meeting their state's standards. (Fountas & Pinnell, 2001; Daniels, 2001)

To be educationally sound, assessment must be ongoing, collaborative, multidimensional, interactive, and reflective. Assessment is undertaken to determine student progress, to identify students' strengths and needs, to make educational decisions, to improve the selection and use of instructional materials and resources, and to communicate what has been learned about the students' growth and progress.

MEASURES OF ASSESSMENT

There are many opportunities that exist throughout the day during regular classroom instruction that can provide valuable information and assistance in instructional planning. Many of the measures take advantage of ongoing interactions with students for purposes of assessing their learning processes, their abilities, and their accomplishments. Some effective assessment measures that teachers should consider include the following:

- Observation/kidwatching
- Rubrics
- Retellings
- Interviews, Surveys, and Inventories
- Student Self-Evaluation
- Think-Alouds
- Analysis of student products and projects (performance assessment) and analysis of student performance on state examinations, which are administered at designated grade levels

Each of these measures is discussed separately. The information provided is intended to be practical in nature to facilitate teachers' incorporation of the measures into their assessment plans.

Observation/Kidwatching

As stated previously, educators have frequently relied on testing to assess their students, which generally occurred at the end of a learning sequence. These postassessments did not provide enough information, because they did not tell teachers how the achievement levels were obtained. Moreover, it was too late to change the fate of the learners. There is a need to pay more attention to evaluating learners who are on the way to these final assessments rather than waiting for the learning to conclude. Assessments are needed that guide teachers while the learning is occurring, because it is believed that assessment should lead to improved instruction.

Teachers can gain valuable data about their students while the students are engaged in the learning process by moving among them as they work, observing their learning behaviors. Observation, or kidwatching, is the process of observing children as they engage in authentic daily activities, or of looking at the results or products of these activities. As an assessment measure, observation has many advantages. It permits information to be recorded in many different literacy contexts, yielding data about both process and product. Moreover, observation is not obtrusive because it is integrally related to all the authentic learning that students do on a regular basis (Rhodes & Shanklin, 1993).

Teachers must constantly observe their students, asking themselves, "What did that mean?" They should look for their students' strengths, confusions, and difficulties. In addition, teachers should be able to document what the students can do and understand, and the processes and strategies they utilize. Observation ensures that teachers are aware of their students' progress so that students are supported and encouraged while they are engaged in the learning process. Opportunities for observation are unlimited once teachers develop the habit of kidwatching. A sampling includes the following:

- Listening to students read aloud, both in textbooks and other nonfiction materials
- Listening to students retell what they have learned and the strategies they used for the learning
- Watching students while they are conducting research and writing reports
- Observing students in literature response groups, while reading independently, and during content area classes when students are using textbooks
- Listening to students as they plan a literature response activity
- Observing students as they interact with one another, both socially and academically

Just as good coaches want to improve their athletes' performances by analyzing an athletic event for the purpose of changing moves and devising strategies, effective educators want to improve their students' performances by watching, analyzing, and devising strategies to help increase learning. Observing students is an integral part of the instructional process, and teachers must become careful and efficient observers of their students.

Observations can be recorded in various ways, such as using checklists and writing anecdotal records. A checklist (Figure 8.2) is a listing of items with a place to note if a particular behavior is present, and sometimes to what degree

Figure 8.2	Checklist for Observing Literature Circles

Checklist for Observing Literature Circles

Student _____

	sometimes		usually		always
Was prepared for literature circle	1	2	3	4	5
Participated in the circle discussions	1	2	3	4	5
Was an attentive listener	1	2	3	4	5
Made interesting connections	1	2	3	4	5
Gave supporting ideas	1	2	3	4	5
Asked meaningful questions	1	2	3	4	5
Voiced his/her opinion appropriately	1	2	3	4	5
Responded politely to peers	1	2	3	4	5
Stayed focused on task	1	2	3	4	5

the behavior exists. Checklists help teachers organize their observations, plan their instruction, and compare evidence of behavior over time, thereby documenting student progress (Cooper & Kiger, 2001). Checklists also are useful as a means of recording teachers' observations. They guide and remind teachers of what to observe, as well as inform all the stakeholders in the assessment process of what kinds of behaviors are valued.

Another way to observe students is through the use of anecdotal records. Anecdotal records are brief notes about students that can result in rich, illuminating information. Anecdotal records help identify patterns and themes in students' learning behaviors. They are highly descriptive, capturing events in sufficient detail that can be revisited at a subsequent time.

Because a major purpose of anecdotal records is to capture students' development as learners, teachers have to learn to look and listen differently. To help teachers focus their observations, they might consider the following questions:

- What does the student already know?
- What is the student capable of doing?
- What does the student know about reading, writing, listening, and speaking?
- How does the student approach and solve problems?
- How does the student approach planning, organizing, and completing tasks and activities?

● What remarks does the student make while working independently or interacting with others? (Church, 1991)

Rubrics

Teachers can also use rubrics to note how well a student is performing during an activity (process) or with a project. Rubrics are sets of guidelines and criteria that are used to determine the extent to which a student has learned or accomplished something. Rubrics can be teacher-made or created collaboratively with students. Rubrics are particularly effective when students participate in their creation, because the process gives students greater insights into what is expected of them and increases student ownership into their own learning. A rubric for literature discussions can be seen in Figure 8.3.

Figure 8.3   Rubric for Literature Discussions

1	2	3	4
usually does not bring response log or book to discussion (unprepared)	brings book and response log to discussion group	brings book and response log to discussion group with some passages marked and has written in journal	brings book and response log to discussion group with insightful response log entries and passages marked
generally does not participate in the discussions	participates once in a while, generally when prompted	participates willingly in discussions	makes significant contributions to discussions
is frequently off-task during discussions	sometimes listens and shares and responds during discussions	usually helps keep discussion moving by sharing and responding appropriately and thoughtfully	very effective at sharing and responding, and keeping the discussion going
provides few, if any, response log entries that can enhance discussions	response logs are incomplete or have few examples to support opinions	response log entries are varied with sufficient support for opinions or thoughts	response log entries are thoughtful, insightful, with many documentations, connections, and analyses provided

Try This

Find Someone Who

Find Someone Who is an excellent strategy to activate and assess prior knowledge, or to determine what was learned about a topic. Using a prepared worksheet with prompts about content they are learning, students find other students who can respond successfully to the prompt. They write down the correct answer as well as name of the student who gave them the answer. Generally, students are given a designated amount of time to interact with their peers, with a goal of locating a different person for each prompt. Once the activity is concluded, the class can share its findings. A variation of this activity is to have students document or verify their responses by using their textbooks or other nonfiction material. An example of this activity can be seen in Figure 8.4.

Figure 8.4   Find Someone Who

Social Studies People Search

Find someone who . . .

- Has visited Washington, D.C.

- Knows the Vice President's name

- Can name the capital of our state

- Remembers the name of Columbus' 3 ships

- Was born in another state

- Can tell you the newest state

- Knows the name of the mountain range in New York

- Remembers the date of America's independence

- Can tell you how many stripes are on our flag

- Is able to recite the opening to the Preamble to the Constitution of the United States of America

- Came to the United States from another country

Retellings

Another effective assessment measure for determining the depth and breadth of understanding of text is retellings (Hoyt, 1999; Fountas & Pinnell, 2001). Retellings are widely used to collect evidence of comprehension after reading. After reading (either orally or silently), students can retell what they have read in their own words, with teachers recording the retellings. Teachers can script the retelling or they can use a rubric to assess the extent that readers summarize, include main ideas and supporting details, sequence, and make sense of the text in general. To assist with recording retellings, teachers could prepare coding sheets beforehand, listing the key concepts and relevant details, and then check them off as the students state them. An advantage to scripting is that teachers can note how much was recalled and the order it which it was recalled. Once the free recall is complete, teachers can prompt for further information: "Tell me more about . . . ," "You mentioned . . . ," "Explain what you meant by . . . ," "Can you remember anything else about . . . ?" Teachers can also collect multiple samples of retellings, order them by degree of understanding, and then use them as exemplars for future retellings with students.

Comprehension questions also can be prepared to determine the kinds of information remembered by the students (e.g., main idea, comparison/contrast, cause/effect, etc.). There are commercial inventories available, such as *The Qualitative Reading Inventory* and *The Basic Reading Inventory*, that have selections already prepared for teachers to use.

Interviews, Surveys, and Inventories

Student interviews provide opportunities for students to talk about their learning, both what they are learning and how they are learning. By sharing their thinking, students are actively involved in the teaching/learning process. Students should be given ample opportunities to discuss the content that is being learned and the processes involved in the learning. Students could share their thinking while involved in such activities as K-W-Ls, Semantic Feature Analysis, or Anticipation/Reaction Guides, which could then be noted by teachers on observation sheets or through anecdotal records. An example of a content area interview can be seen in Figure 8.5.

Try This

Mark the Spot

Mark the Spot is an activity that provides students with a purpose for reading, by giving them specific things to locate and read about. Students are given codes to identify important information, interesting information, and information that is confusing or unclear. For example, codes that might be used could be:

X   Important information

!   Interesting information

?   This is unclear, or I have a question about . . .

Teachers can tell their students to mark three important pieces of information, two interesting facts, and three questions. If students are not allowed to mark their texts, Post-its® can be used to indicate the desired information.

(Stevens & Brown, 2000)

| *Figure 8.5* | Content Area Interview |

1. Tell me exactly what you do when you read nonfiction (trade book, article, textbook)?

2. What types of things in a nonfiction book (chapter, article, etc.) can be good clues to help you understand and remember what you are reading?

3. What are the purposes of . . .?
   - a table of contents
   - a glossary
   - the index
   - the boxed information
   - the illustrations, diagrams, charts
   - the bibliography
   - the copyright date

4. What do you do . . .?
   - before you begin to read nonfiction (look at headings, diagrams, summaries, etc.)
   - while you are reading (e.g., take notes, mark places with Post-Its, etc.)
   - once you have finished reading (summarize, make a graphic organizer, take notes)

5. When you are reading nonfiction, what do you do when you come to something you don't understand?

6. How do you prepare for tests?

7. What do you do to get ready for writing a research project? (Probe for use of note-taking, multiple sources, including the Internet, organizational techniques, etc.)

8. How could you improve your reading (or writing) in social studies, science, math, etc.?

9. How can you use the Internet to help you with school projects? (Can also probe for use of e-mail, presentation tools such as PowerPoint, etc.)

NOTE: Additional questions can be added to obtain knowledge of areas that are of concern and interest, as well as those that relate to skills and processes stressed in state standards.

Student Self-Evaluation

An important element in the assessment process is having students evaluate their own learning. If the ultimate goal for schooling is to produce independent and reflective learners, then teachers must provide opportunities for students to look at themselves as learners and to evaluate their own progress and development. Self-evaluation encourages students to observe themselves constantly.

Initially, students are similar to Pinocchio, who needed Jiminy Cricket to be his conscience. Although Jiminy Cricket's help and guidance were necessary for Pinocchio to learn to live in society, there came a time when Pinocchio had to learn to think for himself and to make his own decisions. The same goes for students in the content area classroom. Students ultimately will have to make their own decisions, and the classroom is the ideal place for them to undertake learning how to self-evaluate. There are many opportunities throughout the day and throughout the year for students to self-evaluate. Students can self-evaluate during conferences, on checklists, on questionnaires, and in their learning logs.

During conferences, interviews, or community share following literature circles, students can be asked the following questions:

- What worked well in . . . ?
- What did you have difficulty with?
- What skills or strategies did you use while reading (or writing) . . . ?
- Which ones worked for you?
- What skills or strategies do you need to learn (or review)?

Students also can be asked to retell and reconstruct their learning in order to help them gain insights into themselves as learners.

Students can be given questionnaires or checklists, which can guide their self-evaluations. They also can be taught to self-evaluate through the use of learning logs, which are suitable for any subject area. At the end of an instructional period, students write comments in their learning logs pertaining to what they learned during the session, what they don't understand, and what they would still like to know.

Self-evaluation requires that teachers model the process, involve their students in discussions about self-evaluation and self-reflection, and provide their students with practice. Students do not come to school armed with metacognitive knowledge and vocabularies to be able to articulate how they are learning and what they can do to improve their learning. But the benefits are many, because student self-evaluation encourages students' responsibility for their own learning, promotes critical reflection, and enables students to become actively involved in their own learning. Self-evaluation gives students opportunities to recognize their strengths and areas needing improvement, and as a result, set realistic goals.

Think-Alouds

Another means of gathering information about how students are performing using expository text is to have students think aloud, that is, verbalize their thoughts as they read or write and make sense of text. This can be likened to a sports announcer giving a play-by-play account of an athletic event. Students give play-by-play accounts of their own reading and writing behaviors using nonfiction texts.

Students will not naturally think aloud as they read and write. They must first be shown how to think aloud, and this can be accomplished through teacher modeling. If teachers use think-alouds as they demonstrate how to read or write nonfiction, this procedure will become familiar to students. Using short texts, such as those in *Time for Kids*, provides an excellent opportunity to demonstrate the think-aloud process. In addition, teachers can ask such probing questions as

- What do you already know about . . . ?
- Why did the author use bolded print to say . . . ?
- What features did the author use to help explain . . . ?
- Where can you find the meaning of that term?
- What strategies would work while reading . . . ?

Helping students get in touch with their own thinking (metacognition) will provide both students and teachers with information that is useful for instruction and student growth.

Student Products, Projects, and Other Work Samples

Work samples provide evidence of students' actual work in a classroom. Samples of students' authentic work yield evidence of student performance. They may include projects, research reports, entries in literature response journals or math learning logs, and so forth. By collecting and analyzing work samples, teachers can

- look at the actual products that result from learning;
- compare the level and quality of the students' efforts and work over time, thereby noting student progress and growth; and
- use what they have learned from the students' performance on the project or activities to help plan future instruction (Cooper & Kiger, 2001).

 Try This

My Learning Notebooks

My Learning notebooks are logs or journals that are designed to help students think about and reflect on their own learning. Students can respond to prompts about *what* they are learning, or they can respond to prompts about *how* they are learning. Some examples of prompts that can be used for this activity are as follows:

What is being learned

- Describe in your own words what you have learned.
- Explain what you have learned to someone who is not in this class.

- Describe what you can do with the information you have learned.
- Explain why it is important to learn this information

How it was learned

- Describe what you did to read this successfully.
- What did you do when the learning became difficult?
- Explain what you did to prepare for . . .
- Explain how you figured out this problem.

Figure 8.6 Rubrics for a Work Sample or Product

Rubric for Nonfiction Projects

SCORE	CRITERIA
3	EXCELLENT: _____ _____ _____
2	SATISFACTORY_____ _____ _____
1	WEAK _____ _____ _____
0	UNACCEPTABLE_____ _____ _____

Rubric for Scoring Nonfiction Work

SCORE	CRITERIA
3	• Identifies the main ideas, themes, and issues • Effectively uses material from the text, resources, and/or personal experience to support ideas • Answers most of the *who, what, where, when, why, or how* questions
2	• Identifies some main ideas, themes, and issues • Uses some material from the text, resources and/or personal experience to support ideas • Answers only some of the *who, what, where, when, why, or how* questions
1	• Makes few references to the main ideas, themes, and issues • Uses little material from the text or other resources to support ideas
0	• Weak response with little or no reference to the main ideas, themes, and issues • Refer to details that are irrelevant • Does not answer the *who, what, where, when, why, or how* questions

Typically, work samples were given to the teacher, who assigned a grade. Students often were not given reasons for the grade, nor were they provided with constructive advice so that they could improve on their performance. However, today, many teachers use these work samples as opportunities to continue the instructional process by involving students in determining their own "grades" (generally through the use of a rubric). This gives the students ownership in the process, and results in instructional improvement. An example of a rubric for student products can be seen in Figure 8.6. If need be, rubrics can be translated into a letter grade, for example, with the various scale points assigned a letter grade, the top performance being an A, the next level a B, and so on.

A FINAL NOTE

Your journey has concluded and now you may be ready to embark on a similar journey in your own classrooms. We hope you can map out your course of action, taking into account your subject matter, your students, and the strategies and processes necessary for successfully undertaking the journey. Before you depart, you must also be cognizant of your own state's frameworks, expectations of learning outcomes, and the assessments that measure these. You need to examine the curricular guidelines and proficiency tests to be sure that you know what is expected and be able to align them with your own classroom teaching and assessment.

A Kid's Guide to the White House

by Betty Debnam

Book Talk

This lively, kid-friendly guide to our presidents' home takes kids on a virtual field trip to Washington, D.C. Written in collaboration with the White House Historical Association, the author leads her readers on a tour of the public rooms of the White House and the huge back yard. The history of the White House is presented, as are descriptions of some of the first families. There is an abundance of nonfiction access features—photographs, cutaways, insets, maps, historic pictures, and primary source documents—that add to the readability of the text and increase the interest of the readers. This book is filled with facts, photographs, and puzzles, making it a family book for readers of all ages.

Instructional Activities for the Classroom

1 *Chapter-Beginning Activity*

To help students realize how much they have changed and learned over the years, share the book *When I Was Little* by Jamie Lee Curtis. This simple picture book compares the "author" as a child and later as she grew up. She describes some of the activities and beliefs she had as a young child, and how she feels when she is older. The text is predictable and is easily adapted to students' own interpretations of things they could do (or couldn't do) when they were young, and what they can do now. This is an excellent lead-in to self-evaluation and goal setting, because students can think about what they could do when they were younger (either physically or academically) and how much they have progressed and learned.

2 *Collecting Testing-Related Literature*

Although much of what is available is fiction, collecting and sharing books about testing and testing situations can alleviate testing fears and even act as a springboard for a discussion on effective test-taking tips and techniques. Some examples include *Testing Miss Malarkey* and *First Grade Takes a Test*.

3 *Student Advice on Test Taking*

Take advantage of the "experts" in your classroom who can give advice to future students regarding being successful on certain tests: standardized tests, state assessments, local exams, and so forth. After taking such a test, students can be given a sheet to fill out that allows them to reflect on how they did, what they did to prepare, and how others could be successful. Some key prompts could include the following:

- I think my performance was . . .
- I prepared by . . .
- Next time, I would . . .
- Advice I would give to next year's students would be . . .

Book Talk and Beyond

The Egyptian News

by Scott Steedman

Using a newspaper format, the author presents information celebrating more than 3,000 years of Egyptian civilization. Written as if it were the time period of the ancient Egyptians, this newspaper-like book is filled with fascinating features of everyday life in ancient Egypt, from

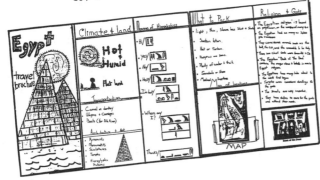

an interview with a royal embalmer to advice on choosing the perfect pet and how to behave at an Egyptian party. There are feature stories, advice, advertising, maps, timelines and more—all revealing the fascinating lifestyle of this historical period. This book, presented as a newsworthy text, is just one of a series dealing with news. If students are hooked on this format, they can read *The Aztec News, The Greek News, The History News: Medicine,* to name a few. They can also create their own versions, featuring topics that they are studying in school—the Olympics, the rain forest, the Revolutionary War, Earth Day, weather, and so on. A variation of this activity could be to explore other formats for presenting information, such as the brochure created by a sixth grader about Ancient Egypt.

Insects—Science Nature Guide

by Dr. George McGavin

Did you know that insects can be found on top of the highest mountain, under water in ponds and rivers, and on every continent in the world? This book will introduce you to amazing insects from everywhere. It gives you clues on how to find them and how to identify them after you locate them. The drawings are in color, and several pages are devoted to double-paged habitat illustrations. These pages have lots of insects in them, so you can practice spotting them and making identifications. It teaches you to be an insect detective! It also teaches you how to study insects with respect, so you do not harm them and you don't get harmed either. If you enjoy doing science projects, this book has fifteen easy-to-do projects about the six-legged creatures that cover our earth.

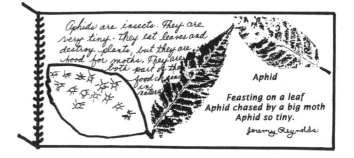

Aphid

Feasting on a leaf
Aphid chased by a big moth
Aphid so tiny.

Jeremy Reynolds

After reading many entries in *Insects—Science Nature Guide,* the class explored the area surrounding their school. The students drew the insects in their habitat, wrote some important information, and created Haiku poetry. The pages were published in a class book.

Nonfiction Books: A Recommended List

An asterisk following a book title indicates that the book is cited in the text.

MATH, SCIENCE, AND TECHNOLOGY
Series of Merit (with sample titles)

■ **All About . . . Series** (Scholastic—New York)

DESCRIPTION AND ORGANIZATIONAL FEATURES: Each book of the series contains informative facts about animals; detailed illustrations, labels, captions, About the Author.

SAMPLE TITLES: *All About Owls; All About Deer*

■ **Alphabet Books Series—Jerry Pallotta** (publishers vary)

DESCRIPTION AND ORGANIZATIONAL FEATURES: Each letter of the alphabet is used to describe some aspect of a scientific topic; informative illustrations accompany facts about a topic for each letter of the alphabet

SAMPLE TITLES: *The Underwater Alphabet Book; The Dinosaur Alphabet Book; The Freshwater Alphabet Book; The Icky Bug Alphabet Book; The Yucky Reptile Alphabet Book*

■ **Are You A . . . Series** (Kingfisher—New York)

DESCRIPTION AND ORGANIZATIONAL FEATURES: Books provide factual information, answering the question, "Are you a ___? If you are . . . "; witty text, colorful illustrations, additional facts provided

SAMPLE TITLES: *Are You a Spider?; Are You A Butterfly?; Are You a Ladybug?; Are You a Snail?*

■ **Eyewitness Juniors** (Alfred Knopf—New York)

DESCRIPTION AND ORGANIZATIONAL FEATURES: Each book gives a real-life look at amazing, but true behavior in the animal world; table of contents, photographs and illustrations, diagrams, index

SAMPLE TITLES: *Amazing Crocodiles & Reptiles*

■ **Fascinating Facts About . . .** (The Millbrook Press—Brookfield, CT)

DESCRIPTION AND ORGANIZATIONAL FEATURES: An exciting new series that is designed to pique the interest of young readers in a wide variety of subjects; vocabulary-controlled texts, colorful illustrations, introduction, table of contents, insets, diagrams, maps, sidebars, more fascinating facts, glossary, index, photo credits

SAMPLE TITLES: *Fascinating Facts About Volcanoes; Fascinating Facts About the Solar System; Fascinating Facts About the Seashore*

■ **First Discovery** (Scholastic—New York)

DESCRIPTION AND ORGANIZATIONAL FEATURES: Outstanding science books that give fascinating overviews of topics; see-through plastic pages, overlays, labels, colorful illustrations

SAMPLE TITLES: *Whales; The Tree; Weather; Vegetables in the Garden; The Camera*

■ **Informania** (Candlewick Press—Cambridge, MA)

DESCRIPTION AND ORGANIZATIONAL FEATURES: Facts about a variety of topics; creative table of contents, About the Author, photographs, insets, diagrams and labels, index, afterword, glossary, maps

SAMPLE TITLES: *Sharks; Ghosts; Aliens; Vampires*

■ **Let's Read and Find Out Science** (HarperCollins—New York)

DESCRIPTION AND ORGANIZATIONAL FEATURES: Each book introduces basic science concepts and builds on them; colorful illustrations, some books contain diagrams, maps, more facts, additional information

SAMPLE TITLES: *The Big Dipper; The International Space Station; Baby Whales Drink Milk; Where Does the Garbage Go?**

■ **Life Cycle of . . . A Bobbie Kalman Book** (Crabtree Publishing Company—New York)

DESCRIPTION AND ORGANIZATIONAL FEATURES: Descriptions of the life cycles of animals; table of contents, illustraions, photographs, inserts, captions, cross-sections, glossary, index, photograph and illustration credits

SAMPLE TITLES: *The Life Cycle of a Bird; The Life Cycle of a Butterfly; The Life Cycle of a Frog; The Life Cycle of a Whale; The Life Cycle of a Sea Turtle*

■ **Life Science Wonder Book** (PowerKids Press—New York)

DESCRIPTION AND ORGANIZATIONAL FEATURES: The books introduce the physical characteristics, habits, and behavior of animals; table of contents, captions, photographs, enlarged text, bold print, glossary, pronunciation guide, index, web sites

SAMPLE TITLES: *I Wonder What It's Like to Be a Grasshopper; I Wonder What It's Like to Be a Bee; I Wonder What It's Like to Be a Spider; I Wonder What It's Like to Be a Butterfly; I Wonder What's Like to Be an Earthworm*

■ **The Magic School Bus Series** (Scholastic—New York)

DESCRIPTION AND ORGANIZATIONAL FEATURES: This magical series blends narrative and non-fiction using a central character, Miss Frizzle, a teacher who takes her students on incredible field trips; the books are immersed with facts, which are often placed and interspersed around the illustrations.

SAMPLE TITLES: *The Magic School Bus at the Waterworks; The Magic School Bus in the Time of the Dinosaurs; The Magic School Bus Inside a Hurricane; The Magic School Bus Inside a Beehive; The Magic School Bus Explores the Senses*

■ **New True Book** (Children's Press—Chicago)

DESCRIPTION AND ORGANIZATIONAL FEATURES: Science series that introduces concepts to young readers; colorful photographs, photo credits, table of contents, words you should know, pronunciation guide, index, About the Author

SAMPLE TITLES: *A New True Book of the Oceans*

■ **One Small Square . . . Series** (McGraw-Hill—New York)

DESCRIPTION AND ORGANZATIONAL FEATURES: This series describes all the living things that can live in one small square of the environment; colorful, illustrated picture guide, diagrams, index, labels, experiments and activities, sidebars, diagrams

SAMPLE TITLES: *One Small Square: Backyard; One Small Square: Woods; One Small Square: Cactus Desert; One Small Square: Swamp*

■ **Our Wild World Series** (NorthWood Press—Minnetonka, MN)

DESCRIPTION AND ORGANIZATIONAL FEATURES: Books about nature in the wild; bolded sidebar information, colorful photos, Fun Facts, index, Internet sites

SAMPLE TITLES: *Sea Turtles; Wolves; Moose; WhiteTail Deer; Black Bears*

■ **Questions and Answers About . . .** (Scholastic—New York)

DESCRIPTION AND ORGANIZATIONAL FEATURES: Describes scientific phenomena using a question-and-answer format; vivid illustrations, table of contents, introduction, diagrams, index, About the Author and Illustrator, key to abbreviations

SAMPLE TITLES: *Do Stars Have Points?: Questions and Answers About Stars and Planets; Did Dinosaurs Live In Your Backyard?: Questions and Answers About Dinosaurs; How Do Flies Walk Upside Down?: Questions and Answers About Insects; Why Do Volcanoes Blow Their Tops?: Questions and Answers About Volcanoes and Earthquakes; Can You Hear a Shout in Space?: Questions and Answers About Space Exploration*

■ **Rookie Read-About Science Series** (Children's Press—New York and Chicago)

DESCRIPTION AND ORGANIZATIONAL FEATURES: Science texts for young readers; simple text, colorful photographs, Words You Know (with accompanying photos), index, About the Author, photo credits

SAMPLE TITLES: *It Could Still Be a Mammal; It Could Still Be a Dinosaur; Busy, Buzz Bees; Of Mice and Rats; Mammals of Long Ago*

■ **Science In . . .** (Franklin Watts—New York)

DESCRIPTION AND ORGANIZATIONAL FEATURES: Describes scientific achievements of the past, using many illustrations

SAMPLE TITLES: *Science in Ancient China; Science in Ancient Greece; Science in Colonial America; Science in Ancient Egypt; Science in Ancient Rome*

■ **Voyages of Discovery** (Scholastic—New York)

DESCRIPTION AND ORGANIZATIONAL FEATURES: This series is a groundbreaking approach to the arts and sciences. The interactive books guide readers back to the source of knowledge about a specific topic; interactive elements, table of contents, cut-aways, flaps, colorful illustrations, captions, insets, graduated pages with additional facts, Words to Know, time line, index

SAMPLE TITLES: *Exploring Space*; Musical Instruments; Paint and Painting; Taming Fire*

■ **What About? Series** (Raintree Steck-Vaughn)

DESCRIPTION AND ORGANIZATIONAL FEATURES: The *What About?* series presents general science topics simply, using clear concise text; striking photographs and illustrations, table of contents, headings, captions, glossary, Things to Do, useful addresses, index

SAMPLE TITLES: *What About? Oceans; What About? Hearing; What About? Fire; What About? Birth and Growth; What About? Pollution*

■ **Wildlife for Kids Series** (Creative Publishing—Minnetonka, MN)

DESCRIPTION AND ORGANIZATIONAL FEATURES: This scientific series, endorsed by *Ranger Rick* and the National Wildlife Federation, showcases a variety of wildlife; each page is accompanied by incredible photographs with descriptive captions

SAMPLE TITLES: *Koalas for Kids; Moose for Kids; Bears for Kids; Sharks for Kids; Eagles for Kids*

Titles of Interest

Adler, David. (1990). *Mathematics*. New York: Doubleday.

Adler, David. (1996). *Fraction Fun*. New York: Holiday House.

Adler, David. (1998). *Shape Up! Fun with Triangles and Other Polygons.* New York: Holiday House.

Adler, Irving. (1990). *Mathematics.* New York: Doubleday.*

Allaby, Michael. (2001). *Tornados: And Other Dramatic Weather Systems.* New York: Dorling Kindersley.

Ancona, George. (1998). *Let's Dance!* New York: Morrow.*

Arnold, Caroline. (1994). *Fireflies.* New York: Scholastic.

Arnold, Caroline. (2001). *Did You Hear That? Animals with Super Hearing.* Watertown, MA: Charlesbridge.

Arnosky, Jim. (1998). *Watching Desert Wildlife.* Washington, DC: National Geographic Society.*

Arnosky, Jim. (2001). *One Whole Day: Wolves.* Washington, DC: National Geographic.

Baker, Lucy. (1997). *Life in the Rainforest.* New York: Scholastic.*

Barnes, Bob. (2001). *Dinosaur Bones.* San Francisco: Chronicle Books.

Bash, Barbara. (1989). *Desert Giant: The World of the Saguaro Cactus.* San Francisco, CA: Sierra Club Books.*

Berman, Ruth. (1999). *Watchful Wolves.* New York: Pull Ahead Books.*

Bennett, Andrea & Kessler, James. (1996). *Apples, Bubbles, and Crystals: Your Science ABCs.* New York: Learning Triangle Press.*

Benson, Laura. (1994). *This is Our Earth.* Watertown, MA: Charlesbridge.*

Berger, Melvin. (1997). *Flies Taste with Their Feet: Weird Facts About Insects.* New York: Scholastic.*

Berger, Melvin & Berger, Gilda. (2001). *How Do Bats See in the Dark? Questions and Answers about Night Creatures.* New York: Scholastic.*

Blashfield, Jean. (1994). *Rescuing Endangered Species.* Chicago: Children's Press.*

Bradley, Catherine. (1998). *Life in the Mountains.* Chicago: World Book.

Bradley, Kimberly. (2001). *Pop! A Book about Bubbles.* New York: Harper.

Butterfield, Moira. (1993). *1000 Facts About the Earth.* New York: Scholastic.*

Caron, Lucille & St. Jacques, Phil. (2000). *Fractions and Decimals.* Berkeley Heights, NJ: Enslow.

Charles, Oz. (1988). *How Is a Crayon Made?* New York: Scholastic.

Cherry, Lynne. (1990). *The Great Kapok Tree.* New York: Trumpet Club.

Chester, Jonathan. (1995). *A is for Antartica.* Berkeley, CA: Tricycle Press.*

Cole, Joanna. (1992). *The Magic School Bus on the Ocean Floor.* New York: Scholastic.*

Cowcher, Helen. (1988). *Rain Forest.* New York: Farrar, Straus, & Giroux.

Direct, D.K. (1991). *What's Inside My Body?* New York: Dorling Kindersley.*

Earthworks Group, The. (1990). *50 Simple Things Kids Can Do to Save the Earth.* New York: Scholastic.

Facklam, Margery. (1992). *Bees Dance and Whales Sing: The Mysteries of Animal Communication.* San Francisco, CA: Sierra Club Books for Children.*

Fleisher, Paul & Keeler, Patricia. (1990). *Looking Inside Machines and Constructions.* New York: Scholastic.

Geisert, Arthur. (1996). *Roman Numerals I to MM.* Boston: Houghton Mifflin.

Gibbons, Gail. (1993). *Spiders.* New York: Holiday House.

Gibbons, Gail. (1995). *The Reasons for the Seasons.* New York: Holiday House.

Gibbons, Gail. (1996). *Deserts.* New York: Holiday House.*

Gibbons, Gail. (2001). *Ducks.* New York: Holiday House.

Greene, Rhonda. (1997). *When a Line Bends . . . A Shape Begins.* New York: Houghton Mifflin.

Guiberson, Brenda. (2001). *The Emperor Who Lays an Egg.* New York: Holt.

Hart, Avery. (2001). *Who Really Discovered America? Unraveling the Mystery and Solving the Puzzle.* Charlotte, VT: Williamson.

Haven, Kendall. (2000). *Marvels of Math: Fascinating Reads and Awesome Activities.* New York: John Wiley & Sons.

Heller, Ruth. (1992). *How to Hide a Butterfly and Other Insects.* New York: Grosset & Dunlap.*

Hooper, Meredith. (2000). *Antarctic Journal.* Washington, DC: National Geographic.*

Hooper, Rosanne. (1998). *Life in the Woodlands.* Chicago: World Book.

Kerley, Barbara. (2001). *The Dinosaurs of Waterhouse Hawkins.* New York: Scholastic.

Kitchen, Bert. (1992). *Somewhere Today.* Cambridge, MA: Candlewick Press.*

Kitchen, Bert. (1993). *And So They Build.* Cambridge, MA: Candlewick Press.*

Koomen, Michele. (2001). *Fractions: Making Fair Shares.* Mankato, MN: Capstone Press.

Lasky, Kathryn. (1997). *The Most Beautiful Roof in the World.* San Diego: Harcourt Brace.

Ledwon, Peter. (2000). *Midnight Math: Twelve Terrific Math Games.* New York: Holiday House.

Leedy, Loreen. (1993). *Postcards from Pluto: A Tour of the Solar System.* New York: Holiday House.*

Leedy, Loreen. (1994). *The Edible Pyramid: Good Eating Every Day.* New York: Holiday House.

Leedy, Loreen. (1994). *Fraction Action.* New York: Holiday House.

Lester, Alison. (1989). *Imagine.* Boston: Houghton Mifflin.*

Levy, Elizabeth. (2000). *Who Are You Calling a Woolly Mammoth?* New York: Scholastic.*

Lowery, Linda. (1991). *Earth Day.* Minneapolis, MN: Carolrhoda Books.

Jenkins, Steve. (2001). *Slap, Squeak, & Scatter.* Boston, MA: Houghton Mifflin.

Lehne, Judith. (2000). *Kangaroo for Kids.* Minnetonka, MN. Creative Publishing.*

Manning, Mick. (2001). *Wash, Scrub, Brush!* New York: Whitman.

Markle, Sandra & Markle, William. (1999). *Gone Forever.* New York: Scholastic.*

Maynard, Thane. (1994). *Animal Olympians.* New York: Franklin Watts.

McGavin, George. (1995). *Insects of North America.* San Diego: Thunder Bay Press.*

McMillan, Bruce. (1991). *Eating Fractions.* New York: Scholastic.

Micucci, Charles. (1992). *The Life and Times of the Apple.* New York: Orchard.*

Miller, David. (2001). *Just Like You and Me.* New York: Dial.

Morrison, Meighan. (1993). *Long Live Earth.* New York: Scholastic.

Mound, L. (1993). *Amazing Insects.* New York: Knopf.

Napoli, Donna & Tchen, Richard. (2001). *How Hungry Are You?* New York: Atheneum.

National Geographic Society. (2000). *The World Beneath Your Feet.* Washington, DC: National Geographic Society.*

Pallotta, Jerry. (1986). *The Icky Bug Alphabet Book.* Watertown, MA: Charlesbridge.*

Pallotta, Jerry & Bolster, Rob. (1999). *The Hershey's Milk Chocolate Fractions Book.* New York: Scholastic.

Parker, Nancy & Wright, Joan. (1987). *Bugs.* New York: Scholastic.

Patent, Hinshaw. (1998). *Bold and Bright.* New York: Walker.

Peterson, Cris. (1994). *Extra Cheese Please! Mozzarella's Journey from Cow to Pizza.* Honesdale, PA: Boyds Mills Press.

Pratt, Kristin. (1996). *A Fly in the Sky.* Nevada City, CA: Dawn.

Pratt-Serafina, Kristen Joy. (2000). *Salamander Rain: A Lake and Pond Journey.* Nevada City, CA: Dawn.

Rabe, Trish. (2001). *Oh, The Things You Can Do That Are Good for You!: All About Staying Healthy.* New York: Random House.*

Reid, Keith. (2001). *Natural World Penguins.* Austin, TX: Raintree.

Resnick, Jane. (1994). *Eyes on Nature: Cats.* Chicago: Kidsbooks.*

Rey, Luis. (2001). *Extreme Dinosaurs.* San Francisco: Chronicle Books.

Ride, Sally & O'Shaughnessy, Tam. (1994). *The Third Planet: Exploring the Earth from Space.* New York: Crown.

Rubin, Susan Goldman. (1998). *Toilets, Toasters, & Telephones: The How & Why of Everyday Objects.* Orlando, FL: Harcourt Brace.

Ruurs, M. (1996). *A Mountain Alphabet.* Toronto: Tundra Books.

Schwartz, David. (2001). *Q is for Quark: A Science Alphabet Book.* Berkeley, CA: Tricycle Press.

Scieszka, Jon & Smith, Lane. (1995). *Math Curse.* New York: Viking Press.*

Showers, Paul. (1994). *Where Does the Garbage Go?* New York: Harcourt.

Singer, Marilyn. (1998). *Bottoms Up!* New York: Holt.

Singer, Marilyn. (2001). *Tough Beginnings: How Baby Animals Survive.* New York: Holt.

Siy, Alexandra. (2001). *Footprints on the Moon.* Watertown, MA: Charlesbridge.

Soldheim, James. (1998). *It's Disgusting and We Ate It!* New York: Simon & Schuster.*

Stonehouse, Bernard. (1999). *Camouflage.* New York: Tangerine Press.

Stonehouse, Bernard. (1999). *Predators.* New York: Tangerine Press.

Stutson, Caroline. (1993). *On the River ABC.* Boulder, CO: Roberts Rinehart Publishers.

Swinburne, Stephen. (1999). *Guess Whose Shadow?* Honesdale, PA: Boyds Mills Press.*

Taylor, Barbara. (1992). *Rivers and Oceans.* New York: Kingfisher Books.*

Warrick, Karen Clemens. (2001). *If I Had a Tail.* Hong Kong: Rising Moon.

Willow, Diane. (1991). *At Home in the Rainforest.* Watertown, MA: Charlesbridge.

World Conservation Monitoring Center. (2000). Cambridge, England: *Endangered Birds.*

Worth, Bonnie. (2001). *Oh, Say Can You Seed? All About Flowering Plants.* New York: Random House.*

Wray, Paul. (2000). *It's a Bug's World: A Directory of Awesome Insects.* New York: Viking.*

Yolen, Jane. (1991). *Welcome to the Green House.* New York: Scholastic.

Math, Science, Technology, and Poetry

Asch, Frank. (1998). *Cactus Poems.* New York: Harcourt.

Brenner, Barbara. (1994). *Earth is Painted Green: A Garden of Poems About Our Planet.* New York: Scholastic.

Cyrus, Kurt. (2001). *Oddhopper Opera: A Bug's Garden of Verses.* New York: Harcourt.

Florian, Douglas. (1996). *On the Wing.* Orlando, FL: Harcourt Brace.

Florian, Douglas. (1998). *Insectlopedia: Poems and Paintings.* Orlando, FL: Harcourt Brace.

Florian, Douglas. (2000). *In the Swim.* Orlando, FL: Harcourt Brace.

Florian, Douglas. (2000). *Lizards, Frogs, and Polliwogs.* Orlando, FL: Harcourt Brace.

Florian, Douglas. (2000). *Mammalabilia: Poems and Paintings.* Orlando, FL: Harcourt Brace.

George, Kristine. (1998). *Old Elm Speaks: Tree Poems.* New York: Clarion.

Harley, Avis. (2001). *Leap into Poetry.* Honesdale, PA: Boyds Mills Press.

Hines, Anna Grossnickle. (2001). *Pieces: A Year in Poems and Quilts.* New York: Greenwillow.*

Hopkins, Lee Bennett. (1997). *Marvelous Math: A Book of Poems.* New York: Simon & Schuster.

Hopkins, Lee Bennett. (1999). *Spectacular Science: A Book of Poems.* New York: Simon & Schuster.

Lewis, J. Patrick. (1998). *The Little Buggers.* New York: Dial.

Lyon, George Ella. (1998). *Counting on the Woods.* New York: DK.

McKelvey, Douglas. (2001). *Locust Pocus!* New York: Philomel.

Paolilli, Paul & Brewer, Dan. (2001). *Silver Seeds.* New York: Viking.*

Schnur, Steven. (1997). *Autumn: An Alphabet Acrostic Book.* Boston, MA: Houghton Mifflin.*

Schnur, Steven. (2001). *Summer: An Alphabet Acrostic Book.* New York: Clarion.*

Yolen, Jane. (1996). *Bird Watch.* New York: Penguin Putnam Books for Young Readers.

Yolen, Jane. (1998). *The Originals.* New York: Philomel.

Zahares, Wade. (2001). *Big, Bad and a Little Bit Scary: Poems That Bite Back.* New York: Viking.

SOCIAL STUDIES

Series of Merit (with sample titles)

■ **Adventures in Colonial America.** (Troll—New York)

DESCRIPTION AND ORGANIZATIONAL FEATURES: Taking readers back in time, this series explores the world as it once was; black and white illustrations, some captions, index

SAMPLE TITLES: *The Winter at Valley Forge: Survival and Victory; Seventh and Walnut: Life in Colonial Philadelphia; Sailing to America: Colonists at Sea; Blue Feather's Vision*

■ **Alphabet Series—Jerry Pallotta** (Charlesbridge—Watertown, MA)

DESCRIPTION AND ORGANIZATIONAL FEATURES: Using each letter of the alphabet, information is provided about a variety of social studies topics; informative and dramatic illustrations accompany each letter of the alphabet

SAMPLE TITLES: *The Boat Alphabet Book; The Airplane Alphabet Book; The Jet Alphabet Book*

■ **Black Americans of Achievement Series** (Chelsea House—New York)

DESCRIPTION AND ORGANIZATIONAL FEATURES: Biographies of famous Black Americans; table of contents, index, chronology, further reading, black and white photos

SAMPLE TITLES: *Kareem Abdul-Jabbar—Basketball Great; Louis Farrakhan—Political Activist; Langston Hughes—Poet; Alex Haley—Author; Matthew Hensen*

■ **Children of Genius** (Barron's Education Series)

DESCRIPTION AND ORGANIZATIONAL FEATURES: Biographies about unusual children who later were recognized as people of genius; clever illustrations

SAMPLE TITLES: *Albert Einstein; Leonardo da Vinci; Amadeus Mozart; Pablo Picasso*

■ **Childhood of Famous Americans Series** (Aladdin Paperbacks—New York)

DESCRIPTION AND ORGANIZATIONAL FEATURES: This historical series chronicles the childhood of many famous Americans; chapter books, black and white illustrations, dialogue, table of contents, fictionalized details and conversations added to make stories alive

SAMPLE TITLES: *John Glenn: Young Astronaut; Louisa May Alcott: Young Novelist; Jim Hensen: Young Puppeter; Rosa Parks: Young Rebel; Eleanor Roosevelt: Fighter for Social Justice.*

■ **Cornerstones of Freedom Series** (Children's Press—New York)

DESCRIPTION AND ORGANIZATIONAL FEATURES: Series describes places and times of historical interest; includes photos, glossaries, and time lines

SAMPLE TITLES: *The Industrial Revolution; The National Mall; African-Americans in the Thirteen Colonies; The Liberty Bell; The Great Depression*

■ **Creative Minds Biographies** (Carolrhoda Books—Minneapolis, MN)

DESCRIPTION AND ORGANIZATIONAL FEATURES: The lives and times are described in this series, featuring creative individuals who have made extraordinary contributions to society

SAMPLE TITLES: *Walking the Road to Freedom: A Story About Sojourner Truth; Mr. Blue Jeans: A Story About Levi Strauss; Oh, the Places He Went: A Story About Dr. Seuss; Voice of Freedom: A Story About Frederick Douglass; We Will Race You, Henry: A Story About Henry Ford*

■ *Gateway Biography Series* (Millbrook Press—Brookfield, CT)

DESCRIPTION AND ORGANIZATIONAL FEATURES: Stories of fascinating people for young readers; photographs, boxed text, important dates listed at end of book, index, For Further Reading

■ *If You . . .* (Scholastic—New York)

DESCRIPTION AND ORGANIZATIONAL FEATURES: Transports readers to different times, and different places, emphasizing what it would have been like if the readers had been there; bold-faced questions are answered with many accompanying illustrations.

SAMPLE TITLES: *. . . If Your Name Was Changed at Ellis Island; . . . If You Lived in the Alaska Territory; . . . If You Were There When They Signed the Constitution; . . . If You Lived in the Days of the Knights; . . . If You Lived at the Time of the American Revolution*

■ *In Their Own Words* (Scholastic—New York)

DESCRIPTION AND ORGANIZATIONAL FEATURES: Biographical reference books; use of primary sources, quotes from the person being featured, as well as facts to bring an historical figure to life, black and white illustrations, table of contents, chronology, bibliography of primary and secondary sources, Further Reading, For More Information, photo credits

SAMPLE TITLES: *Christopher Columbus; Paul Revere; Abraham Lincoln*

■ *Lives and Times Series* (Heinemann Library—Chicago)

DESCRIPTION AND ORGANIZATIONAL FEATURES: Series introduces readers to the lives of many famous historical figures

SAMPLE TITLES: *The Wright Brothers; Dr. Seuss; Martin Luther King, Jr.; Thomas Edison*

■ *Lives of . . .* (Harcourt Brace—Orlando, FL)

DESCRIPTION AND ORGANIZATIONAL FEATURES: Presents interesting tidbits, information, accomplishments, etc., of various professions

SAMPLE TITLES: *Lives of Extraordinary Women: Rules, Rebels (And What the Neighbors Thought); Lives of the Artists: Masterpieces, Messes (And What the Neighbors Thought); Lives of the Athletes; Lives of the Musicians: Good Times, Bad Times . . . And What the Neighbors Thought; Lives of the Presidents: Fame, Shame (And What the Neighbors Thought)*

■ *Look What Came From . . .* (Franklin Watts—New York)*

DESCRIPTION AND ORGANIZATIONAL FEATURES: Describes many things, both familiar and unfamiliar, that originally came from certain places around the world; table of contents, maps, photos, captions, labels, glossary, index, To Find Out More, Meet the Author

SAMPLE TITLES: *Look What Came from Egypt; Look What Came from the United States; Look What Came from Australia; Look What Came from China; Look What Came from Italy*

■ *A New True Book* (Children's Press—Chicago)

DESCRIPTION AND ORGANIZATIONAL FEATURES: Informational books on a variety of social studies topics; photo credits, table of contents, photographs, chapters, enlarged text, words you should know, pronunciation guide, index, about the author

SAMPLE TITLES: *The Constitution; The Navajo; Pioneers; Explorers; Yellowstone National Park*

■ *A Picture Book of . . .* (Holiday House—New York)

DESCRIPTION AND ORGANIZATIONAL FEATURES: Biographical picture books; many illustrations to complement the text; Author's Note, Important Dates in back of books

SAMPLE TITLES: *A Picture Book of Benjamin Franklin; A Picture Book of Rosa Parks; A Picture Book of Jesse Owens; A Picture Book of Florence Nightingale; A Picture Book of Paul Revere*

■ *Postcards From . . . Series* (Steck-Vaughn—Austin, TX)*

DESCRIPTION AND ORGANIZATIONAL FEATURES: Describes places around the world using a postcard format; single page information accompanied by a photograph

SAMPLE TITLES: *Postcards from Israel; Postcards from Mexico; Postcards from Spain; Postcards from Kenya; Postcards from China*

■ *Rookie Read-About Holidays* (Grolier—New York)

DESCRIPTION AND ORGANIZATIONAL FEATURES: Informational texts about holidays; simple text and photographs

SAMPLE TITLES: *Independence Day; Martin Luther King, Jr. Day*

■ *Scholastic Biography* (Scholastic—New York)

DESCRIPTION AND ORGANIZATIONAL FEATURES: chapter biographies; a few small illustrations, table of contents, occasional photographs

SAMPLE TITLES: *Mark Twain; The Secret Soldier: The Story of Deborah Sampson; Sojourner Truth: Ain't I a Woman?; Mr. President: A Book of United States Presidents; Rosa Parks*

■ *Sleeping Bear Press Alphabet Series* (Sleeping Bear Press—Chelsea, MI)

DESCRIPTION AND ORGANIZATIONAL FEATURES: Alphabet books that capture each state with entertaining rhymes, rich history, and fun facts; in addition to the rhymes, the alternate page provides facts about the alphabet letter being described; illustrations include scenery, artifacts, maps, drawings of famous people; information about items in the book is also found at the end of the book.

SAMPLE TITLES: *A is for America**; *L is for Lobster: A Maine Alphabet*; *M is for Maple: A Canadian Alphabet**; *S is for Sunshine: A Florida Alphabet*

■ *The Lands, People, and Culture Series—Bobbie Kalman Books* (Crabtree—New York)*

DESCRIPTION AND ORGANIZATIONAL FEATURES: Three books for each country featured, providing information on the lands, the people, and the cultures; table of contents, headings, many colorful and black and white photos, maps, captions, glossary

SAMPLE TITLES: *India: The Land*; *India: The People*; *India: The Culture* (also available for South Africa, Mexico, Germany, Argentina, etc.)

■ *The Time Traveling Twins Series* (Joanna Cotler Books, HarperCollins—New York)

DESCRIPTION AND ORGANIZATIONAL FEATURES: Author blends humor and historical detail into this series, which features word balloons packed with comedy and lots of information; author's note, maps, illustrations in the end papers depict artifacts then and now (e.g., plumbing, communication tools such as the quill pen and cellphones)

SAMPLE TITLES: *Joining the Boston Tea Party: Jumping Back in Time with the Time Traveling Twins*

■ *True Book Series* (Children's Press—New York)

DESCRIPTION AND ORGANIZATIONAL FEATURES: Large print and many photographs accompany text about a variety of historical topics.

SAMPLE TITLES: *True Book of: The Thirteen Colonies*; *True Book of: Colonial Life*; *True Book of: American Indian Games*; *True Book of: The Declaration of Independence*; *True Book of: The Presidency*

■ *Ultimate Field Trip Books* (Aladdin Paperbacks—New York)

DESCRIPTION AND ORGANIZATIONAL FEATURES: Chapter picture book; table of contents, Glossary, further reading, more information, color photographs

SAMPLE TITLES: *Ultimate Field Trip 1: Adventures in the Amazon River Forest*; *Ultimate Field Trip 2: Digging into Southwest Archaeology*; *Ultimate Field Trip 3: Wading into Marine Biology*; *Ultimate Field Trip 4: A Week in the 1800s*

■ *Usborne Timetours* (Usborne—London)

DESCRIPTION AND ORGANIZATIONAL FEATURES: These comprehensive guides of life long ago are packed with information on everyday life, from fashions to schools, and where to stay. Many drawings, charts, illustrations, and detailed maps of the ancient places being visited

SAMPLE TITLES: *A Visitor's Guide to Ancient Rome*; *A Visitor's Guide to Ancient Egypt.**

■ *We Came to North America* (Crabtree—New York)*

DESCRIPTION AND ORGANIZATIONAL FEATURES: Stories about the triumph of the human spirit, adapting to America, and the contributions of various immigrant groups; table of contents, photos, captions, insets, headings, maps, glossary, index

SAMPLE TITLES: *We Came to North America—The Hispanics*; *We Came to North America—The Africans*; *We Came to North America—The Chinese*; *We Came to North America—the Jews*; *We Came to North America—The French*

■ *Yearling Biography* (Dell—New York)

DESCRIPTION AND ORGANIZATIONAL FEATURES: Chapter book biographies; a few black and white illustrations, time lines

SAMPLE TITLE: *The Story of Benjamin Franklin, Amazing American*

Titles of Interest

Adler, Jeanne Winston. (1998). *In the Path of War: Children of the American Revolution Tell Their Stories*. Peterborough, NH: Cobblestone.*

Ajmera, Maya & Ivanke, John. (2001). *Back to School*. Watertown, MA: Charlesbridge.*

Armstrong, Jennifer. (1998). *Shipwreck at the Bottom of the World: The Extraordinary True Story of Shackelton and the Endurance*. New York: Crown.*

Ancona, George. (1995). *Fiesta USA*. New York: Lodestar.*

Angeli, Carole. (1996). *Celebrations Around the World: A Multicultural Handbook*. Golden, CO: Fulcrum.*

Barabas, Kathy. (1997). *Let's Find Out About Making Money*. New York: Scholastic.

Bateman, Teresa. (2001). *Red, White, Blue, and Uncle Who?: The Story Behind Some of America's Patriotic Symbols*. New York: Holiday.*

Beeler, Selby. (1998). *Throw Your Tooth on the Roof: Tooth Traditions from Around the World*. Boston: Houghton-Mifflin.

Begay, S. (1995). *Navajo: Visions and Voices Across the Mesa*. New York: Scholastic.

Bouchard, David. (1995). *If You're Not From the Prairie . . .* New York: Aladdin Picture Books.

Bowen, Gary. (1994). *Stranded on Plimoth Plantation*. New York: HarperCollins.*

Bray, Rosemary. (1997). *Martin Luther King*. New York: Morrow.*

Bredeson, Carmen. (2001). *Looking at Maps and Globes*. Chicago: Children's Press.*

Brisson, Pat. (1990). *Kate Heads West*. New York: Simon & Schuster.

Brown, Laurie & Brown, Marc. (1998). *How to Be a Friend: A Guide to Making Friends and Keeping Them*. Boston: Little, Brown.

Bruchac, Joseph. (1994). *A Boy Called Slow: The True Story of Sitting Bull*. New York: Philomel.

Bryan, Ashley. (1999). *The Night Has Ears: African Proverbs*. New York: Simon & Schuster.*

Bunting, Eve. (1989). *Terrible Things: An Allegory of the Holocaust*. Philadelphia: Jewish Publication Society.

Carle, Eric, Briggs, Raymond, Popov, Nicolai, Hayashi Akido, Calvi, Gian, Dillon, Leo & Diane, Chengliang, Zhu, Brooks, Ron, & Anno Mitsumasa. (1986). *All in a Day*. New York: Penguin Putnam Books for Young Readers.*

Chapman, Gillian. (1999). *Egyptians*. New York: Harcourt.*

Colbert, Jim & Harms, Ann. (1998). *Dear Dr. King: Letters from Today's Children to Dr. Martin Luther King, Jr.* New York: Hyperion Books.*

Connell, Kate. (1992). *They Shall Be Heard: Susan B. Anthony and Elizabeth Cady Stanton*. Austin, TX: Raintree.*

Conrad, Pam. (1991). *Pedro's Journal*. New York: Scholastic.*

Cox, Clinton. (1993). *The Forgotten Heroes: The Story of the Buffalo Soldiers*. New York: Scholastic.

Curlee, Lynn. (2000). *Liberty*. New York: Atheneum Books for Young Readers.

David, Rosalie. (1998). *Handbook to Life in Ancient Egypt*. New York: Oxford.

Davis, Kevin. (1999). *Look What Came From Australia*. New York: Franklin Watts.*

Denenberg, Barry. (1998). *The Journal of William Thomas Emerson: A Revolutionary War Patriot*. New York: Scholastic.*

Der Manuelian, Peter. (1991). *Hieroglyphs from A to Z*. New York: Scholastic.*

Edwards, Pamela Duncan. (1997). *Barefoot: Escape on the Underground Railroad*. New York: Scholastic.

Edwards, Pamela Duncan. (2001). *Boston Tea Party*. New York: Putnam.*

Enderlin, Cheryl. (1998). *Celebrating Birthdays in Brazil*. Mankato, MN: Capstone.*

Englart, Mindi. (2001). *Newspapers: From Start to Finish*. New York: Blackbirch.

Erickson, Paul. (2001). *Daily Life in the Pilgrim Colony 1636*. New York: Clarion.

Fanelli, Sara. (2001). *My Map Book*. New York: Harper.*

Freedman, Russell. (1987). *Lincoln: A Photobiography*. New York: Clarion.

Freedman, Russell. (1996). *The Life and Death of Crazy Horse*. New York: Holiday House.

Freedman, Russell. (2000). *Give Me Liberty! The Story of the Declaration of Independence*. New York: Holiday House.

Freedman, Russell. (2000). *In the Days of the Vaqueros: America's First True Cowboys*. New York: Clarion.

Fritz, Jean. (1976). *What's the Big Idea, Ben Franklin*. New York: Scholastic.

Fritz, Jean. (1986). *Shh! We're Writing the Constitution*. New York: G.P. Putnams' Sons.

Fritz, Jean. (1992). *George Washington's Mother*. New York: Grosset & Dunlap.

Fritz, Jean. (2001). *Leonardo's Horse*. New York: Putnam.*

Garland, Sherry. (1998). *A Line in the Sand: The Alamo Diary of Lucinda Lawrence*. New York: Scholastic.*

George, Jean Craighead. (1993). *The First Thanksgiving*. New York: Philomel Books.

Giblin, James. (1994). *Thomas Jefferson: A Picture Book Biography*. New York: Scholastic.*

Gold, Alison Leslie. (1997). *Reflections of a Childhood Friend: Memories of Anne Frank*. New York: Scholastic.

Gregory, Kristiana. (2001). *Five Smooth Stones*. New York: Scholastic.*

Guiberson, Brenda. (1998). *Mummy Mysteries*. New York: Holt.

Guthrie, Woodie. (1998). *This Land is Your Land*. New York: Little, Brown.*

Harness, Cheryl. (1995). *The Amazing, Impossible Erie Canal*. New York: Aladdin Paperbacks.

Harness, Cheryl. (1996). *Young Abe Lincoln: The Frontier Days*. Washington, DC: National Geographic Society.

Harper, Charise. (2001). *Imaginative Inventions: The Who, What, Where, When, and Why of Roller Skates, Potato Chips, Marbles, and Pie (and More!)* New York: Little, Brown.

Hart, G. (1990). *Ancient Egypt*. New York: Alfred A. Knopf.

Hazell, R. (2000). *The Barefoot Book of Heroic Children*. New York: Barefoot Books.

Herman, John. (1998). *Red, White, and Blue: The Story of the American Flag*. New York: Grosset & Dunlap.*

High, Linda Oatman. (2001). *Under New York*. New York: Holiday House.

Hooper, Meredith. (2001). *Who Built the Pyramid?* New York: Candlewick.*

Hurwitz, Johanna. (1994). *A Word to the Wize and Other Proverbs*. New York: Morrow Junior.

Kalman, Bobbie. (1999). *The United States from A to Z*. New York: Crabtree.*

Kalman, Bobbie. (1999). *Mexico from A to Z*. New York: Crabtree.*

Keller, Laurie. (1998). *The Scrambled States of America*. New York: Holt.

Kindersley, Barnabus & Kindersley, Anabel. (1997). *Celebrations*. New York: D.K.*

Knotts, Bob. (2000). *The Summer Olympics*. New York: Children's Press.

Kroll, Steven. (1999). *The Story of the Star-Spangled Banner*. New York: Scholastic.*

Krull, Kathleen. (1994). *Lives of the Writers*. New York: Harcourt, Brace.*

Krull, Kathleen. (1997). *Wish You Were Here: Emily's Guide to the 50 States*. New York: Doubleday.*

Krupp, Robin Rector. (1992). *Let's Go Traveling*. New York: Morrow Junior Books.*

Hill, Sandi. (1999). *Celebrating Cinco De Mayo: Fiesta Time*. Huntington Beach, CA: Learning Works.*

Hoyt-Goldsmith, Diane. (1994). *Day of the Dead: A Mexican-American Celebration*. New York: Holiday House.*

Lavender, D. (1995). *The Santa Fe Trail*. New York: Scholastic.

Lasky, Kathryn. (1983). *Sugaring Time*. New York: Aladdin Paperbacks.*

Lasky, Kathryn. (1996). *A Journey to the New World: The Diary of Remember Patiences Whipple, Mayflower 1620*. New York: Scholastic.*

Lauber, Patricia. (1998). *What You Never Knew About Fingers, Forks, and Chopsticks*. New York: Simon & Schuster.*

Lauber, Patricia. (2001). *What You Never Knew About Tubs, Toilets, & Showers*. New York: Simon & Schuster.

Leacock, Elspeth & Buckley, Susan. (2001). *Places in Time*. Boston, MA: Houghton Mifflin.

Leedy, Loreen. (1999). *Celebrate the 50 States*. New York: Holiday House.*

Leedy, Loreen. (2000). *Mapping Penny's World*. New York: Henry Holt and Company.*

Leigh, Nila. (1993). *Learning to Swim in Swaziland: A Child's Eyeview of a Southern African Country*. New York: Scholastic.*

Lourie, Peter. (1992). *Hudson River: An Adventure from the Mountains to the Sea*. Honesdale, PA: Boyds Mills Press.

Lourie, Peter. (1997). *Erie Canal: Canoeing America's Great Waterway*. Honesdale, PA: Boyds Mills Press.*

Luenn, Nancy. (1998). *Celebrations of Light: A Year of Holidays Around the World*. New York: Simon & Schuster.*

Maestro, Betsy & Giulio. (1987). *A More Perfect Union: The Story of Our Constitution*. New York: Mulberry.

Macaulay, David. (1973). *Cathedral: The Story of Its Construction*. Boston: Houghton Mifflin.

Macaulay, David. (1977). *Castle*. Boston: Houghton Mifflin.*

Mathias, Sharon. (1975). *The Hundred Penny Box*. New York: Puffin Books.

Matthaei, Gay & Grutman, Jewel. (1997). *The Ledgerbook of Thomas Blue Eagle*. New York: Lickle.

Milford, Susan. (1999). *Hands Around the World*. New York: Williamson.*

Miller, Millie & Nelson, Cyndi. (1999). *The United States of America: A State-by-State Guide*. New York: Scholastic.

Moehn, Heather. (2000). *World Holidays: A Watts Guide for Children*. New York: Franklin Watts.*

Murphy, Jim. (1995). *The Great Fire*. New York: Scholastic.

Murphy, Jim. (1996). *A Young Patriot: The American Revolution as Experienced by One Boy*. New York: Clarion.

Murphy, Jim. (1998). *The Journal of James Edmond Pease: A Civil War Soldier*. New York: Scholastic.*

Nelson, Ray, Kelly, Douglas, Adams, Ben, & McLane, Mike. (1995). *Wooden Teeth and Jelly Beans*. New York: Scholastic.*

Nichol, Barbara. (1993). *Beethoven Lives Upstairs*. New York: Orchard.*

Nicholson, Robert & Watts, Claire. (1991). *The Vikings*. New York: Scholastic.*

Nikola-Lisa, W. (2000). *The Year with Grandma Moses*. New York: Henry Holt.*

O'Neill, Catherine & Bruchac, Margaret. (2001). *1621: A New Look at Thanksgiving*. Washington, DC: National Geographic.

Osborne, Mary Pope. (1990). *Ben Franklin*. New York: Penguin Books.*

Osborne, Mary Pope. (1998). *Standing in the Light: The Captive Diary of Catherine Carey Logan*. New York: Scholastic.*

Parker, Nancy Winslow. (1995). *Money, Money, Money: The Meaning of the Art and Symbols of United States Paper Currency*. New York: HarperCollins.

Parks, Rosa. (1996). *A Dialogue with Today's Youth*. New York: Lee & Low.*

Platt, Richard. (2001). *Pirate Diary: The Journal of Jake Carpenter*. Cambridge, MA: Candlewick Press.*

Provensen, Alice. (1997). *The Buck Stops Here: The Presidents of the United States*. New York: Harper & Row.*

Turner, Ann. (1987). *Nettie's Trip South*. New York: Aladdin Picture Books.*

Rau, Dana. (2000). *Harriet Tubman*. Mankato, MN: Capstone.*

Robb, Don. (2000). *Hail to the Chief: The American Presidency*. Watertown, MA: Charlesbridge.

Roop, Peter & Connie. (1989). *Keep the Lights Burning, Abbie*. Boston: Houghton Mifflin.

Roop, Peter & Connie. (2000). *Benjamin Franklin*. New York: Scholastic.*

Ryan, Carrie. (1993). *Louisa May Alcott: Her Girlhood Diary*. New York: Troll.*

Ryan, Pam Munoz. (1996). *The Flag We Love*. Watertown, MA: Charlesbridge.*

Sabuda, Robert. (1994). *The Christmas Alphabet*. New York: Orchard Books.*

Safransky, Sy. (1990). *Sunbeams: A Book of Quotations*. Berkeley, CA: North Atlantic Books.*

Schanzer, Rosalyn. (1997). *How We Crossed the West: The Adventures of Lewis and Clark*. Washington, DC: National Geographic Society.*

Schimmel, Schim. (1994). *Dear Children of the Earth: A Letter from Home*. Minnetonka, MN: NorthWood Press.*

Scholastic Publishers. (2000). *The Pledge of Allegiance*. New York: Scholastic.

Simmons, Lesley. (1996). *Meet Kofi, Maria, & Sunita: Family Life in Ghana, Peru, & India*. Peterborough, NH: Cobblestone Press.*

Sis, Peter. (1991). *Follow the Dream: The Story of Christopher Columbus*. New York: Alfred Knopf.*

Sis, Peter. (1996). *Starry Messenger*. New York: Farrar, Straus & Giroux.*

Sobel, Syl. (1999). *How the United States Government Works*. New York: Barron's Educational Series.

Spencer, Eve. *A Flag for Our Country*. (1993). Austin, TX: Raintree, Steck-Vaughn.*

St. George, Judith. (2000). *So You Want to Be President*. New York: Philomel.

Stanley, Diane. (1994). *Cleopatra*. New York: Mulberry.

Steedman, Scott. (1997). *The Egyptian News*. Cambridge, MA: Candlewick Press.*

Stewart, David. (2001). *You Wouldn't Want to Be an Egyptian Mummy! Disgusting Things You'd Rather Not Know*. New York: Scholastic.*

Tapahonso, Luci & Schick, Eleanor. (1995). *Navajo ABC*. New York: Aladdin Paperbacks.*

Tsuchiya, Yukio. (1988). *Faithful Elephants*. Boston: Houghton Mifflin.

van der Roul, Ruud & Verhoeven, Rian. (1992). *Anne Frank Beyond the Diary: A Photographic Remembrance*. New York: Scholastic.

Wade, Mary. (1994). *Amelia Earhart*. Brookfield, CT: Millbrook Press.*

Washington, George. (2000). *George-isms: The 110 Rules George Washington Wrote When He Was 14—and Lived By All His Life*. New York: Atheneum Books for Young Readers.

West, Delno & West, Jean. (2000). *Uncle Sam and Old Glory: Symbols of America*. New York: Atheneum Books for Young Readers.*

Wilcox, Charlotte. (1999). *Mummies & Their Secrets*. Boston: Houghton Mifflin.*

Wilcox, Charlotte. (2000). *Mummies, Bones, & Body Parts*. New York: Scholastic.*

Winnick, Karen. (1996). *Mr. Lincoln's Whiskers*. Honesdale, PA: Boyds Mills Press.

Yip, Dora. (2001). *Welcome to Ireland*. Milwaukee, WI: Gareth Stevens.*

Yolen, Jane. (1992). *Encounter*. New York: Harcourt Brace.

Yorinks, Arthur. (1999). *The Alphabet Atlas*. New York: Winslow Press.*

Younger, Barbara. (1998). *Purple Mountain Majesties*. New York: Penguin Putnam.

Poetry and Social Studies

Foster, John. (1989). *Let's Celebrate: Festival Poems*. Cary, NC: Oxford University Press.*

Hopkins, Lee Bennett. (1994). *Hand in Hand: An American History through Poetry*. New York: Simon & Schuster.

Hopkins, Lee Bennett. (1999). *Lives: Poems About Famous Americans*. New York: HarperCollins.

Hopkins, Lee Bennett. (2000). *My America: A Poetry Atlas of the United States*. New York: Simon & Schuster.

Janecxzko, Paul. (1998). *That Sweet Diamond: Baseball Poems*. New York: Atheneum.

Longfellow, Henry. (2000). *Midnight Ride of Paul Revere*. Washington, DC: National Geographic Press.

Olaleye, Isaac. (1995). *Distant Talking Drum: Poems from Nigeria*. Honesdale, PA: Boyds Mills Press.*

Nye, Naomi Shihab. (1998). *The Space Between Our Footsteps*. New York: Simon & Schuster.*

Panzer, Nora. (1994). *Celebrate America in Poetry and Art*. New York: Warner Books.*

Sierra, Judy. (1998). *Antarctic Antics*. New York: Harcourt.*

Yolen, Jane. (1995). *Ballad of the Pirate Queens*. New York: Harcourt Brace.

THE ARTS

Series of Merit (with sample titles)

■ **Art Around the World Series** (Copper Beech Books—Brookfield, CT)

DESCRIPTION AND ORGANIZATIONAL FEATURES: This series introduces the major art eras and artists who contributed to their development; introduction, table of contents, insets, captions, chronology of the era, colorful reproductions, narrative text

SAMPLE TITLES: *In the Time of Renoir (The Impressionist Era); In the Time of Michelangelo (The Renaissance)*

■ **Famous Artists Series** (Barron's Educational Series—Hauppauge, NY)

DESCRIPTION AND ORGANIZATIONAL FEATURES: Introduces readers to world's celebrated painters and sculptors. Each title assesses the achievements of the artists, focusing on the most famous works. Hands-on projects allow readers to try some of the artist's materials and techniques; table of contents, introduction, labels, captions, colorful reproductions of artwork, insets, index, afterword, time line, glossary

SAMPLE TITLES: *Cezanne; Matisse; Van Gogh; Picasso; Monet*

■ **Getting to Know the World's Greatest Artists** (Children's Press—Chicago)

DESCRIPTION AND ORGANIZATIONAL FEATURES: Famous artists are featured in this biographical series; photographs, color art prints, cartoons, sketches, captions

SAMPLE TITLES: *Paul Klee; Michelangelo; Georgia O'Keeffe; Marc Chagall; Dorothea Lang*

■ **Getting to Know the World's Greatest Composers** (Children's Press—Chicago)

DESCRIPTION AND ORGANIZATIONAL FEATURES: Using paintings and photographs, this series explores the lives of famous composers; paintings, photographs, captions, cartoons

SAMPLE TITLES: *George Gershwin; Aaron Copland; Duke Ellington; Frederic Chopin; Johannes Brahms*

■ **How Artists Use . . .** (Heinemann—Chicago)

DESCRIPTION AND ORGANIZATIONAL FEATURES: Art techniques are featured in this art series; bold type, glossary, photographs, index, art prints, captions

SAMPLE TITLES: *How Artists Use Shape; How Artists Use Pattern and Texture; How Artists Use Line and Tone; How Artists Use Perspective; How Artists Use Color*

■ **The Life and Work of . . .** (Heinemann—Chicago)

DESCRIPTION AND ORGANIZATIONAL FEATURES: This series explores the contributions of various artists; table of contents, time line, photographs, art prints, sketches, bold print, glossary, index

SAMPLE TITLES: *Leonardo da Vinci; Vincent van Gogh; Frederic Remington; Auguste Rodin; Michelangelo Buonarroti*

■ **Sounds of Music Discovery Library** (Rourke—Vero Beach, FL)

DESCRIPTION AND ORGANIZATIONAL FEATURES: Gives an understanding and appreciation of American music

SAMPLE TITLES: *Classical; Country; Folk; Jazz and Blues; Rap*

Titles of Interest

Barboza, Steven. (1992). *I Feel Like Dancing.* New York: Crown.

Brenner, Barbara. (1999). *The Boy Who Loved to Draw: Benjamin West.* Boston: Houghton Mifflin.

Cooper, Elisha. (2001). *Dance!* New York: Greenwillow.

Cumming, Robert. (1982). *Just Imagine: Ideas in Painting.* New York: Scribner.

Cumming, Robert. (1998). *Great Artists.* New York: Dorling-Kingsley

Davidson, Rosemary. (1994). *Take a Look: An Introduction to the Experience of Art.* New York: Viking.

Duggleby, John. (1996). *Artist in Overalls: The Life of Grant Wood.* New York: Chronicle.

Freedman, Russell. (1998). *Martha Graham: A Dancer's Life.* New York: Clarion.

George-Warren, Holly. (2001). *Shake, Rattle, & Roll.* New York: Houghton Mifflin.

Gherman, Beverly. (2000). *Norman Rockwell: Storyteller with a Brush.* New York: Simon & Schuster.

Gibbons, Gail. (1998). *The Art Box.* New York: Holiday House.

Grau, Andree. (1998). *Dance.* New York: Alfred A. Knopf.

Greenway, Shirley. (2000). *Art: An A to Z Guide.* New York: Franklin Watts.

Hausherr, Rosemarie. (1992). *What Instrument Is This?* New York: Scholastic.

Hebach, Susan. (2001). *Tap Dancing.* Chicago: Children's Press.

Horee, Jeffrey. (1992). *O'Keeffe: The Life of an American Legend.* New York: Bantam Books.

Husain, Shahrukh. (1999). *Stories from the Opera.* New York: Barefoot Books.

Jessel, Camilla. (2000). *Ballet School: What It Takes to Make a Dancer.* New York: Harcourt.

Kalman, Bobbie & Gentile, Petrina. (1994). *Ballet School. New York:* Crabtree.

Kalman, Esther. (1994). *Tschaikovsky Discovers America.* New York: Orchard.*

Knapp, Brian. (1991). *Sounds and Music.* Danbury, CN: Grolier.

Koscielniak, Bruce. (2000). *The Story of the Incredible Orchestra.* Boston: Houghton Mifflin.

Krull, Kathleen. (1995). *Lives of the Artists: Masterpieces, Messes (and What the Neighbors Thought).* New York: Harcourt.*

Laden, Nina. (1998). *When Pigasso Met Mootise.* New York: Chronicle.

Landmann, Bimba. (2000). *The Genius of Leonardo Guido Visconti.* New York: Barefoot Books.

Langley, Andrew. (1999). *Shakespeare's Theatre.* New York: Oxford University Press.

Lauber, Patricia. (1998). *Painters of the Caves.* Washington, DC: National Geographic.

Levine, Robert. (2001). *The Story of the Orchestra.* New York: Black Dog & Leventhal.

Marceau, Marcel & Goldstone, Bruce. (2001). *Bip in a Book.* New York: La Martiniere.

Marcus, Leonard. (1998). *A Caldecott Celebration: Six Artists and Their Paths to the Caldecott Medal.* New York: Walker.

Micklethwait, Lucy. (1999). *A Child's Book of Art: Discover Great Paintings.* New York: DK.

Morley, Jacqueline. (1994). *Entertainment: Screen, Stage, and Stars.* New York: Franklin Watts.

Muhlberger, Richard. (1993). *What Makes a Degas a Degas?* New York: Metropolitan Museum of Art.

Nikola-Lisa, W. (2000). *The Year with Grandma Moses.* New York: Holt.*

Roche, Denis. (1998). *Art Around the World.* Boston: Houghton Mifflin.*

Stanley, Diane. (1996). *Leonardo Da Vinci.* New York: Morrow.

Tallchief, Maria with Wells, Rosemary. (1999). *Tallchief: America's Prima Ballerina.* New York: Puffin.

Weatherford, Carol. (2000). *Sound that Jazz Makes.* New York: Walker & Son.

Winter, Jeanette. (1998). *My Name is Georgia.* New York: Harcourt.

Zeri, Federico. (1999). *100 Paintings: Van Gogh.* Toronto, Ontario, Canada: NDE.

NONFICTION MAGAZINES: A RECOMMENDED LIST

Calliope World History for Kids

Cobblestone: The History Magazine for Young People

3-2-1 Contact

Dolphin Log

Kids Discover

Muse

National Geographic for Kids

Ranger Rick

Smithsonian

Sports Illustrated for Kids

Time for Kids

The Weekly Reader

Zillions: Consumer Reports for Kids

Zoobooks

WEB SITES OF INTEREST

www2.scholastic.com/teachers/authorsandbooks/authorstudies/authorstudies.jhtml

Features authors for chats

www.acs.ucalgary.ca/~dkbrown/authors.html

Photos, biographical information, and lists of published books

www.authorchats.com

Features several author chats each month

Kids.si.edu/collecting/

Provides tips for creating collections and displays some of the Smithsonian's "Amazing Collections"

www.usmint.gov/kids/

History in Your Pocket site that shows how coins can be used across the curriculum

www.infomall.org/kidsweb/geography.html

Kids Web—Geography

info.er.usgs.gov/fact-sheets/finding-your-way/finding-your-way.html

Finding your way with maps and compass

funnelweb.utcc.utk.edu/~hoemann/cwarht.html

American Civil War home page

www.earthcamforkids.com

Visit many of the world's most stunning landmarks

www.sci.muc.mn.us/greatestplaces

Global highlights that give a taste of traveling

now2000.com/kids/zoos.shtml

Information on common and unusual animals

www.teachervision.com

Lists "Best Social Studies sites for kids"

Bibliography

Allen, J. (1999). *Words, Words, Words: Teaching Vocabulary in Grades 4–12*. Portland, ME: Stenhouse.

Allen, J. (2000). *Yellow Brick Roads: Shared and Guided Paths to Independent Reading 4–12*. Portland, ME: Stenhouse.

Anders, P. & Bos, C. (1986). Semantic features analysis: An interactive strategy for vocabulary and text comprehension. *Journal of Reading*, 29, 610–616.

Armbruster, B., Anderson, T., & Ostertag, J. (1989). Teaching text structure to improve reading and writing. *The Reading Teacher, 43*, 130–137.

Armstrong, T. (2000). *Information Transformation*. Portland, ME: Stenhouse.

Baltas, J. & Nessel, D. (1999). *Easy Strategies & Lessons That Build Content Area Reading Skills*. New York: Scholastic.

Bamford, R. & Kristo, J. (2000). *Checking Out Nonfiction K–8: Good Choices for Best Learning*. Norwood, MA: Christopher-Gordon.

Bamford, R. & Kristo, J. (Eds.). (2003). *Making Facts Come Alive: Choosing Quality Nonfiction Literature K–8*. Norwood, MA: Christopher-Gordon.

Barrentine, Shelby. (1996). Storytime plus dialogue equals interactive read-alouds. In Gambrell, L. & Almasi, J. (Eds.). *Lively Discussions! Fostering Engaged Reading*. Newark, DE: International Reading Association, 52–62.

Beck, I., McKeown, M., Hamilton, R., & Kucan, L. (1997). *Questioning the Author: An Approach for Enhancing Student Engagement with Text*. Newark, DE: International Reading Association.

Booth, D. (1998). *Guiding the Reading Process: Techniques and Strategies for Successful Instruction in K–8*. York, ME: Stenhouse.

Brabham, E. & Villaume, S. (2000). Questions and answers: Continuing conversations about literature circles. *The Reading Teacher, 54*, 278–280.

Bridges, L. (1995). *Assessment: Continuous Learning*. York, ME: Stenhouse.

Bromley, K., Irwin-DeVitis, L., & Modlo, M. (1995). *Graphic Organizers*. New York: Scholastic.

Bromley, K., DeVitis, L., & Modlo, M. (1995). *Graphic Organizers: Visual Strategies for Active Learning*. New York: Scholastic.

Bromley, K., DeVitis, L., & Modlo, M. (1999). *50 Graphic Organizers for Reading, Writing, and More*. New York: Scholastic.

Brozo, W. & Simpson, M. (1995). *Readers, Teachers, Learners: Expanding Literacy in Secondary Schools*. Columbus, OH: Merrill.

Buehl, D. (2001). *Classroom Strategies for Interactive Learning*. Newark, DE: International Reading Association.

Burke, E. & Glazer, S. (1994). *Using Non-Fiction in the Classroom*. New York: Scholastic.

Campbell Hill, B., Johnson, N., & Schlick Noe, J. (1995). *Literature Circles and Response*. Norwood, MA: Christopher-Gordon.

Campbell Hill, B., Johnson, N., & Schlick Noe, J. (2001). *Literature Circles Resource Guide*. Norwood, MA: Christopher-Gordon.

Campbell Hill, B., Schlick Noe, J., & King, J. (2003). *Literature Circles in Middle School: One Teacher's Journey*. Norwood, MA: Christopher-Gordon.

Carr, E. & Ogle, D. (1987). K-W-L Plus: A strategy for comprehension and summarization. *The Reading Teacher, 30*, 626–631.

Church, J. (1991). Record keeping in whole language classrooms. In B. Harp (Ed.), *Assessment and Evaluation in Whole Language Classrooms*, 177–200. Norwood, MA: Christopher-Gordon.

Cooper, D. (2000). *Literacy: Helping Children Construct Meaning*. Boston: Houghton Mifflin.

Cooper, D. & Kiger, N. (2001). *Literacy Assessment: Helping Teachers Plan Instruction*. Boston: Houghton Mifflin.

Cudd, E. & Roberts, L. (1989). Using writing to enhance content area learning in the primary grades. *The Reading Teacher, 42*, 392–404.

Cullinan, B. & Galda, L. (1994). *Literature and the Child*. Orlando, FL: Harcourt Brace.

Daniels, H. (2001). *Looking into Literature Circles*. (Video). Portland, ME: Stenhouse.

Daniels, H. (2002). *Literature Circles: Voice and Choice in Book Clubs & Reading Groups*. York, ME: Stenhouse.

Day, J., Spiegel, D., McLellan, J., & Brown, V. (2002). *Moving Forward with Literature Circles*. New York: Scholastic.

Doiron, R. (1994). Using nonfiction in a read-aloud program: Letting the facts speak for themselves. *The Reading Teacher, 47*, 616–624.

Dorn, L. & Soffos, C. (2001). *Scaffolding Young Writers: A Writers' Workshop Approach*. Portland, ME: Stenhouse.

Drapeau, P. (1998). *Great Teaching with Graphic Organizers*. New York: Scholastic.

Dreher, J., Davis, K. , Waynant, P. & Clewell, S. (2000). *Easy Steps to Writing Fantastic Research Reports*. New York: Scholastic.

Dufflemeyer, F. & Baum, D. (1992). The Extended Anticipation Guide revisited. *Journal of Reading, 35*, 654–656.

Duthie, C. (1996). *True Stories: Nonfiction Literacy in the Primary Classroom*. York, ME: Stenhouse.

Edinger, M. & Fins, S. (1998). *Far Away and Long Ago: Young Historians in the Classroom*. Portland, ME: Stenhouse.

Education Department of Western Australia. (1994). *Writing Resource Book*. Portsmouth, NH: Heinemann.

Eeds, M. & Wells, D. (1989). Grand conversations: An exploration of meaning construction in literature study groups. *Research in the Teaching of English, 23*, 4–29.

Evans, K. (2001). *Literature Discussion Groups in the Intermediate Grades: Dilemmas and Possibilities*. Newark, DE: International Reading Association.

Fountas, I. & Pinnell, G. (2001). *Guiding Readers and Writers Grades 3–6*. Portsmouth, NH: Heinemann.

Freeman, M. (2001). *Nonfiction Writing Strategies: Using Science Big Books as Models*. Gainesville, FL: Maupin House.

Grolier Classroom Publishing Company. (1995). *Using Nonfiction Effectively in Your Classroom*. New York: Grolier.

Harvey, S. (1998). *Nonfiction Matters: Reading, Writing, and Research in Grades 3–8*. York, ME: Stenhouse.

Harvey, S. & Goudvis, A. (2000). *Strategies That Work: Teaching Comprehension to Enhance Understanding*. Portland, ME: Stenhouse.

Hayes, Jacobs, H. (1997). *Mapping the Big Picture: Integrating Curriculum & Assessment K–12*. Alexandria, VA: Association for Supervision and Curriculum Development.

Heimlich, J. & Pittleman, S. (1986). *Semantic Mapping: Classroom Applications*. Newark, DE: International Reading Association.

Hepler, S. (1998). Nonfiction books for children: New directions, new challenges. In R. Bamford & J. Kristo (Eds.). *Making Facts Come Alive: Choosing Quality Nonfiction Literature K–8*, Norwood, MA: Christopher-Gordon, 3–17.

Horowitz, R. (1985a). Text patterns: Part 1. *Journal of Reading, 28*, 448–454.

Horowitz, R. (1985b). Text patterns: Part 2. *Journal of Reading, 28*, 534–541.

Hoyt, L. (1999). *Revisit, Reflect, Retell: Strategies for Improving Reading Comprehension*. Portsmouth, NH: Heinemann.

Hoyt, L. (2000). *Snapshots: Literacy Minilessons Up Close*. Portsmouth, NH: Heinemann.

Hoyt, L. (2002). *Make It Real: Strategies for Success with Informational Texts*. Portsmouth, NH: Heinemann.

Johns, J. (2001). *Basic Reading Inventory*. Dubuque, IA: Kendall/Hall.

Johnson, D., Pittelman, S. & Heimlich, J. (1986). Semantic mapping. *The Reading Teacher, 39*, 778–783.

Johnson, H. & Freedman, L. (2001). Talking about content knowledge at the middle level: Using informational trade books in content-area literature circles. *The Language and Literacy Spectrum, 11*, 52–62.

Johnson, Paul. (2000). *Making Books*. Portland, ME: Stenhouse.

Johnston, Peter. (1992). *Constructive Evaluation of Literate Activity*. New York: Longman.

Kerper, R. (1998). Choosing quality nonfiction literature: Features for accessing and visualizing information. In R. Bamford & J. Kristo (Eds.). *Making Facts Come Alive: Choosing Quality Nonfiction Literature*, Norwood, MA: Christopher-Gordon, 55–74.

Kretzer, M., Slobin, M., & Williams, M. (1996). *Making Social Studies Come Alive: 65 Classroom-Tested Activities and Projects*. New York: Scholastic.

Kuta, K. (1992). Teaching text patterns to remedial readers. *Journal of Reading, 35*, 657–658.

Leal, Dorothy. (1996). Transforming grand conversations into grand creations: Using different types of text to influence student discussion. In Gambrell, L. & Almasi, J. (Eds.) *Lively Discussions! Fostering Engaged Reading*. Newark, DE: International Reading Association, 149–168.

Lenski, S. & Johns, J. (2000). *Improving Writing: Resources, Strategies, Assessments*. Dubuque, IA: Kendall/Hunt Publishing Company.

Lenski, S., Wham, M., & Johns, J. (1999). *Reading & Learning Strategies for Middle & High School Students*. Dubuque, IA: Kendall/Hunt.

Leslie, L. & Caldwell, J. (2001). *Qualitative Reading Inventory -III*. New York: Longman.

Levy, E. (2000). *Who Are You Calling a Woolly Mammoth?* New York: Scholastic.

Lubliner, S. (2001). *A Practical Guide to Reciprocal Teaching*. Bothell, WA: Wright Group/McGraw Hill.

Manzo, K. (1998). More dollars for textbooks draws sellers. *Education Week* (September 30): 1,12.

Mazzuchi, D. (1994). Map-making and neighborhood exploration in a multi-age classroom. In S. Steffey & W. Hood (Eds.), *If This Is Social Studies, Why Isn't It Boring?* York, ME: Stenhouse Publishers, 137–152.

McClure, A. (1998). Choosing quality nonfiction literature: Examining aspects of writing style. In R. Bamford & J. Kristo (Eds.), *Making Facts Come Alive: Choosing Quality Nonfiction Literature K–8* . Norwood, MA:

Christopher-Gordon, 39–54.

McGee, L. (1995). Talking about books with young children. In N. Roser & M. Martinez (Eds.), *Book Talk and Beyond: Children and Teachers Respond to Literature*, 105–115. Newark, DE: International Reading Association.

McGee, L. & Richgels, D. (1985). Teaching expository text structure to elementary students. *The Reading Teacher*, *38*, 739–748.

McGee, L. & Richgels, D. (1992). Text structure strategies. In E. Dishner, T. Bean, J. Readence, & D. Moore (Eds.), *Reading in the Content Areas: Improving Classroom Instruction*. Dubuque, IA: Kendall/Hunt, 234–247.

McIntosh, M. & Draper, R. (1995). Applying the Question–Answer Relationship strategy in mathematics. *Journal of Adolescent & Adult Literacy*, *39*, 120–131.

Meinbach, A., Fredericks, A., & Rothlein, L. (2000). *The Complete Guide to Thematic Units: Creating the Integrated Curriculum*. Norwood, MA: Christopher-Gordon.

Meisels, S. (1996/1997). Using work sampling in authentic assessments. *Educational Leadership*, *45*, 60–65.

Miller, K. & George, J. (1992). Expository passage organizers: Models for reading and writing. *Journal of Reading*, *35*, 372–377.

Moline, S. (1995). *I See What You Mean*. Portland, ME: Stenhouse.

Moore, D. & Moore, S. (1992). Possible sentences: An update. In E. Dishner, T. Bean, J. Readence, & D. Moore (Eds.), *Reading in the Content Areas: Improving Classroom Practice*, Dubuque, IA: Kendall/Hunt, 196–202.

Moore, D., Moore, S., Cunningham, P., & Cunningham, J. (1998). *Developing Readers & Writers in the Content Areas K–12*. New York: Longman.

Naughton, V. (1993/1994). Creative mapping for content reading. *Journal of Reading*, *37*, 324–326.

Norwick, L. (1995). Deepening response through the arts. In B. Campbell Hill, N. Johnson, & K. Schlick Noe (Eds.), 131–152. *Literature Circles and Response*. Norwood, MA: Christopher-Gordon.

Nuzum, M. (2001). *Study Skills That Stick*. New York: Scholastic.

Offutt, Elizabeth & Offutt, Charles. (1997). *Multimedia and the Elementary Classroom: Practical Tips and Projects*. Torrance, CA: Good Apple.

Ogle, D. (1986). K-W-L: A teaching model that develops active reading of expository text. *The Reading Teacher*, *39*, 564–570.

Ogle, D. (1989). The know, want to know, learn strategy. In K. Muth (Ed.), *Children's Comprehension of Text: Research into Practice*. Newark, DE: International Reading Association, 205–223.

Palinczar, A. & Brown, A. (1983). *Reciprocal Teaching of Comprehension-Monitoring Activities*. Bethesda, MD: National Institute of Health and Human Development.

Pappas, C., Kiefer, B., & Levstik, L. (1999). *An Integrated Language Perspective in the Elementary School: An Action Approach*. New York: Longman.

Parsons, L. (2001). *Response Journals Revisited*. Portland, ME: Stenhouse.

Peterson, R. & Eeds, M. (1990). *Grand Conversations: Literature Groups in Action*. New York: Scholastic.

Piccolo, J. (1987). Expository text structure: Teaching and learning strategies. *The Reading Teacher*, *40*, 838–847.

Pike, K. & Mumper, J. (1998). *Books Don't Have to Be Flat!* New York: Scholastic.

Pittleman, S., Heimlich, Berglund, J., & French, M. (1991). *Semantic Feature Analysis: Classroom Applications*. Newark, DE: International Reading Association.

Portalupi, J. & Fletcher, R. (2001). *Nonfiction Craft Lessons: Teaching Informational Writing K–8*. Portland, ME: Stenhouse.

Raphael, T. (1982). Question-answering strategies for children. *The Reading Teacher*, *36*, 186–190.

Raphael, T. (1984). Teaching learners about sources of information for answering comprehension questions. *Journal of Reading*, *28*, 303–311.

Raphael, T. (1986). Teaching questions-answer relationships, revisited. *The Reading Teacher*, *39*, 516–522.

Raphael, T., Kehus, M., & Damphousse, K. (2001). *Book Club for Middle School*. Lawrence, MA: Small Planet Communications.

Raphael, T. & McMahon, S. (1994). Book Club: An alternative framework for reading instruction. *The Reading Teacher*, *39*, 561–522.

Raphael, T., Pardo, L., Highfield, K., & McMahon, S. (1997). *Book Club: A Literature-Based Curriculum*. Littleton, MA: Small Planet Communications.

Readence, J., Bean, T., & Baldwin, R. (2000). *Content Area Literacy: An Integrated Approach*. Dubuque, IA: Kendall/Hunt.

Readence, J., Moore, D., & Rickelman, R. (2000). *Prereading Activities for Content Area Reading and Learning*. Newark, DE: International Reading Association.

Redman, P. (1995). Finding a balance: Literature circles and "Teaching Reading." In B. Campbell Hill, N. Johnson, & K. Schlick Noe (Eds.), *Literature Circles and Response*. 55–70. Norwood, MA: Christopher-Gordon Publishers.

Rhodes, L. & Shanklin, N. (1993). *Windows into Literacy: Assessing Learners K–8*. Portsmouth, NH: Heinemann.

Richards, J. & Gipe, J. (1995). What's the structure? A game to help middle school students recognize common writing patterns. *Journal of Reading*, *38*, 667–669.

Robb, L. (1996). *Reading Strategies That Work: Teaching Your Students to Become Better Readers.* New York: Scholastic.

Robb, L. (2000). *Teaching Reading in Middle School.* New York: Scholastic.

Robb, L. (2003). *Teaching Reading in Social Studies, Science, and Math.* New York: Scholastic.

Roser, N. & Martinez, M. (Eds.). (1995). *Book Talk and Beyond: Children and Teachers Respond to Literature.* Newark, DE: International Reading Association.

Roser, N. & Keehn, S. (2002). Fostering thought, talk, and inquiry: Linking literature and social studies. *The Reading Teacher, 55,* 416–426.

Routman, R. (1991). *Invitations.* Portsmouth, NH: Heinemann.

Routman, R. (2000). *Conversations: Strategies for Teaching, Learning, and Evaluating.* Portsmouth, NH: Heinemann.

Routman, R. (2003). *Reading Essentials.* Portsmouth, NH: Heinemann.

Sadler, C. (2001). *Comprehensive Strategies for Middle Grade Learners: A Handbook for Content Area Teaching.* Newark, DE: International Reading Association.

Schlick Noe, K. & Johnson, N. (1999). *Getting Started with Literature Circles.* Norwood, MA: Christopher-Gordon.

Schoenbach, R., Greenleaf, C., Cziko, C., & Hurwitz, L. (1999). *Reading for Understanding: A Guide to Improving Reading in Middle and High School Classrooms.* San Francisco: Jossey-Bass.

Schumm, J., Vaughn, S., & Leavell, A. (1994). Planning pyramid: A framework for planning for diverse student needs during content area instruction. *The Reading Teacher, 47,* 608–615.

Simpson, M. (1994/1995). Talk throughs: A strategy for encouraging active learning across the content areas. *Journal of Reading, 38,* 296–304.

Sims Bishop, R. (1992). Making informed choices. In V. Harris (Ed.), *Teaching Multicultural Literature in Grades K–8,* 41. Norwood, MA: Christopher-Gordon.

Slater, W. (1985). Teaching expository text structure with structural organizers. *Journal of Reading, 28,* 712–718.

Stead, T. (2002). *Is That a Fact? Teaching Nonfiction Writing K–3.* Portland, ME: Stenhouse.

Stevens, E. & Brown, J. (2000). *A Handbook of Content Literacy Strategies: 75 Practical Reading and Writing Ideas.* Norwood, MA: Christopher-Gordon.

Stevenson, C. & Carr, J. (1993). Integrated studies planning framework. In C. Stevenson & J. Carr (Eds.), *Integrated Studies in the Middle Grades: "Dancing through Walls."* New York: Teachers College Press, 26–39.

Strickland, D., Ganske, K., & Monroe, J. (2001). *Supporting Struggling Readers and Writers.* Portland, ME: Stenhouse.

Tierney, R. & Readence, J. (2000). *Reading Strategies and Practices: A Compendium.* Boston: Allyn & Bacon.

Tierney, R., Readence, J., & Dishner, E. (1995). *Reading Strategies and Practices: A Compendium.* Boston: Allyn & Bacon.

Tovani, C. (2000). *I Read It, But I Don't Get It: Comprehension Strategies for Adolescent Readers.* Portland, ME: Stenhouse.

Tower, C. (2000). Questions that matter: Preparing elementary students for the inquiry process. *The Reading Teacher, 53,* 550–557.

United States Department of Labor. (1991). *What Work Requires of Schools: A SCANS Report for America 2000.* Washington D.C.: U.S. Department of Labor.

Walsh, N. (1994). *Making Books Across the Curriculum.* New York: Scholastic.

Wells, D. (1995). Leading grand conversations. In N. Rosner and M. Martinez (Eds.) *Book Talk and Beyond: Children and Teachers Respond to Literature,* 132–139. Newark, DE: International Reading Association.

Whitin, P. (2002). Leading into literature circles through the sketch-to-stretch strategy. *The Reading Teacher, 55,* 444–450.

Wood, K. (1988). Guiding students through informational text. *The Reading Teacher, 41,* 912–920.

Wood, K. (2001). *Literacy Strategies across the Subject Areas.* Boston: Allyn & Bacon.

Young, T. & Vardell, S. (1993). Weaving readers theatre and nonfiction into the curriculum. *The Reading Teacher, 46,* 396–406.

Index

ABCs
   of nonfiction writing, 136–137, 137*f*
   of reading nonfiction, 77, 77*f*
Access features, 4–5, 6*f*–7*f*
Accordion books
   making, 166–167, 168*f*
   for sharing literature, 161, 163*f*
Accuracy, of nonfiction materials, 33
Afterword, 6*f*
Alphabet books, 73, 73*f*, 121
Alphabetical book reports, 158
Amazing Insects: Eyewitness Juniors 26 (Mound), 109
Analyzing, primary source documents, 28, 29*f*
And In That Universe . . . ., 19–20
Anecdotal records, 183–184
Animal Homes: A First Look at Animals (James; Lynn), 108
Anticipation/Reaction Guides, 90–93, 92*f*
Appendix, 6*f*
Apples, Bubbles, and Crystals: Your Science ABCs (Bennett & Kessler), 152
Art
   recommended list of nonfiction books, 205–206
   in sharing literature, 160–161
Artifact books, 166, 167*f*
Artifact-bound books, 166, 166*f*
Assessment, 178–180
   of bookmaking, 173, 175*f*
   effective, elements of-181, 180
   of literature circle, 75, 76*f*, 77
   measures of, 181
      Find Someone Who strategy, 185, 185*f*
      interviews, surveys and inventories, 186, 187*f*
      Mark the Spot strategy, 186
      My Learning Notebooks, 189
      observation/kidwatching, 182–184, 183*f*
      retellings, 185–186
      student self-evaluation, 187–188
      think-alouds, 188–189
      work samples, student, 189–190, 190*f*–191*f*
   purposes of, 180–181
   vs. evaluation, 180
Asterisks, 7*f*
Author and You questions, 94, 95*f*
Author/illustrator notes, 6*f*
Authors, nonfiction, 25*f*
Autobiographies, 25

Background knowledge. *See* Knowledge, prior or background
Backpack metaphor, 3
Bees Dance and Whales Sing: The Mysteries of Animal Communication (Facklam), 177
Ben Franklin and the Magic Square (Murphy), 155
Bibliography, 6*f*

Biographical profile chart, 146, 146*f*
Biographies, 25
Book clubs. *See* Literature circles
Bookmaking, 164
   accordion books, 166–167, 168*f*
   artifact books, 166, 167*f*
   artifact-bound books, 166, 166*f*
   assessment of, 173, 175*f*
   envelope books, 167, 171*f*
   flap books, 171, 173*f*
   framed books, 167, 170*f*
   graduated pages book, 167, 169*f*
   interlocking plastic bag books, 164, 165*f*
   pocket folder books, 171–172, 174*f*
   scroll-like, 164, 165*f*
   slit books, 171, 172*f*
Bookmarks, 71, 71*f*
Book reports
   alphabetical, 158
   shaped, 160, 160*f*
Book reviews/lists, for selecting literature circle materials, 55
Brainstorming, 69
Bullets, 7*f*
A Burst of Firsts: Doers, Shakers, and Record Breakers (Lewis), 85

Cans books, information in, 164, 165*f*
Captions, 7*f*
Cause and effect, 37*f*, 40
Characteristics reports, alphabetical, 159, 159*f*
Charts, 8*f*
Checklists, observational, 182–183, 183*f*
Clarification, 99
Class environment, 11–12, 13*f*
Class journals, 129–130
Cloze procedure, 41
Community share, 55, 57–58
Comparison/contrast pattern
   description of, 34, 38*f*–39*f*
   graphic organizers, 146, 147*f*–148*f*
   identifying, 40
Comprehension questions, 186
Concept books, 24
Concept/definition maps, 105, 106*f*, 145, 145*f*
Conceptual graphic organizers, 144*f*–146*f*, 145–146
Contextual Redefinition strategy, 104–105
Conversations, written, 126, 127
Costume designing, 161
Curriculum areas. *See also specific curriculum areas*
   evaluating nonfiction materials for, 32–33
   nonfiction usage in, 14
   persuasive writing topics for, 119

Decision tree graphic organizer, 118–119, 119*f*
Description, 35*f*, 40
Design, of nonfiction materials, 33
Diagrams, 7*f*
Dialogue journals, 125–126, 127*f*
Diaries, writing in. *See* Journal writing
Discussions, literature
    group roles in, 60–61
    in literature circles, 68–72
    promoting, 69, 69*f*
    strategies for, 70–71, 72*f*
Discussion sheets, 71, 72*f*
Double-entry journal, 131–132, 132*f*
Drama
    literature circles and, 74
    in sharing literature, 161–164
Drawing, 71

Editor, letters to, 74
The Egyptian News (Steedman), 193
E-mail, 133–134
English language arts, 119
Envelope books, 167, 171*f*
Erie Canal: Canoeing America's Great Waterway (Lourie), 181
Evaluation
    of nonfiction materials, 32–33
    vs. assessment, 180
Exposition
    decision tree graphic organizer for, 118–119, 119*f*
    organizational pattern, 117, 117*f*
    purpose of, 117
    topics for, 119
Expository writing. *See* Nonfiction
Extension projects, for literature circles, 72–75

Famous quotes report, 159
Fiction, 3
531 Things That Changed the World and Some That Didn't (West), 16
Find Someone Who strategy, 185, 185*f*
Fish bowl strategy, 60
The Flag We Love (Ryan), 79
Flannel board story, 73–74, 74*f*
Flap books, 171, 173*f*
Flexibility, of literature circles, 58–59
Fly with Poetry (Harley), 42
The Fossil Girl (Brighton), 72
Framed books, 167, 170*f*
Franklin D. Roosevelt; Letters from a Mill Town Girl (Winthrop), 32
Frontloading techniques, 52–53

Getting-to-know-you class quilt, 57, 57*f*
Gist, reading for, 100–101, 101*f*
Glossary, 6*f*
Gradual release model of instruction, 83–84
Graduated pages book, 167, 169*f*

Graphic organizers, 140–141, 141*f*
    advantages of, 153–154
    choosing, 153
    definition of, 142
    description of, 142
    effective usage of, 153–154
    rationale for using, 142
    of text structures, 40
        cause and effect, 37*f*
        comparison/contrast, 39*f*
        description, 35*f*
        listing, 36*f*
        problem/solution, 38*f*
        question and answer, 35*f*
        sequence or time order, 37*f*
    topical, 145
    types of, 143, 145. *See also specific types of graphic organizers*
        comparison/contrast, 39*f*, 146, 147*f*–148*f*
        conceptual, 144*f*–146*f*, 145–146
        cyclical, 150, 150*f*–151*f*
        hierarchical, 149, 149*f*
        sequential, 151, 152*f*, 153
    uses of, 143, 143*f*
Graphs, 8*f*
Groups, effective *vs.* ineffective, 69, 70*t*
Guess Whose Shadow? (Swinburne), 102
Guided topics, 70

Handy tips, for reading nonfiction, 89, 91*f*
Hangers, use in sharing books, 161
Headings, 7*f*
Hierarchical graphic organizers, 149, 149*f*
The History of Counting (Schmandt-Besserat), 175
How-to books, 25, 163
How-to demonstrations, 163

Illustrations, 7*f*
Illustrator
    in literature circle, 61
    notes, 6*f*
Independent reading, 15
Informational storybooks, 8
Informational texts, 4, 8
    access features, 4–5, 6*f*–7*f*
    benefits of, 10*f*
    challenges of, 16, 17*f*
    textual features, 4, 5*f*
    visual features, 4, 5, 7*f*–8*f*
Information sources
    for answering questions, 93–94, 95*f*
    for readers, 80–81
In My Head questions, 94, 95*f*
Inquiry charts or I-charts, 132–133, 134*f*–135*f*
Insects—Science Nature Guide (McGavin), 193
Insets, 7*f*

Instructional approach, for expository text structure, 34, 39–41
Interlocking plastic bag books, 164, 165*f*
Interviews, 186, 187*f*
In the Book questions, 94, 95*f*
Introduction, 6*f*
Inventories, 186

Journal writing
    class journals, 129–130
    dialogue journals and, 125–126, 127*f*
    forms of, 124
    historical aspects of, 122
    inquiry charts or I-charts, 132–133, 134*f*–135*f*
    learning logs, 128, 128*f*
    nonfiction notebooks/wonderbooks, 125, 126*f*
    personal, 124, 124*f*
    Possible Sentences, 131
    purposes of, 122–124
    Quick Writes, 130
    reading response logs, 129
    simulated journals, 129
    topics for, 124, 124*f*
    two-column notes, 131–132, 132*f*
    written conversations and, 126, 127

A Kid's Guide to the White House (Debnam), 191
Kidwatching, 182–184, 183*f*
Knowledge
    of expository text structure, 33–34
    prior or background
        for answering questions, 93, 94–95*f*
        overall, 86–87
        text-specific, 86, 87
K-W-H-L procedure, 87, 89*f*
K-W-L Plus, 87–90, 90*f*
K-W-L procedure, 86–87, 88*f*, 118

Labels, 7*f*
Language, memorable, 70
Learning, from writing, 121
Learning logs, 128, 128*f*
Let's Go Traveling (Krupp), 18
Letters, 74
Letter writing, 158
Lifelines, 74, 161, 163*f*
List-Group-Label-Write strategy, 102–103
Listing pattern
    identifying, 40
    simple, 34, 36*f*
Literary luminary/passage maker, in literature circle, 61
Literature circles, 53–54
    assessment of, 75, 76*f*, 77
    benefits of, 54
    community share in, 55, 57–58
    effective, key features for, 55–56
    effective *vs.* ineffective groups, 69, 70*t*

    establishing, 57–59
    explicit instruction for, 55–56, 56*f*
    extension projects, 72–75
    introducing, 59–61
    literature discussions in. *See* Discussions, literature
    mini-lessons for, 55–56, 56*f*
    nonfiction discussion sheet for, 61, 62*f*
    roles in, 60–61
    selection of reading material for, 55
    text sets, group formations and, 58, 59*f*
    written responses to text, 61, 63*f*–68*f*, 64, 67
Literature response activities, 156*f*, 157–158
Literature response groups. *See* Literature circles
Living books, 162

The Magic School Bus Series, 2, 8, 51
Mapping Penny's World (Leedy), 153
Maps, 8*f*
    concept/definition, 105, 106*f*, 145, 145*f*
    mind maps. *See* Graphic organizers
    semantic. *See* Graphic organizers
    for text organization, 87–88
Mark the Spot strategy, 186
Math
    journals, prompts for, 128, 128*f*
    recommended list of nonfiction books, 195–199
Math Curse (Scieszka; Smith), 79
Memoirs, 25
Mind maps. *See* Graphic organizers
Mini-lessons, for literature circles, 55–56, 56*f*
Mock trials, 163–164
A Mountain Alphabet (Ruurs), 121
Multimedia, for writing program, 133–135
Music, 119
My Learning Notebooks, 189

Narrative information books, 24
Narrative texts
    basic plan of, 3
    vs. nonfiction, 3
News magazines, 30–31, 30*f*, 31*f*
Newspaper reporting, 158
Newspapers, 30–31, 30*f*, 31*f*
Newspapers-in-Education programs, 30, 31*f*
Nonfiction, 1–3
    books, recommended list of, 195–206
    in classroom, 10*f*, 11–16
    definition of, 4
    evaluating, 32–33
    materials, 21, 22*f*. *See also specific nonfiction materials*
    models for, 14
    reading. *See* Reading
    reading aloud. *See* Reading aloud
    role of, 8–11, 10*f*, 11*f*
    style/organization of, 16
    technology and, 28
    types of. *See also* Informational texts; Textbooks

Nonfiction *(Cont.)*
    informational storybooks, 8
    trade books, 24–25
    vs. narrative text, 3
Notebooks
    My Learning Notebooks, 189
    nonfiction, 125, 126*f*
    and wonderbooks, 125, 126*f*
Notetaking, bookmarks for, 71, 71*f*

Observation, 182–184, 183*f*
Oh, The Things You Can Do That Are Good For You! (Rabe),
    18
On Your Own questions, 94, 95*f*
Organization, of nonfiction materials, 33
Overviewing, 51, 52–53

Paragraph frames, 39, 42
Passages, highlighted, 70
Patterned writing, 121, 122*f*, 123*f*
Periodicals, 25–26
Personality reports, 74, 159, 159*f*
Personal journals, 124, 124*f*
Persuasive writing
    characteristics of good arguments in, 118, 118*f*
    forms of, 117. *See also* Exposition
    independent, 120
    introducing to students, 117–118
    purposes of, 116–117
    rubric for, 120*f*
    student-teacher collaboration for, 119
    topics for, 119
Photographs, 7*f*
Picture books, to introduce students to literature circles, 60
Pieces: A Year in Poems and Quilts (Hines), 9
Plastic bag books, interlocking, 164, 165*f*
Pocket folder books, 171–172, 174*f*
Poetry, 25, 121
    concept/definition map, 145*f*
    as literature circle extension, 74, 75*f*
    and science, recommended list of nonfiction books,
        198–199
    and social studies, recommended list of nonfiction books,
        204
Politicians, letters to, 74
Possible Sentences strategy, 131
Postcards from Pluto: A Tour of the Solar System (Leedy),
    139
The Preamble of Constitution, students' artistic renditions of,
    12, 13*f*
Prediction, 99
Preface, 6*f*
Presentations, multimedia, 134
Previewing
    in context strategy, 103–104
    reading aloud and, 51, 52–53
Primary source documents, 26–28, 27*f*, 29*f*
Principal, letters to, 74

Problem/solution pattern, 38*f*, 40
Products, student, 189–190, 190*f*–191*f*
Profile charts, 146, 146*f*
Projects, student, 189–190, 190*f*–191*f*
Pronunciation guides, 6*f*

Question and answer structure, 35*f*, 40
Question-Answer Relationships, 93–94, 95*f*–96*f*
Questioner role, in literature circle, 61
Question Generating strategy, 99
Questions
    literature response, 63, 64*f*–67*f*
    student-generated, 70
Quick Writes, 130
Quilts
    Pieces: A Year in Poems and Quilts (Hines), 9
    plastic bag, 164
    for sharing literature, 161, 162*f*
Quotations collection, building, 159
Quote and question, 71

Read-alouds, 12
Readers
    good, strategies for, 84*f*
    information sources for, 80–81
    proficient, 82, 83*f*
Readers' Theater, 49, 50–51
Reading, 44–45
    ABCs of, 77, 77*f*
    after, strategies for, 84*f*
    Anticipation/Reaction Guides, 90–93, 92*f*
    before, strategies for, 84*f*
    during, strategies for, 84*f*
    for the gist, 100–101, 101*f*
    handy tips, 89, 91*f*
    as interactive process, 81–82
    nonfiction, in school, 3
    Question-Answer Relationships, 93–94, 95*f*–96*f*
    skills development, nonfiction and, 10–11, 11*f*
    strategies, 82–83
Reading aloud, 48
    benefits of, 45–46, 46*f*
    interactive, 48–50
    Readers' Theater, 49, 50–51
    Say Something strategy, 49, 50, 51
    suggestions for, 48
    teacher responses, 46, 47*f*
    think-alouds and, 46
Reading response logs. *See* Response logs
Reciprocal Teaching, 98–100
Recommendations for further reading, 6*f*
Reference aids. *See* Access features
Reports
    alphabetical book reports, 158
    book reports, alphabetical, 158
    characteristics reports, alphabetical, 159, 159*f*
    famous quotes report, 159
    multimedia, 134

personality, 74, 159, 159*f*
shaped book reports, 160, 160*f*
Researcher, in literature circle, 61
Response logs, 129
fabric covered, making of, 63, 63*f*
prompts, 63, 63*f*
purpose of, 64
questions, 63, 64*f*–67*f*
response options, 68*f*
use of, 61, 63
Retellings, 185–186
Richard Orr's Nature Cross-Section (Orr), 176
Right There answers, 93, 95*f*
Right There questions, 94, 95*f*
Role-playing, 163
Rubrics
for assessment, 184
for project-based learning, 175*f*
for work sample/product, 190, 190*f*–191*f*

Say Something strategy, 49, 50, 51
Scaffolded model of instruction, 83–84
Science, 119, 195–199
Self-evaluation, student, 187–188
Semantic Feature Analysis (SFA), 96–98, 98*f*
Semantic maps. *See* Graphic organizers
Semantic webs, 145
Sequence, 36*f*–37*f*, 40
Sequential graphic organizers, 151, 152*f*, 153
SFA (Semantic Feature Analysis), 96–98, 98*f*
Shaped book reports, 160, 160*f*
Sharing literature
through art, 160–161
through bookmaking. *See* Bookmaking
through drama, 161–164
through writing, 158–159, 159*f*
Sidebars, 7*f*
Signal words, 33, 34
Silent reading, in literature circle, 58
Silhouette biographies, 159, 160*f*
Simulated journals, 129
Situational factors, in reading, 81
Sketching, 71
Skills, *vs.* strategies, 82
Slit books, 171, 172*f*
Social factors, in reading, 81
Social sciences, 119
Social studies, recommended list of nonfiction books,
199–204
Stars, 7*f*
Stick-on tags, 70
Story grammar, 3
Strategic instruction, model for, 82–85
Strategic learning, enhancement of, 85
Strategies. *See also specific strategies*
for reading, 82–83
vs. skills, 82
A Street Called Home (Robinson), 136

Structured overviews. *See* Graphic organizers
Student
background knowledge of, 81
choices, in literature circles, 58
collaboration, in literature circles, 54
conversations, in literature circle, 58
dialogue with teacher, interactive read-alouds and, 50
introducing literature circles to, 59–61
self-evaluation, 187–188
Study skills development, nonfiction and, 10–11, 11*f*
Summarization, 99–100
Summarizer role, in literature circle, 61
Summarizing, 99
Summary writing, 88
Surveys, 186

Table of contents, 6*f*
Talking sticks, 69
Tapestries, 161
T-chart, for effective and ineffective groups, 70
Teacher
demonstration of strategic learning, 84–85
dialogue with student, interactive read-alouds and, 50
responses, to nonfiction materials, 46, 47*f*
role in leading literature discussions, 68–69, 69*f*, 72
textbook usage by, 23–24
vocabulary instruction and, 102
Teacher-student dialogue, interactive read-alouds and, 50
Teaching materials, multiple, 23–24
Technology, 28
recommended list of nonfiction books, 195–199
in writing classroom, 133–135
Textbooks, 3–4, 24
advantages of, 21
ancillary materials, 22
considerate features of, 23
disadvantages, 22–23
inconsiderate features of, 23
Texts. *See also specific texts*
expository structure, 33–34, 35*f*–39*f*
identifying, 40–41
instructional approach for, 34, 39–40
insensitivity to patterns in, 33
short, for strategic learning, 85
Textual features, of informational books, 4, 5*f*
Thematic study, 15, 15*f*
Think-alouds, 46, 83, 188–189
Think and Search answers, 93–94, 95*f*
Think and Search questions, 94, 95*f*
Think sheets, 71, 72*f*
Time lines, 7*f*, 151, 152*f*, 153, 161, 163*f*
Time order or sequence, 36*f*–37*f*, 40
Topical graphic organizers, 145
Trade book authors, 25*f*
Trade books, 24–25
Transition words, 117
T-shirts, 161
Two-column notes, 131–132, 132*f*

Videotapes, to introduce students to literature circles, 60

Visual features, 4, 5, 7*f*–8*f*

Vocabulary development, 102

concept/definition maps, 105, 106*f*

Contextual Redefinition strategy, 104–105

List-Group-Label-Write strategy, 102–103

Previewing in Context strategy, 103–104

word walls, 105–107, 107*f*

Vocabulary enricher role, in literature circle, 61

Web pages, 134–135

Webs. *See* Graphic organizers

Web sites, of interest, 206

Whole class reading instruction, 13–14

Wonderbooks, 125, 126*f*

Wooden Teeth and Jelly Beans (Nelson; Kelly; Adams and McLane), 138

Word walls, for vocabulary development, 105–107, 107*f*

Workplace, basic competencies for, 9

Work samples, student, 189–190, 190*f*–191*f*

Writing, 110–111

ABCs of nonfiction writing, 136–137, 137*f*

craft of, 112–113

forms of, 114*f*–115*f*, 115

guidelines for, 115–116

incorporating into content area classes, 120–121

instructional framework for, 116

journal. *See* Journal writing

to learn, 121

to other schools/communities, 136

patterned, 121, 122*f*, 123*f*

persuasive. *See* Persuasive writing

process, overview of, 112–113, 113*f*

purposes of, 114*f*–115*f*

quality examples of, 115

in sharing literature, 158–159, 159*f*

style, of nonfiction materials, 33

Writing classroom, technology in, 133–135

Written conversations, 126, 127

Written responses, to text, 61, 63*f*–68*f*, 64, 67

Yankee Doodle (Kellogg), 164